Wonder-filled WEEKDAYS

for Spring

65 Lesson Plans for Christian Preschool Ministries

Cynthia Gray, B.S.

Abingdon Press
Nashville

Wonder-filled Weekdays for Spring

ISBN 0-687-08994-8

Editor: Daphna Flegal
Designed and Illustrated by: Paige Easter
Sign Language: Illustrated by: Robert S. Jones
Cover Photograph: Ron Benedict
Production Editors: Leslie Johnson and Betsi Smith

00 01 02 03 04 05 06 07 08 09—10 9 8 7 6 5 4 3 2 1

MANUFACTURED IN THE UNITED STATES OF AMERICA

Table of Contents

Introduction

Overview

Wonder-filled Weekdays offers 65 lesson plans for teachers of preschoolers in Christian preschool ministries. These lesson plans integrate developmentally appropriate activities with religious development and are designed to help teachers make faith connections. The lesson plans are organized around monthly seasonal themes with weekly (five-day) lesson plans.

Each lesson contains:

- An outline of the lesson with:
  - Goals
  - Objectives
  - Faith Connections
  - Bible Verse
  - Teacher's Prayer
- Center Time
- Wonder Time
- Group Fun
- Goodbye Circle
- Evaluation

It is expected that teachers will choose from the suggested activities and fit them into their own classroom schedules.

Snack Time

Snack time is an important time for young children. Occasionally you will find a suggestion for a snack that the children make as part of the lesson's activities. These are included because they specifically add to the day's goals and objectives. It is expected that you have a snack as part of your regular schedule. Use it as an opportunity to pray. Talk with the children about the day's lessons as you eat together.

Teacher Talk

Several features of *Wonder-filled Weekdays* will help the teacher make faith connections with their children. Verbalizing our faith as the children work and play is what gives an ordinary preschool activity a Christian value. Looking at sprouting seeds is not just a science lesson. It is an opportunity to talk about God as Creator and about God's plan for the seasons.

Teacher Talk is designed to help the teacher think through the words to say to help children learn about God, Jesus, and our faith in connection to the lesson and to individual activities. Teacher Talk is found on the first page of each lesson, along with the goals and objectives. Teacher Talk is also found with each suggested activity during Center Time.

The Bible

Each lesson has a suggested Bible verse for the children to hear and to experience. You may want to use each Bible verse as suggested. Or you may want to choose one Bible verse for the week and repeat it each day. There are also suggested Bible stories for each unit. Find these Bible stories in Bible storybooks or in your Sunday school curriculum resources to present the stories in ways the children can understand. *Don't Just Sit There, Bible Stories That Move You for Ages 3-5* (ISBN 0-687-12210-4) is an excellent source of age-appropriate Bible stories. You may order *Don't Just Sit There* through your Christian bookstore or by calling 800-672-1789.

As you teach your children Bible stories and Bible verses, let them see you handle the Bible. Give the children opportunities to hold the Bible and open its pages. This is the book of our faith. We want to give our children a love for its teachings.

Christian Values

Throughout *Wonder-filled Weekdays* teachers will find Christian values presented as part of the lessons. These values include:

We are created in the image of God.
God loves us.
We can love God.
We can love others.
God is always with us.
We can trust God.
God's world is good.
Jesus loves us.
Jesus taught us about God's love.

Centers for Spring

Home Living Center

chairs and table
play appliances
pretend food
dishes, pots, and pans
dress-up clothes
accessories: belts, hats, ties, jewelry
phone
computer

Besides the normal pretend food and dishes, include items that are found in today's homes, such as a television set (make one out of a box), a briefcase, and a computer. Some centers include actual living room furniture—soft chairs and sofas. Include items that will represent family chores, such as a plastic waste paper basket, a broom, a stuffed animal with a leash, and pretend pet food and dishes. Also include dress-up clothes that a mother, father, grandmother, and grandfather would wear.

Manipulatives Center

puzzles
play dough
buttons
lacing beads
Duplo blocks
pegboards
pegs
small wooden blocks
foam peanuts
pompons
tongs

This center encourages children to use their small muscles. You will see a marked difference between three-year-olds and five-year-olds in this center. Both younger and older preschoolers need practice using their small muscles.

Manipulating objects also helps children with learning how to pattern, solve problems, and assemble.

Math Center

small items for counting
ruler
measuring cups
items for sorting and matching
a counting line with numbers to 25

Math for young children involves counting, sorting and matching, spatial relationships, estimating, and comparing. Avoid worksheets for preschoolers; instead, use actual objects for counting and matching.

Have the children bring items from home for use in the center. Or use items common to most families, such as Duplo blocks, stickers, paper clips, animal figures, and so forth.

Music/Movement Center

cassettes or CDs
cassette or CD player
scarfs or ribbons
rhythm instruments
headphones

Music can be used for quiet listening or for movement. The activities can be done with one child or with the whole group. Vary the music and movement experiences you provide for your children. Set up a place with headphones, pillows, and blankets for quiet listening. Move furniture out of the way or take the children to a larger space for large muscle play. Remember that music and movement are two important ways children learn.

Art Center

- easel and paintbrushes
- construction paper (different sizes)
- glue
- collage materials
- scissors
- fabric scraps
- crayons
- magazines
- markers
- rubber stamps
- plain paper
- mural paper
- manila drawing paper
- colored pencils
- watercolors
- art tissue
- smocks
- table covering

Slowly include items in the Art Center as children learn how to use the items, to care for them, and to put them back after the children have used them. Children need the opportunity to experiment with a variety of art mediums without trying to create any specific project. The Art Center can also be used for group activity projects.

Cover the table with rolled paper, newspaper, or a plastic tablecloth to make cleanup easier. Have the children wear smocks to protect their clothing.

Cooking Center

- mixing bowls
- mixing spoons
- measuring cups
- baking trays
- muffin tins
- cupcake liners
- plastic bags
- oven (or access to one)

Preschoolers love to cook! Have a separate Cooking Center or combine cooking activities with the Home Living Center. Let the children mix, stir, squish, pound, knead, and of course—taste.

Building Center

- large wooden blocks
- Lincoln Logs building toys
- small wooden blocks
- Kinex interlocking building toys
- small sticks
- Duplo blocks

Preschool boys and girls love to construct buildings, houses, roadways, boats, airplanes, and so forth. As with other centers this center needs close supervision. Be sure children know the rules for fun in the center. If play becomes too rough, close the center and tell the children why.

Some children will want to stay in the Building Center every day for center time. Be sure to have a way of encouraging them to enjoy other centers and to let other children play with building materials. Limit the number of children who can play in the center at one time. This can be done by giving each child a center card. The child puts his or her card in a plastic pocket you have made. Place five pockets in the center, and when they are filled, no one else can come in until a child leaves.

The Building Center encourages creative thought as children seek to solve problems in their building. It is a wonderful place for children to learn social skills and to work together. The Building Center promotes growth of fine and gross motor skills and is a good place for children to practice language skills.

You can reinforce your lesson theme in the Building Center by using characters that go along with the theme. For example, put plastic snakes, lizards, alligators, and turtles in the Building Center the week you are learning about reptiles.

Centers for Spring

Writing Center

- pencils of different lengths and widths
- erasers
- plain writing paper
- lined writing paper
- envelopes of different sizes
- rulers
- posters of the alphabet
- stickers
- mailboxes for each child and teacher

Basics in this center are paper and pencils. Ask parents to recycle paper from their businesses. Use stamps from magazine promotionals for pretend stamps. Have pencils of varying sizes available so each child can choose the one that feels most controllable and comfortable.

You might want to make a post office as part of the center so children can send messages to others in their class. Be sure to include a name on each box, including each of the adults in the class. Remember, the purpose of this center is for the child to practice writing. For younger children this will probably mean scribbling or writing letters that have no meaning for you. If you are teaching five-year-olds, you may want to have lined paper available and a poster of the alphabet for them to see.

To use the center as a reinforcement for your lessons in the “Colors and More” unit, encourage children to “write”with crayons that match the color of the day. School-age children are encouraged to write in their journals; therefore, you might want to help older preschoolers get used to this idea by making little books in which children can draw and write. Posting the name of each child, printed so they can copy it, will help older preschoolers with writing their names.

Water/Sand Play Center

- water or sand table
- dishpan
- water
- sand
- plastic cups and bowls
- plastic pitchers
- turkey basters
- plastic spoons
- towels
- plastic animals
- plastic boats
- coffee scoops
- colanders
- combs
- egg beaters
- funnels
- plastic pails
- shells
- rocks
- sponges
- watering cans

Water and sand play is great fun for young children. It can also provide a calming effect and help the children relax. It promotes creativity and provides tactile experiences.

Have towels on hand to clean up water from the floor and from hands and arms. Always sweep up and throw away any sand that lands on the floor.

Color Center

- objects brought from home
- objects that are the color of the day

This a special center for the unit on “Colors and More.” Send notes home asking parents to send objects that are the color of the day with the children. Place the objects in this center. Have some extra objects available for children who are not able to bring objects from home.

Science Center

magnifying glass
nature items (rocks, bugs, leaves, and so forth)
class pet
magnets
experiments
writing paper and pencil
photographs of people

Science for young children includes active involvement in collecting specimens, viewing specimens, and talking and writing about what they see. Encourage children to contribute items to the Science Center, and be sure all children get a chance to participate in experiments at the center.

Show and Tell Center

objects brought from home
objects that match the shape of the day

Have a place for the children to put objects they bring from home that match the shape of the day. Send notes asking parents to send these objects with their children.

Dramatic Play Center

clothing and fabrics to represent clothing
farmers
gardening tools
artificial plants
seed packets

Encourage the children to pretend to be farmers and gardeners. Let the children pretend to plant and take care of growing seeds, plants, flowers, and trees. Or let the children have a pretend garden store to buy and sell seeds and garden tools.

Book Center

books
pictures

Give the Book Center a little extra attention. Add pillows, blankets, and sleeping bags. Put up a tent or make a reading house from a large appliance box. Hang stars or brightly colored leaves from the ceiling. Rotate stuffed animal characters through the center as you highlight the books they come from. Make this center a special space for the children to enjoy.

Worship Center

Bible
Bible storybook
nature items (rocks, leaves, shells, and so forth)
flowers or plants
worship cloth
pictures

Worship for young children happens in the midst of everyday life. It is the moment of wonder when a child examines a leaf that has changed from green to red, or the moment of delight when warm, freshly baked bread is tasted on the tongue. Worship happens at Wonder Time, on the playground, and in the Science Center. If this is true, then why is a Worship Center suggested each week? The Worship Center is designed to give the teacher a planned opportunity to talk and pray with the children. The activities suggested in the Worship Center will range from art projects to science experiments to games. But each activity has an extra-special ingredient. It suggests ways for you to connect the day's lessons with the faith.

Having a Worship Center gives your classroom a sacred space. It reminds parents, teachers, and children that God is important in this place.

Preschoolers

Each child in your class is a one-of-a-kind child of God. Each child has his or her own name, background, family situation, and set of experiences. It is important to remember and celebrate the uniqueness of each child. Yet all of these one-of-a-kind children of God have some common needs.

- All children need love.
- All children need a sense of self-worth.
- All children need to feel a sense of accomplishment.
- All children need to have a safe place to be and to express their feelings.
- All children need to be surrounded by adults who love them.
- All children need to experience the love of God.

Preschoolers (children ages 3-5 years old) also have some common characteristics.

Their Bodies

- They do not sit still for very long.
- They have lots of energy.
- They enjoy moving (running, galloping, dancing, jumping, hopping).
- They are developing fine motor skills (learning to cut with scissors, learning to handle a ball, learning to tie their shoes).
- They enjoy using their senses (taste, touch, smell, hearing, sight).

Their Minds

- They are learning more and more words.
- They enjoy music.
- They are learning to express their feelings.
- They like to laugh and be silly.
- They enjoy nonsense words.
- They are learning to identify colors, sizes, and shapes.
- They have an unclear understanding of time.
- They have a wonderful imagination.

Their Relationships

- They are beginning to interact with others as they play together.
- They are beginning to understand that other people have feelings.
- They are learning to wait for their turn.
- They can have a hard time leaving parents, especially mother.
- They want to help.
- They love to feel important.

Their Hearts

- They need to handle the Bible and see others handle it.
- They need caring adults who model Christian attitudes and behaviors.
- They need to sing, move to, and say Bible verses.
- They need to hear clear, simple stories from the Bible.
- They can express simple prayers.
- They can experience wonder and awe at God's world.
- They can share food and money and make things for others.
- They can experience belonging at church and preschool.

Unit 1

Colors and More

Goals:

1. The children will practice identifying and naming colors.
2. The children will have the opportunity to learn the names and characteristics of different shapes.
3. The children will have the opportunity to learn about letter names and sounds.
4. The children will have the opportunity to participate in a variety of number activities through learning center activities, games, songs, and books.
5. The children will be exposed to a variety of children's literature.

This four-week unit focuses on several basic skills preschoolers need to learn. These include identifying and naming colors, shapes, letters, and numbers. These lessons are not designed to teach the children all the colors, all the shapes, the whole alphabet, and how to count to a hundred. Rather, the lessons will reinforce the learnings that are part of your ongoing program and then introduce some new concepts.

Invite the parents and other caregivers to become involved in these lessons. Send home notes to let the parents and caregivers know what concepts are being explored each week. Ask the parents and caregivers to to practice naming and identifying colors, shapes, letters, and numbers with their children.

Bible Stories for This Unit:

Genesis 1 (The Creation)
Genesis 6, 9 (The Ark, The Rainbow)
Psalm 23 (The Lord Is My Shepherd)
Psalm 54:4 (God Is My Helper)
Psalm 98 (Sing to the Lord)
Psalm 100 (Worship the Lord)
Proverbs 17:17 (A Friend Loves)
Matthew 15:32-38 (Feeding of the Four Thousand)
Luke 2:52 (Jesus Grew)
Philippians 4:13 (Christ Strengthens Me)

COLORS

This week the children will focus on colors, with a special emphasis on one color each day. The week's activities will culminate in "Rainbow Day," when the children will be able to enjoy participating in activities that involve all the colors of the rainbow. Send home to parents a list of each day's color prior to this week's activities, and encourage the children to wear clothes in the color of the day (see page 222). One of the learning centers for the week will be a collection of objects in the day's colors. Ask parents to send with their child an object each day that is the color of the day to put in the learning center display.

Lesson 1

Red Day

Teacher Talk:

God made many different colors.

Each color is special.

Each one of us is special.

Red is one of the colors God made.

Red is a color we can see in God's world.

Goals:

To identify and name colors.

To understand that God made colors.

To help the children enjoy a variety of colors.

Objectives:

By the end of this session the children will:

Point out red objects.

Listen to a story about the color red.

Faith Connections

Bible verse: When the sun is setting, you say, "We are going to have fine weather, because the sky is red." (Matthew 16:2, *Good News Bible*)

Red is a color we often associate with joy and with parties. Preschool children recognize that there are different colors, and they need the opportunity to recognize and to name specific colors. Children need to know that God created all the colors in the world and that all the colors are important.

Teacher's Prayer

Dear God, help me to share the magic of the colors of the world with the children in my care. Amen.

Center Time

Set up your centers as described on pages 6–9. For this lesson add the following:

As children arrive, place a red sticker on their clothing or on the backs of their hands.

Writing Center

Teacher Talk
God made the color red.

Resources
index cards, tracing paper, red crayons

Write the word *red* on index cards. Set out the cards, tracing paper, and red crayons. Let the children trace the word *red* on the paper provided.

Worship Center

Teacher Talk
Red is a color we can see in God's world.

Resources
children's Bible; selection of "natural" red objects: apple, strawberry, red flowers, and so forth

Set the children's Bible on a table with the red objects. Have the children look at the stories in the Bible and name the objects and their color.

Say: These are some things that God made that are red. God made many wonderful things in this world for you and me to enjoy.

Pray: Thank you, God, for the color red. Amen.

Color Center

Teacher Talk
Red is one of the colors God made.

Resources
collection of red objects that the children have brought from home

Set out the red objects. Encourage the children to name the objects and their color.

Art Center

Teacher Talk
Each color is special.

Resources
washable red paint, paintbrushes, red crayons, red glitter, red construction paper, paint smocks

Set out the red art materials and the brushes and paint smocks. Encourage the children to create artwork in red using the materials provided.

Math Center

Teacher Talk
God made the color red.

Resources
Several sets of red objects, such as crayons, buttons, beads, blocks (whatever is available)

Set out the red objects. Encourage the children to create patterns with the objects

Cooking Center

Teacher Talk
Red is a color God made.

Resources
small paper plates, napkins, plate with a variety of red foods (tomatoes, strawberries, sliced pieces of apples), plastic knives

Set out the foods, plates, napkins, and knives. Encourage the children to cut, serve, and taste the variety of red foods provided.

Mural Center

Teacher Talk
God made many different colors.

Resources
large sheet of paper, marker, magazines, scissors, glue sticks

Place a large sheet of paper on a table. Write the word *red* in large letters at the top of the paper. Encourage the children to find red objects in the magazines, cut or tear them out, and glue them to the paper.

Manipulatives Center

Teacher Talk
Red is one of the colors God made.

Resources
cardboard tubes cut into sections, pieces of red cellophane, tape

Encourage the children to cover one end of their tubes with the red cellophane and tape the pieces in place. The children can look around the room with the new "red explorer tubes."

Open the Bible to Matthew 16:2.

Say: "When the sun is setting, you say, 'We are going to have fine weather, because the sky is red'" (Matthew 16:2, *Good News Bible*).

Have the children repeat the Bible verse.

Wonder Time

Call the children together for wonder time.

Wonder Question: I wonder why God made the color red?

Say: We are learning about colors this week. Today's color is red. Let's look around the room and see if we can find something in the room that is red.

Sing: "Who is Wearing Red Today?" to the tune of "London Bridge." Repeat the song as desired, adding other actions, such as touch your nose, turn all around, and so forth.

Who is wearing red today,
Red today, red today.
Who is wearing red today?
Hop up and down.

Read the Bible verse.

Say: God made many wonderful colors, and one of the colors that God made is red.

Pray: Thank you, God, for making so many beautiful colors like the color red. Amen.

Group Fun

Resources

bottom parts of cardboard boxes (a box for a case of soda would work well), white construction paper (8- by 11-inch), marbles, red tempera paint, tablespoon, smocks

Have the children wear smocks. Explain to the children that they are going to "paint" with marbles. Place a piece of paper in the bottom of each box and put approximately one tablespoon of red paint on the paper or in a corner of the box. (Let each child choose where the paint should go.) Give each child a marble to put in the box. Encourage the children to roll the marble back and forth in the box. Allow the pictures to dry flat. Be sure to mark each child's paper with his or her name.

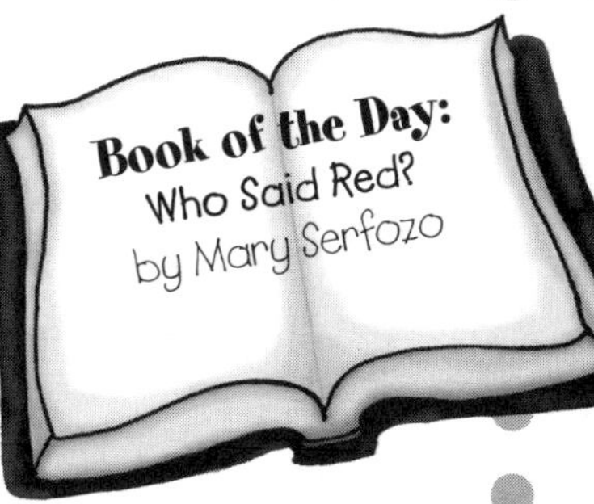

Goodbye Circle

Let the children talk about the things they enjoyed doing today. Hold up a red object and ask the children to name the color of the object. Ask each child to point out something in the room that is red.

Pray: Thank you, God, for special colors like red and special people like all the children in this room. Amen.

Evaluation

Was each child able to identify and name the color red? If a child did not participate in wearing the color or bringing in an object of the color, make plans to provide objects so each child can participate.

Lesson 2

Yellow Day

Goals:

To identify and name colors.

To understand that God made colors.

To help the children enjoy a variety of colors.

Objectives:

By the end of this session the children will:

Point out yellow objects.

Listen to a story about the color yellow.

Faith Connections

Bible verse: The dove's wings glittered with yellow gold.

(Psalm 68:13, *Good News Bible*, adapted)

Yellow is a color that we associate with bright and shiny things. Preschool children need the opportunity to know that God created many colors and that the Bible often describes the colors of the things God created.

Teacher's Prayer

Thank you, God, for this opportunity to help the children in my care shine with the brilliance of your love. Amen.

Teacher Talk:

God made many different colors.

Each color is special.

Each one of us is special.

Yellow is a color that God made.

Yellow is a color we can see in God's world.

Center Time

Continue the centers from Lesson 1. For this lesson add or change the following:

As children arrive, place a yellow sticker on their clothing or on the backs of their hands.

Writing Center

Teacher Talk

Yellow is a color that God made.

Resources

index cards, tracing paper, yellow crayons

Write the word *yellow* on index cards. Set out the index cards, tracing paper, and yellow crayons. Let the children trace the word *yellow*.

Art Center

Teacher Talk

Each color is special.

Resources

"yellow pages" from old phone book, yellow crayons and markers, gold glitter, glue, cotton swabs, shallow container

Set out yellow art materials. Place glue in a shallow container. Let the children create artwork in yellow, using the materials provided.

Manipulatives Center

Teacher Talk

Yellow is a color that God made.

Resources

sections of cardboard tubes, pieces of yellow cellophane or plastic wrap, tape

Have the children cover one end of their tubes with yellow cellophane and tape the pieces in place. The children can look around the room with their "yellow explorer tubes."

Mural Center

Teacher Talk

God made many different colors.

Resources

large sheet of paper, marker, magazines, scissors, glue sticks

Write the word *yellow* in large letters at the top of a large piece paper. Encourage the children to find yellow objects in the magazines, cut or tear them out, and glue them to the paper.

Math Center

Teacher Talk

Yellow is a color God made.

Resources

several sets of yellow objects: crayons, buttons, beads, blocks (whatever is available)

Set out the yellow objects. Encourage the children to create patterns with the objects.

Cooking Center

Teacher Talk

Yellow is a color we can see in God's world.

Resources

small paper plates, napkins, pineapple rings on a plate, plastic knives

Set out pineapple, plates, napkins, and knives. Encourage the children to cut, serve, and taste the pineapple chunks.

Color Center

Teacher Talk

Yellow is a color that God made.

Resources

collection of yellow objects, objects children have brought from home

Set out the yellow objects. Encourage the children to name the objects and their color.

Worship Center

Teacher Talk

Yellow is a color we can see in God's world.

Resources

children's Bible; selection of natural yellow objects such as bananas, flowers, and feathers

Set the children's Bible and yellow objects on a table. Let the children look at the stories in the Bible and name the objects and their color.

Say: These are some things that God made that are yellow. God made many wonderful things in this world for everyone to enjoy.

Pray: Thank you, God, for the color yellow. Amen.

Wonder Time

Call the children together for wonder time.

Wonder Question: I wonder why God made the color yellow?

Say: Today we are learning about the color yellow. Let's look around the room and see if we can find something in the room that is yellow.

Give the children yellow crepe paper streamers. Play music from a cassette or CD and encourage the children to wave the streamers.

Read the Bible verse.

Say: Yellow is a bright shiny color, the color of the sun. It is one of the beautiful colors in the world that God made.

Pray: Thank you, God, for making bright beautiful colors like the color yellow. Amen.

Open the Bible to Psalm 68:13.

Say: "The dove's wings glittered with yellow gold" (Psalm 63:13, *Good News Bible*, adapted).

Have the children repeat the Bible verse.

Group Fun

Resources

paper plates, yellow crepe paper streamers, sunflower seeds, green construction paper strips (approximately one-by-six inches), scissors, glue

Tell the children that they are going to make bright yellow sunflowers. Give each child a paper plate. Encourage the children to cut or tear the yellow crepe paper into strips approximately one to two inches long. Have the children glue the yellow crepe paper around the outside of the paper plate. The children can glue sunflower seeds to the center of the plate and a green paper strip to the back for the stem.

Goodbye Circle

Let the children talk about the things they enjoyed doing today. Hold up a yellow object and ask the children to name the color of the object. Ask each child to point out something in the room that is yellow.

Pray: Thank you, God, for bright colors like yellow. Amen.

Evaluation

Was each child able to identify and name the color yellow? Are there children who are having difficulty finding objects that are the color of the day? Make plans to help each child meet the day's objectives.

Lesson 3

Blue Day

Teacher Talk:

God made many different colors.

Each color is special.

Each one of us is special.

Blue is a color that God made.

We can see the color blue in God's world.

Goals:

To identify and name colors.

To understand that God made colors.

To help the children enjoy a variety of colors.

Objectives:

By the end of this session the children will:

Point out blue objects.

Listen to a story about the color blue.

Faith Connections

Bible verse: Spread a blue cloth over the table for the bread offered to the LORD.

(Numbers 4:7, *Good News Bible*)

Blue is the color of the sky and the water. It is a color we often associate with peace. Preschool children need the opportunity to learn the names of colors. They also need to learn that the Bible tells us ways to praise and honor God.

Teacher's Prayer

Dear God, help me to remember to give you thanks for everything you have given me. Be with me as I strive to teach the children in my care to thank you for the blessings you have given them. Amen.

Center Time

Continue the centers from Lessons 1 and 2. For this lesson add or change the following:

Writing Center

Teacher Talk

Blue is a color that God made.

Resources

index cards, tracing paper, blue crayons

Write the word *blue* on several index cards. Set out the index cards, tracing paper, and blue crayons. Encourage the children to trace the word *blue* on the paper provided.

Manipulatives Center

Teacher Talk

Blue is a color that God made.

Resources

cardboard tube sections, pieces of blue cellophane or plastic wrap, tape

Encourage the children to cover one end of their tubes with the blue cellophane and tape the pieces in place. The children can look around the room with their new "blue explorer tubes."

Math Center

Teacher Talk

Blue is a color that God made.

Resources

several sets of blue objects, such as crayons, buttons, beads, blocks (whatever is available)

Set out the blue objects. Encourage the children to sort the objects and to describe how they decided where to put each object.

Mural Center

Teacher Talk

God made many different colors.

Resources

large sheet of paper, marker, magazines, scissors, glue sticks

Lay the large sheet of paper on a table and write the word *blue* in large letters at the top of the paper. Let the children find blue objects in the magazines, cut or tear them out, and glue them to the paper.

As children arrive, place a blue sticker on their clothing or on the backs of their hands.

Color Center

Teacher Talk

Blue is a color that God made.

Resources

collection of blue objects, objects children have brought from home

Set out the blue objects. Encourage the children to name the objects and their color.

Art Center

Teacher Talk

Each color is special.

Resources

washable blue paint, paintbrushes, blue crayons, blue construction paper, paint smocks

Set out the blue art materials, brushes and paint smocks. Encourage the children to create artwork in blue, using the materials provided.

Cooking Center

Teacher Talk

Blue is a color that God made.

Resources

small paper plates, napkins, plate with blueberries

Set out the plates and napkins. Encourage the children to taste the blueberries.

Worship Center

Teacher Talk

God made many different colors.

Resources

children's Bible, blue tablecloth (plastic or cloth), table, pictures of sky and water

Say: God gave us some special things that are blue, such as sky and water. This blue cloth on the worship table will help us remember to thank God for all the beautiful colors.

Pray: Thank you, God, for the color blue. Amen.

Open the Bible to Numbers 4:7.

Say: "Spread a blue cloth over the table for the bread offered to the LORD" (Numbers 4:7, *Good News Bible*).

Have the children repeat the Bible verse.

Wonder Time

Call the children together for wonder time.

Wonder Question: I wonder why God made the sky blue?

Say: Today we are learning about the color blue. Let's look around the room and see if we can find something in the room that is blue.

Have the children play a game called "Jump the River." Cut blue yarn into two lengths, approximately five or six inches long. Place the two lengths of yarn on the floor about one inch apart to form a "river." Encourage each child to jump over. Widen the river a few inches and see if the children can still jump across. Continue in this way, widening the river, as long as there is time and the children enjoy the activity.

Read the Bible verse.

Say: God made many beautiful colors. Blue is the color that God chose for the sky and the water.

Pray: Thank you, God, for giving us beautiful blue skies and blue water. Amen.

Group Fun

Resources

hand-held grater, old blue crayons, five-inch wax paper squares, towels, iron, craft sticks, glue, blue yarn

Let the children make blue suncatchers. Have the children rub crayons on the grater to make shavings. Supervise the children closely as they use the grater. Give each child a piece of wax paper, and have the children sprinkle shavings on the paper. Place a second wax paper square over the first. Place both pieces on a towel. Place a second towel over the paper and iron with warm iron on the cloth. Remove the wax paper. The children can then glue craft sticks around the edges of the suncatcher. If desired, let the children suspend their suncatchers from blue yarn.

Note: Only adults should handle the iron.

Goodbye Circle

Let the children talk about the things they enjoyed doing today. Hold up a blue object and ask the children to name the color of the object. Ask each child to point out something in the room that is blue.

Pray: Thank you, God, for giving us the color blue. Amen.

Evaluation

Was each child able to identify and name the color blue? If a child is having difficulty meeting the objectives, make plans to help the child.

Lesson 4

Green Day

Goals:

To identify and name colors.

To understand that God made colors.

To help the children enjoy a variety of colors.

Objectives: By the end of this session the children will:

Point out green objects.

Listen to a story about the color green.

Discover that blue and yellow make green.

Faith Connections

Bible verse: God lets me rest in fields of green grass.

(Psalm 23:2, *Good News Bible*, adapted)

Green is the color of growing things, a color we often associate with spring. Preschool children need the opportunity to learn that God created every growing thing and every color in the world. They can learn to appreciate and enjoy the gifts that God has given us.

Teacher's Prayer

Dear God, grant me the tranquillity that a rest in a field of green grass can bring. Help me bring that tranquillity of spirit into the classroom as I work with the children in my class. Amen.

Teacher Talk:

God made many different colors.

Each color is special.

Each one of us is special.

Green is a color that God made.

We can see the color green in God's world.

Center Time

Continue the centers from Lessons 1-3.
For this lesson add or change the following:

As children arrive, place a green sticker on their clothing or on the backs of their hands.

Writing Center

Teacher Talk

Green is a color that God made.

Resources

index cards, tracing paper, green crayons

Write the word *green* on index cards. Set out the cards, tracing paper, and green crayons. Let the children trace the word *green* on the paper.

Manipulatives Center

Teacher Talk

Green is a color that God made.

Resources

cardboard tube sections, pieces of green cellophane or plastic wrap, tape

Have the children cover one end of the tubes with the green cellophane and tape the pieces in place. The children can look around the room with their "green explorer tubes."

Mural Center

Teacher Talk

God made many different colors.

Resources

large sheet of paper, marker, magazines, scissors, glue sticks

Write the word *green* in large letters at the top of a large sheet of paper. Have the children find green objects in the magazines, cut or tear them out, and glue them to the paper.

Art Center

Teacher Talk

Each color is special.

Resources

green paint, shallow container, cookie cutters, white paper, table covering, smocks

Pour paint in a shallow container. Have the children wear smocks. Let the children dip the cookie cutters into the paint and then onto their papers to make prints.

Color Center

Teacher Talk

Green is a color that God made.

Resources

collection of green objects, objects children have brought from home

Set out the green objects. Encourage the children to name the objects and their color.

Cooking Center

Teacher Talk

Green is a color God made.

Resources

small paper plates, napkins; plate with a variety of green foods, such as kiwi, peas, celery, and so forth; plastic knives

Set out plates, napkins, and knives with the foods. Encourage the children to cut, serve, and taste the variety of green foods.

Science Center

Teacher Talk

We can see the color green in God's world.

Resources

collection of green plants, magnifying glass

Set the plants on a table with the magnifying glass. Let the children look at, touch, and explore the plants by studying them with the binoculars.

Worship Center

Teacher Talk

God made many different colors.

Resources

children's Bible, selection of "natural" green objects such as plants and vegetables

Set out the children's Bible and the green objects. Have the children look at the stories in the Bible and name the objects and their color.

Say: These are some things that God made that are green.

Pray: Thank you, God, for the color green. Amen.

Wonder Time

Call the children together for wonder time.

Wonder Question: I wonder why God made the grass green?

Say: Today we are learning about the color green. Let's look around the room and see if we can find something in the room that is green.

Play a game called "Go, Frog, Go." Say: Frogs are animals that God made that are green. What do frogs like to do? They like to hop. We are going to line up and hop like frogs and make "frog noises." Hop and make frog noises as long as time allows and children enjoy the activity.

Read the Bible verse.

Say: God made many beautiful things that are green. Everything that God made was made because God loves us.

Pray: Thank you, God, for loving us and for giving us so many wonderful green things like frogs and grass. Amen.

Open the Bible to Psalm 23:2.

Say: "God lets me rest in fields of green grass" (Psalm 23:2, *Good News Bible*, adapted).

Have the children repeat the Bible verse.

Group Fun

Resources

yellow and blue tempera paint, resealable plastic bags (optional: water, blue and yellow food coloring, clear glass bowl; or blue and yellow transparent report covers, scissors, glue, paper)

Help the children discover green. Give each child a resealable plastic bag. Pour a small amount of blue paint and yellow paint into each child's bag, and help each child seal his or her bag carefully. Encourage the children to manipulate the bag to mix the colors.

Say: What colors did I put in the bags? What color is in your bag now? What do you think happened?

If desired, expand the discovery time by mixing blue and yellow food coloring with water in a clear glass bowl. You could also purchase blue and yellow transparent report covers (available at office supply stores) and cut circles out of the covers. Give each child a circle of each color to glue on paper, slightly overlapping the circles.

Goodbye Circle

Let the children talk about the things they enjoyed doing today. Ask the children what happens when they mix blue and yellow. Ask each child to point out something in the room that is green.

Pray: Thank you, God, for giving us the color green. Amen.

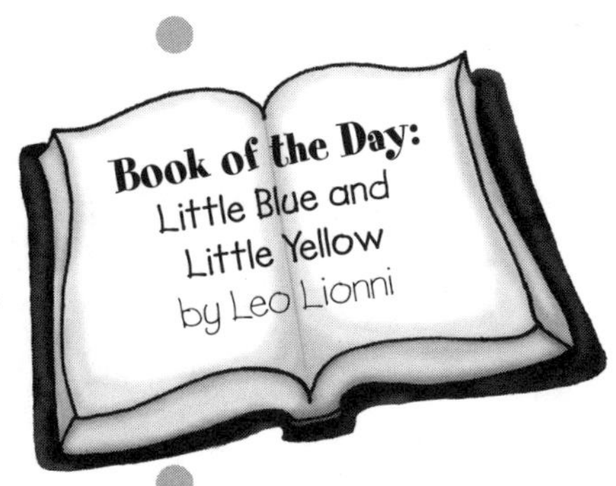

Evaluation

Was each child able to identify and name the color green? If a child is having difficulty meeting the objectives, make plans to help the child.

Lesson 5

Rainbow Day

Teacher Talk:

God made many different colors.

Each color is special.

Each one of us is special.

God made rainbows.

Goals:

To identify and name colors.

To understand that God made colors.

To help the children enjoy a variety of colors.

Objectives: By the end of this session the children will:

Point out and name an object's color.

Listen to a story about colors.

Faith Connections

Bible verse: God said, "When the rainbow appears in the clouds, I will remember my promise to you."

(Genesis 9:16, *Good News Bible*, adapted)

Rainbows are a symbol of happiness. We see them after a storm and know that sunshine is on its way. God made the first rainbow as a promise to Noah that God would never again destroy the world with a flood. Each time we see a rainbow, we can remember God's promise. Preschool children need the opportunity to see, appreciate, and understand the meaning of rainbows.

Teacher's Prayer

Dear God, thank you for the promise you made to Noah and to each of us. Help me to share the joy of that promise with the children in my care. Amen.

Center Time

Continue the centers from Lessons 1-4.
For this lesson add or change the following:

As children arrive, place a rainbow sticker on their clothing or on the backs of their hands.

Writing Center

Teacher Talk
God made rainbows.

Resources
index cards, tracing paper, rainbow-colored crayons

Write the word *rainbow* on index cards. Set out the index cards, tracing paper, and crayons. Encourage the children to trace the word *rainbow* on the paper.

Manipulatives Center

Teacher Talk
God made rainbows.

Resources
variety of multicolored pompons or large beads, tweezers or tongs, containers

Set out a container of pompons or beads. Place tweezers or tongs and empty containers nearby. Have the children use the tweezers or tongs to pick up and sort the pompons or beads by color. (Supervise closely.)

Color Center

Teacher Talk
God made rainbows.

Resources
collection of objects children brought from home

Arrange the objects in rainbow color order (red, orange, yellow, green, blue, indigo, violet). Encourage the children to name the objects and their colors.

Mural Center

Teacher Talk
God made rainbows.

Resources
large sheet of paper, marker, scraps of multi-colored construction paper, glue sticks

Lay the large sheet of paper on a table. Draw a rainbow shape on the paper. Encourage the children to tear and glue the paper to the rainbow shape.

Art Center

Teacher Talk
Each color is special.

Resources
craft sticks, ice cube tray, water, plastic wrap, paper, food coloring

Set out freezie paints and paper. Encourage the children to "draw" with the freezie paints.

Freezie Paints
Fill an ice cube tray with water. Add drops of food coloring to each section. The color needs to be fairly strong. Cover with plastic wrap. Poke craft sticks through the plastic into the water. Put them in the freezer for several hours.

Math Center

Teacher Talk
God made rainbows.

Resources
paper plates, eight-inch colored crepe paper strips (rainbow colors), tape, tongue depressors

Before class, prepare one paper plate by taping rainbow strips in order: red (top), orange, yellow, green, blue, purple. Hang so the children can see it. Set out the materials above. The children can tape colored streamers to the plate following the pattern, then attach a tongue depressor to make a "rainbow kite."

Worship Center

Teacher Talk
God made many different colors.

Resources
children's Bible, prisms, light source (or set near window)

Set out the children's Bible and the prisms. Encourage the children to explore the rainbows they can make when they hold the prisms in front of the light source.

Say: God made rainbows as a promise to Noah and to each one of us that God would take care of us.

Pray: Thank you, God, for rainbows and for many different colors. Amen.

Open the Bible to Genesis 9:16.

Say: God said, "When the rainbow appears in the clouds, I will remember my promise to you" (Genesis 9:16, *Good News Bible*, adapted).

Have the children repeat the Bible verse.

Wonder Time

Call the children together for wonder time.

Wonder Question: I wonder why God made rainbows?

Say: This week we have been learning about colors. Rainbows are made of seven different colors: red, orange, yellow, green, blue, indigo, and violet (purple).

Play: Build a Rainbow (see box at right).

Read the Bible verse.

Say: God made the rainbow as a promise to Noah and all of us that God would care for us and the earth.

Pray: Thank you, God, for rainbow colors and rainbows. Amen.

Build a Rainbow

You will need construction paper in various colors. Have the children sit in a circle. Give each child a piece of construction paper. Have the children hold their sheets of paper up in the air. Choose one child to be the "Rainbow Builder." That child stands in the middle of the circle. Sing "The Rainbow Needs a Red" to the tune of "The Farmer in the Dell." The rainbow builder taps the shoulder of the child holding the red construction paper, who joins the rainbow builder in the center of the circle. Continue the game singing the colors of the rainbow until everyone is in the circle.

Group Fun

Resources

egg cartons cut in half lengthwise (making strips of six cups), scraps of construction paper (red, orange, yellow, green, blue, purple), scissors, chenille stems, black marker or crayon, yarn pieces twelve to sixteen inches long, paper punch

Encourage the children to make rainbow caterpillars. Help the children cut circles out of the paper, one of each color. If desired, draw the circles ahead of time for the children to cut. Have the children glue a circle of each color to the "humps" of the egg carton. Each child can bend his or her chenille stem in half, insert it into the first cup of the carton to make the antennae, then use the marker or crayon to make eyes. If desired, the children can put the yarn into a hole made in the front of the first cup. (Teachers can make the holes, or the children can use a paper punch). The yarn can be knotted and used as a pull handle.

Goodbye Circle

Let the children talk about the things they enjoyed doing today. Hold up an object for each color of the rainbow, and ask the children to name the color. Ask each child to point out an object and name its color.

Pray: Thank you, God, for loving us and giving us colorful rainbows. Amen.

Evaluation

Was each child able to identify and name the colors of the rainbow? If a child had difficulty with any of the colors during the week, make plans to help the child.

SHAPES

This week the children will focus on shapes, with a special emphasis on one shape each day. The children will participate in a variety of activities that will help the children learn the names and characteristics of each of the shapes being taught.

To help reinforce the learning, encourage parents to talk with their children about the shapes being studied. Send home a list of each day's shape prior to this week's activity (see page 222). Ask parents to send with their children an object each day that is the shape of the day to put in the learning center display.

Lesson 6

Rectangles

Goals:

To identify and name shapes.

To understand that there are many different shapes in God's world.

Objectives: By the end of this session the children will:

Name an object that is a rectangle.

Listen to a story about rectangles.

Faith Connections

Bible verse: The door and the windows of the palace had rectangular frames. (1 Kings 7:5, *Good News Bible*, adapted)

We see rectangles in use every day. This verse describes King Solomon's palace, but it could describe most buildings and churches we see. Preschool children are familiar with doors and windows, but they can learn that their shape has a name—rectangle.

Teacher's Prayer

Dear God, be with me today as I work with the children in my care. Give me the wisdom of Solomon as I deal with any crises that may come my way. Amen.

Teacher Talk:

There are many different shapes in God's world.

A rectangle has four sides.

We can use shapes to make many things.

Center Time

Set up your centers as described on pages 6–9. For this lesson add the following:

As children arrive, have them place any rectangles they brought from home in the Show-and-Tell Center.

Show-and-Tell Center

Teacher Talk

God made many different shapes.

Resources

rectangles children brought from home

Provide a table for the children to place the rectangles they bring from home. Encourage the children to look at the rectangles and describe them.

Writing Center

Teacher Talk

A rectangle has four sides.

Resources

stencils of a variety of rectangles or paper plates, paper, pencils

Provide stencils of rectangles or make stencils by cutting rectangular shapes out of the center of paper plates. Encourage the children to trace the rectangles on the paper.

Building Center

Teacher Talk

A rectangle has four sides.

Resources

variety of rectangular boxes, rectangles cut from construction paper, paper, glue

Set out the boxes, rectangle cutouts, paper, and glue. The children can use the materials to make any type of "construction" they choose.

Art Center

Teacher Talk

There are many different shapes in God's world.

Resources

rectangular blocks, tempera paint, paper, shallow containers, smocks, table covering

Cover the table and have the children wear smocks. Pour paint into a shallow containers. Let the children use the rectangle blocks as stamps. Show the children how to dip the blocks in the paint and then onto the paper to create designs.

Shape Center

Teacher Talk

A rectangle has four sides.

Resources

pieces of yarn, paper, glue, pictures of rectangles (or rectangle cutouts)

Set out the rectangles, yarn, paper, and glue. Have the children to use yarn to create the shape displayed. Let the children glue the yarn in place.

Cooking Center

Teacher Talk

A rectangle has four sides.

Resources

graham crackers, paper plates, napkins, plastic knives, peanut butter or icing

Set out graham crackers, napkins, plates, and knives. Let the children spread peanut butter or icing on their graham cracker rectangles.

Math Center

Teacher Talk

A rectangle has four sides.

Resources

rectangles (blocks, boxes, and so forth)

Set out the rectangles. Encourage the children to sort and arrange the objects by size.

Worship Center

Teacher Talk

There are many different shapes in God's world.

Resources

children's Bible, picture of church (your building, if in a church, or any picture of a church)

Set out the Bible. Hang the picture of the church, or set it next to the Bible.

Say: Churches are places to learn about God. The doors and windows of churches and other buildings are often in the shape of a rectangle.

Pray: Thank you, God, for all the different shapes we can see. Amen.

Wonder Time

Call the children together for wonder time.

Wonder Question: I wonder what rectangles we can find in this room?

Say: We are learning about shapes this week. The special shape we are learning about today is a rectangle. Let's make a rectangle shape with our hands. (Demonstrate and have the children try.)

Sing: "It's a Rectangle" to the tune of "B-I-N-G-O."

Read the Bible verse.

Say: We can use rectangles to make doors and windows, just like the doors and windows in the palace in the Bible verse.

Pray: Thank you, God, for all the different shapes we can see in your world. Amen.

There is a shape that
has four sides,
It is not a square, No!
It's a rectangle,
It's a rectangle,
It's a rectangle,
A shape that has four
sides-O.

Two sides are short,
Two sides are long.
They are not the same-O.
It's a rectangle,
It's a rectangle,
It's a rectangle,
A shape that has four
sides-O.

Open the Bible to 1 Kings 7:5.

Say: "The door and the windows of the palace had rectangular frames" (1 Kings 7:5, *Good News Bible*, adapted).

Have the children repeat the Bible verse.

Group Fun

Resources

permanent markers, beanbags, old sheet, large piece of paper, plastic tablecloth, or old shower curtain

Before class, draw a variety of shapes—rectangles, circles, squares, triangles, and diamonds—on the sheet (or whatever material you are using). Point out the shape outlines on the "target," and have the children name them. Give each child a chance to toss a beanbag at a shape and to name the shape the beanbag lands on. As an alternative activity, call out a shape, and have the children take turns trying to toss the beanbag on the shape you named.

Goodbye Circle

Let the children talk about the things they enjoyed doing today. Hold up a rectangle and ask the children to name the shape. Ask each child to point out a rectangle in the room.

Pray: Thank you, God, for rectangles. Amen.

Evaluation

Was each child able to identify a rectangle? If a child had difficulty learning the shape, make plans to help the child. Make note of each child's ability to manipulate the yarn to make the shape and, if necessary, find ways to help the child with his or her fine motor skills.

Lesson 7

Circles

Teacher Talk:

There are many different shapes in God's world.

A circle is round.

We can use shapes to make many things.

Goals:

To identify and name shapes.

To understand that there are many different shapes in God's world.

Objectives:

By the end of this session the children will:

Name an object that is a circle.

Listen to a story about a circle.

Faith Connections

Bible verse: God sits above the circle of the earth.

(Isaiah 40:22, adapted)

A circle is a globe and a sun—and a happy face symbol. We see circles every day. Preschool children can learn the names of shapes, and they can learn that the earth is in the shape of a giant circle.

Teacher's Prayer

Thank you, God, for this beautiful earth you created. Help me to share the joy of that creation with the children in my care. Amen.

Center Time

Continue the centers from Lesson 6.
For this lesson add or change the following:

As children arrive, place a circle sticker on the back of each child's hand or on the child's clothing.

Show-and-Tell Center

Teacher Talk

A circle is round.

Resources

circles children bring from home

Provide a table for the children to place the circles they bring from home. Encourage the children to look at the circles and to describe their characteristics.

Shape Center

Teacher Talk

A circle is round.

Resources

pieces of yarn, paper, glue, pictures of circles (or circle cutouts)

Set out the circles, yarn, paper, and glue. Encourage the children to use the yarn to create the shape displayed. Let the children glue the yarn in place.

Manipulatives Center

Teacher Talk

We can use shapes to make many things.

Resources

plastic lids, milk jug tops, circular oatmeal containers, circles cut from construction paper, paper, glue

The children can use the materials to make any type of "construction" they choose.

Art Center

Teacher Talk

We can see different shapes in God's world.

Resources

empty thread spools, soft drink bottle caps, milk jug caps, tempera paint, paper, smocks, table covering, shallow trays

Cover the table and have the children wear smocks. Pour paint into shallow containers. Set out the circular items and the paper. Let the children use the circles as stamps. Show the children how to dip the circles into the paint and then onto the papers.

Writing Center

Teacher Talk

A circle is round.

Resources

templates or stencils of circles, paper, pencils

Set out the templates/stencils, paper, and pencils. Let the children trace the circles and create designs.

Cooking Center

Teacher Talk

A circle is round.

Resources

paper plates, napkins, plastic knives, plain round cookies, frosting

Set out cookies, napkins, plates, and knives. Let the children spread the frosting on their cookie circles.

Math Center

Teacher Talk

A circle is round.

Resources

collection of different-sized circles (cans, thread spools, coffee can lids, and so forth)

Set out the collection of circles. Encourage the children to sort and arrange the objects by size.

Worship Center

Teacher Talk

We can see different shapes in God's world.

Resources

children's Bible, globe

Set out the Bible and globe. Have the children look through the Bible and explore the globe.

Say: This globe is like a picture of the earth. It is the shape of a giant circle. God created the earth and all the things on the earth for you and all the people in the world to enjoy.

Pray: Thank you, God, for making such a beautiful world for (*name each child*). Amen.

Open the Bible to Isaiah 40:22.

Say: "God sits above the circle of the earth" (Isaiah 40:22, adapted).

Have the children repeat the Bible verse.

Wonder Time

Call the children together for wonder time.

There is a shape that has no sides;
It just goes round and round-O.
It's a circle-O,
It's a circle-O,
It's a circle-O,
It just goes round and round-O.

Wonder Question: I wonder where we could find a circle in this room?

Say: The special shape we are learning about today is called a circle. It is different from the rectangle shape we learned yesterday because it has no sides—it is round.

Sing: "A Circle" to the tune of "B-I-N-G-O."

Read the Bible verse.

Say: God made the earth in the shape of a circle. God made this special shape for each of us to use and enjoy.

Pray: Thank you, God, for making the earth and for all the circles we can see in your world. Amen.

Group Fun

Resources

large hula hoops, cassette/CD player and cassette/CD

Play a game of musical circles. Set the hula hoops on the floor and play the music. Tell the children that they are to dance and move to the music. When the music stops, they are to stand inside a hula hoop circle. Continue to play the game, but each time you start the music, take away one hula hoop. When it gets crowded inside the hoop, have the children put only a part of their body, such as their hand, foot, head, or elbow, inside the hoop.

Teacher's Note: As the game continues, encourage the children to play this cooperatively instead of competitively. The object is for everyone to be able to be inside the hoop, not to find a "winner."

Goodbye Circle

Let the children talk about the things they enjoyed doing today. Hold up a circle and ask the children to name the shape. Ask each child to point out a circle in the room.

Pray: Thank you, God, for making circles. Amen.

Evaluation

Was every child able to identify a circle? If not, make plans to help the child. If any children had difficulties playing the game cooperatively, find additional activities for the children to do to help them learn to work together.

Lesson 8

Squares

Goals:

To identify and name shapes.

To understand that there are many different shapes in God's world.

Objectives: By the end of this session the children will:

Name an object that is a square.

Listen to a story about squares.

Faith Connections

Bible verse: The city was perfectly square, as wide as it was long.

(Revelations 21:16, *Good News Bible*)

This verse describes the "new Jerusalem" and also defines a square. A square is a perfect shape, to be used in a perfect world that is yet to come. It allows preschool children to learn what a square is in the context of a scriptural situation.

Teacher's Prayer

Dear God, be with me today as I work with the children in my class. Help me to teach them with patience and love. Amen.

Teacher Talk:

We can see many different shapes in God's world.

A square has four sides that are the same size.

We can use shapes to make many things.

Center Time

Continue the centers from Lessons 6-7. For this lesson add or change the following:

> **As children arrive,** tape precut paper squares on the children's clothing.

Math Center

Teacher Talk

A square has four sides that are all the same size.

Resources

squares in a variety of colors and sizes cut out of construction paper

Set out the squares. Encourage the children to sort the squares by color and by size. The children can make patterns with the squares, if they desire.

Writing Center

Teacher Talk

A square has four sides that are all the same size.

Resources

templates or stencils of a variety of squares, paper, pencils

Set out templates/stencils, paper, and pencils. Let the children trace the squares to create a design.

Manipulatives Center

Teacher Talk

A square has four sides that are all the same size.

Resources

play dough, pictures of squares or square blocks, plastic knives

Set out the play dough, plastic knives, and squares. Have the children try to form the play dough into square shapes.

Art Center

Teacher Talk

We can use shapes to make many things.

Resources

variety of square blocks, tempera paint, glitter, paper, shallow trays, table covering, smocks

Cover the table and have the children wear smocks. Pour paint into shallow containers. Set out blocks and paper. Encourage the children to use the squares as stamps by dipping them into the paint and then onto the paper to create designs. Children who want to can sprinkle glitter on the wet paint.

Shape Center

Teacher Talk

A square has four sides that are all the same size.

Resources

pieces of yarn, paper, glue, pictures of squares (or square cutouts)

Display the squares. Set out yarn, paper, and glue. Let the children use yarn to create the shape displayed. Let the children glue the yarn in place.

Cooking Center

Teacher Talk

God made many different shapes.

Resources

paper plates, napkins, slices of toast (squares)

Have each child take a piece of toast and discuss its shape. How does the shape change when they take a bite out of the toast? What shapes can they make as they eat the toast?

Show-and-Tell Center

Teacher Talk

A square has four sides that are all the same size.

Resources

squares children brought from home

Provide a table for the children to place the squares they brought from home. Encourage the children to look at the squares and describe them.

Worship Center

Teacher Talk

God made many different shapes.

Resources

children's Bible, collection of different blocks

Set out the Bible and blocks on a small table.

Say: Each one of these blocks is different, but each is important. Each one of the children in this room is different, but each of you is important to God. God loves you and every person in this room and in the world.

Pray: Thank you, God, for so many different shapes and different people. Amen.

Wonder Time

Call the children together for wonder time.

My four sides are just the same,
Just the same,
Just the same.
My four sides are just the same.
I'm a square.

Wonder Question: I wonder where we can find a square shape in this room?

Say: The special shape we are learning about today is a square. *(Hold up a square block.)* Squares are different than rectangles because all the sides are the same size.

Sing: "I'm a Square" to the tune of "London Bridge". Have the children hold their fingers in the shape of a square while they sing the song together.

Read the Bible verse.

Say: God can see many different shapes and people in God's world. Every shape and person is important.

Pray: Thank you, God, for things that are different. Amen.

Open the Bible to Revelations 21:16.

Say: "The city was perfectly square, as wide as it was long" (Revelations 21:16, *Good News Bible*).

Have the children repeat the Bible verse.

Group Fun

Resources

large collection of half-inch squares cut from various colors of construction paper, uncut construction paper, glue, cotton swabs, shallow containers

Let the children make mosaics. Set out the squares in a large pile, and put the glue in shallow containers. Give each child a piece of uncut construction paper. Encourage the children to choose a variety of squares and to arrange them on their paper as desired. When the children are pleased with their design, they can glue the squares in place.

As you are working, discuss the shapes being used: The bottom paper is a rectangle, and the mosaic pieces are squares. How are the pieces the same? How are they different?

Goodbye Circle

Let the children talk about the things they enjoyed doing today. Hold up a square and ask the children to name the shape. Ask each child to point out a square in the room.

Pray: Thank you, God, for squares. Amen.

Evaluation

Was each child able to identify a square? If a child is having difficulty learning the shapes or meeting the objectives, make plans to help the child.

Lesson 9

Triangles

Teacher Talk:

We can see many different shapes in God's world.

A triangle has three sides.

We can use shapes to make many things.

Goals:

To understand that there are many different shapes in God's world.

A triangle has three sides.

We can use shapes to make many things.

God helps us.

Objectives:

By the end of this session the children will:

Name an object that is a triangle.

Listen to a story about triangles.

Faith Connections

Bible verse: I can do all things through Christ who strengthens me.

(Philippians 4:13, adapted)

Preschool children may get frustrated as they try to learn new things, such as shapes and letters. They need the opportunity to learn that they can learn and that God, through Jesus, is always there to help them.

Teacher's Prayer

Dear God, be with me as I try to help the children in my class learn new things. Give me the words to teach them that you are with them at all times. Amen.

Center Time

Continue the centers from Lessons 6-8. For this lesson add or change the following:

As children arrive, tape precut paper triangles on the children's clothing

Show-and-Tell Center

Teacher Talk:
A triangle has three sides.

Resources:
triangles children bring from home

Provide a table for the children to place the triangles they bring from home. Encourage the children to look at the triangles and describe their characteristics.

Manipulatives Center

Teacher Talk:
A triangle has three sides.

Resources:
play dough, pictures of triangles or triangular blocks, plastic knives

Set out the play dough, plastic knives, and triangles. Encourage the children to try to form the play dough into triangle shapes.

Math Center

Teacher Talk:
We can use shapes to make many things.

Resources:
craft sticks, pictures of triangles

Set out the crafts sticks and the pictures of triangles. Encourage the children to use the craft sticks to form different sizes of triangles.

Worship Center

Teacher Talk:
God helps us.

Resources:
children's Bible, squares, rectangles, triangles

Set out the Bible and the shapes.

Say: We are learning about shapes. Sometimes it is hard to remember all the different shapes, but God planned for you to have a mind that can learn. God will always be with you and help you too.

Pray: Thank you, God, for helping us learn. Amen.

Writing Center

Teacher Talk:
A triangle has three sides.

Resources:
templates or stencils of a variety of triangles, paper, pencils

Set out the templates/stencils, paper, and pencils. Encourage the children to trace the rectangles and use them to create a design.

Art Center

Teacher Talk:
We can use shapes to make many things.

Resources:
selection of different shapes cut out of construction paper, glue, paper

Set out the shapes, glue, and paper. Let the children create a collage by gluing the shapes to the paper in any design they choose.

Shape Center

Teacher Talk:
A triangle has three sides.

Resources:
pieces of yarn, paper, glue, pictures of triangles (or triangle cutouts)

Display the triangles. Set out the yarn, paper, and glue. Encourage the children to use the yarn to create the shape displayed. Have the children glue the yarn in place.

Cooking Center

Teacher Talk:
A triangle has three sides.

Resources:
paper plates, napkins, plastic knives, slices of cheese, triangular crackers

Set out the plates, napkins, knives, cheese, and crackers on the table. Show the children how to use the knives to cut the cheese in half to create two triangles. Let the children eat their triangular snack.

Open the Bible to Philippians 4:13.

Say: "I can do all things through Christ who strengthens me" (Philippians 4:13, adapted).

Have the children repeat the Bible verse.

Wonder Time

There is a shape that has three sides,
It is not a square, No!
It's a triangle,
It's a triangle,
It's a triangle,
A shape that has three sides-O.

Call the children together for wonder time.

Wonder Question: I wonder where we can find a triangle in this room?

Say: Today's special shape is a triangle. It has only three sides. Let's make a triangle shape with our hands. (Demonstrate for the children.)

Sing: "It's a Triangle" to the tune "B-I-N-G-O."

Read the Bible verse.

Say: We have been learning many new shapes and new things. Sometimes when we learn new things, it seems hard, but we are lucky because God loves us and will help us when we need it. God loves us so much that God gave us Jesus.

Pray: Thank you, God, for loving us and helping us. Amen.

Group Fun

Resources

triangle shape cut from foam core or plastic foam (with hole punched in center), skein of yarn

Cut a large piece of yarn, long enough that when the ends are tied together, it will fit around your class when they sit in a circle. Thread the triangle shape onto the yarn, and tie the ends together.

Have the children sit in a circle around the yarn circle. Each child holds onto a section of the yarn with their hands. Sing the following song as the children push the shape around the circle from child to child.

Sing: "Round and Round the Triangle Goes" to the tune of "Pop Goes the Weasel."

Round and round the triangle goes,
Pass it 'round the circle.
Where it stops, nobody knows.
STOP!
Where's the triangle?

Whoever has the triangle stands at the end of the song, makes a triangle shape with his or her hands, and says: "triangle." Continue playing as long as time allows and as long as the children enjoy the activity.

Goodbye Circle

Let the children talk about the things they enjoyed doing today. Hold up a triangle and ask the children to name the shape. Ask each child to make a triangle with their hands and name the shape.

Pray: Thank you, God, for triangles. Amen.

Evaluation

Was each child able to identify a triangle? Were all the children able to meet the objectives? Make plans to help any children who are having difficulty learning the names of the shapes.

Lesson 10

Diamonds

Goals:

To identify and name shapes.

To understand that there are many different shapes in God's world.

Objectives: By the end of this session the children will:

Name an object that is the shape of a diamond.

Listen to a story about shapes.

Faith Connections

Bible verse: God traveled on the wings of the wind.

(Psalm 18:10, *Good News Bible*, adapted)

Preschool children are able to learn that while we can't see God or the wind, we know that they exist. We know the wind is there because of what it does (like making kites fly), and we know God is there because of everything God created. Use today's lesson as an opportunity to talk about God as the children learn about diamond shapes and kites.

Teacher's Prayer

Thank you, God, for always being with me. Like the wind, you surround me, an invisible but constant presence. Amen.

Teacher Talk:

There are many different shapes in God's world.

A diamond has four sides. It is the shape of a kite.

We can use shapes to make many things.

Center Time

Continue the centers from Lessons 6-9. For this lesson add the following:

As children arrive, tape precut paper diamonds on the children's clothing.

Show-and-Tell Center

Teacher Talk
There are many different shapes in God's world.

Resources
diamond shapes children brought from home

Encourage the children to look at the diamond shapes and to describe their characteristics.

Art Center

Teacher Talk
A diamond has four sides. It is the shape of a kite.

Resources
sturdy paper cut into the shape of a kite, straws, tape, yarn, markers

Have the children decorate their kites with markers. When they are done, help them tape straws to the back, horizontally and lengthwise. Help the children tie string to the back where the straws cross, leaving a piece long enough so that the children can fly their kites.

Writing Center

Teacher Talk
A diamond has four sides. It is the shape of a kite.

Resources
templates or stencils of a variety of diamond shapes, paper, pencils

Let the children trace the diamond shapes and use them to create a design.

Shape Center

Teacher Talk
A diamond has four sides. It is the shape of a kite.

Resources
pieces of yarn, paper, glue, pictures of diamonds (or diamond cutouts)

Set out the diamond shapes, yarn, paper, and glue. Let the children use the yarn to create the shape displayed. Let the children glue the yarn in place.

Math Center

Teacher Talk
There are many different shapes in God's world.

Resources
collection of the five shapes discussed this week cut from different colors of construction paper

Let the children sort the shapes by type or color. They can use the shapes to make patterns.

Manipulatives Center

Teacher Talk
A diamond has four sides. It is the shape of a kite.

Resources
play dough, pictures of diamonds, plastic knives

Have the children try to form the play dough into the shape of a diamond.

Cooking Center

Teacher Talk
A diamond has four sides. It is the shape of a kite.

Resources
paper plates, napkins, plastic knives, bread cut into diamond shapes, jam

Let the children use knives to spread jam on their "diamonds" and then eat their creations.

Worship Center

Teacher Talk
There are many different shapes in God's world.

Resources
children's Bible, landscape-type pictures that show effects of blowing wind

Encourage the children to look at the pictures and discuss what is happening.

Say: We can't see the wind, but we know it is there because we can feel it or see leaves and kites blowing. God is like the wind. We can't see God, but we know God is there.

Pray: Thank you, God, for wind and for being with us all the time, even if we can't see you. Amen.

Wonder Time

A diamond can fly high,
A diamond can fly high,
It has four sides
and looks like a kite,
A diamond can fly high.

Call the children together for wonder time.

Wonder Question: I wonder what makes kites stay up in the sky?

Say: Today is the last day of shapes week. The shape we are learning about today is a diamond. A diamond has four sides, like a rectangle and a square, but it looks like a kite. (*Hold up a rectangle, square, and diamond to compare.*)

Sing: "A Diamond Can Fly High" to the tune of "The Farmer in the Dell." Have the children hold their kites (made in the Art Center) up in the air and wave them back and forth as they sing.

Read the Bible verse.

Say: We can't see the wind, and we can't see God, but we know they are there. The wind makes our diamond-shaped kites fly high, and God loves us every day.

Pray: Thank you, God, for diamond-shaped kites and for the wind. Thank you for loving us. Amen.

Open the Bible to Psalm 18:10.

Say: "God traveled on the wings of the wind" (Psalm 18:10, *Good News Bible*, adapted).

Have the children repeat the Bible verse.

Group Fun

Resources

posterboard cut into five- by three-inch diamonds, five-inch squares of aluminum foil, 24-inch lengths of yarn; plastic "jewels," sequins, or glitter; glue, paper punch

Let the children make diamond necklaces. Give each child a diamond shape and a square of aluminum foil. Have the children wrap the foil around the diamond shape. The children can punch a hole at the top of the shape and string the yarn through the hole. Encourage the children to decorate their diamond necklaces as desired with the glue and "jewel" items.

Optional: Extend the activity by making crowns to wear. Give each child additional diamonds to decorate with foil and "jewels." Provide posterboard cut into rectangles to fit the children's heads or use "sentence strips." The children can glue their "diamonds" on the crowns. Teachers can staple the crowns in place. (Make sure the staples point away from the child's head.)

Goodbye Circle

Let the children talk about the things they enjoyed doing today. Hold up a diamond and ask the children to name the shape. Ask each child to point out a shape in the room and to name the shape.

Pray: Thank you, God, for so many different shapes and people. Amen.

Evaluation

Was each child able to identify a diamond? Is each child able to identify and name the shapes focused on this week? Make plans to provide additional learning time with those children who had difficulties, because being able to name basic shapes is a skill that will be helpful for children when they begin kindergarten.

ALPHAPHABET FUN WITH BOOKS

This week's lessons are about letter names and sounds. The children will participate in a variety of alphabet activities by focusing on a specific children's book each day. Each day will include five or six special letters of the day. Encourage the children to bring in objects from home that start with those special letters. This lesson is not intended to teach the alphabet in one week, but to reinforce the ongoing language arts program in your classroom.

Lesson 11

Clifford

Teacher Talk:

When we put letters together, they can make words.

Every letter has a special sound.

The letter __ sounds like ___.

The Bible uses letters and words to tell stories that teach us about God.

Goals:

To help the children learn letter names and letter sounds.

To help children learn that letters are put together to make words.

To expose the children to a variety of children's literature.

Objectives:

By the end of this session the children will:

Listen to the "Book of the Day."

Write or trace a "letter of the day."

Name an object that begins with a "letter of the day."

Faith Connections

Bible verse: Friends always show their love. (Proverbs 17:17, *Good News Bible*)

Preschool children are developing their minds as they learn about letters and words. They also are developing relationships with other children and need opportunities to work together and to think of others.

Teacher's Prayer

Dear God, help me to think of the needs of my children above my own needs. Be with me as I try to model love and caring for others. Amen.

Center Time

Set up your centers as described on pages 6–9. For this lesson add the following:

As children arrive, ask the children to bark like a very small dog. Then have the children bark like a very big dog.

Art Center

Teacher Talk

Every letter has a special sound.

Resources

Clifford ears (see page 210), paper, markers, posterboard, scissors, stapler, glue

Encourage the children to pretend to be *Clifford, the Big Red Dog*. Before class, photocopy the "Clifford ears" (see page 210) for each child. Cut posterboard into one- or two-inch strips long enough to fit around each child's head. Set out the ears, markers, scissors, staplers, and glue. The children can color the ears and headbands. Help the children staple the ears to the headband. Then staple the headband around each child's head.

Letters Center

Teacher Talk

The letter __ sounds like __ .

Resources

paper, markers, table, objects from home (or collected by teacher) starting with the letters of the day

Write the letters A, B, C, D, E, one letter per sheet of paper. Hang the letters over a table. Encourage the children to name the objects and tell what letter they start with. The children can move the objects near the letter they start with.

Worship Center

Teacher Talk

The Bible uses letters and words to tell stories that teach us about God.

Resources

children's Bible, assortment of children's books about God and the Bible

Set out the children's Bible and books. Let the children look at the books and pictures.

Say: One way we can learn about God is by reading or hearing stories about God. The Bible is full of stories that teach us about God and what God wants us to do.

Pray: Thank you, God, for giving us a special book to learn about you. Amen.

Writing Center

Teacher Talk

When we put letters together, they can make words.

Resources

paper, postcards, old greeting cards, pencils, index cards, marker

Write the following words on index cards: *Clifford, big, dog, Emily Elizabeth*. Underline the C, b, d, and E. Hang the cards over the writing table. The children can write letters or cards to Clifford or a friend, or they can copy the words on the cards.

Math Center

Teacher Talk

When we put letters together, they can make words.

Resources

paper, marker, assortment of dog bones, 2 to 3 dog dishes (or dog bones cut from a variety of construction paper, and cereal bowls)

Write the words *dog bones* on paper and hang them over the center. Set out the dog bones and the bowls. Let the children sort the dog bones by color or size, and put them into the bowls.

Dramatic Play Center

Teacher Talk

When we put letters together, they can make words.

Resources

old white shirts, doctor kits, stuffed dogs, blankets

The children can use the materials provided to pretend to be veterinarians and help "sick" dogs.

Science Center

Teacher Talk

When we put letters together, they can make words.

Resources

paper, books about different kinds of dogs or pets

Write the word *dog* and *pet* and hang over the center. Let the children look through the books.

Open the Bible to Proverbs 17:17.

Say: "Friends always show their love" (Proverbs 17:17, *Good News Bible*).

Have the children repeat the Bible verse.

Wonder Time

Call the children together for wonder time.

Wonder Question: I wonder how we can show love to a friend?

Say: Today's book is about a girl named Emily Elizabeth who has a pet named Clifford. Clifford is a big red dog who is Emily Elizabeth's friend.

Play: "Doggie, Doggie, Where's Your Bone?". You will need a cardboard dog bone with the letter "B" written on it. Have the children sit in a circle with one child sitting in the center of the circle. That child is the "doggie." Place the bone on the floor behind the doggie. The doggie should have his or her eyes closed. Motion to a child to pick up the bone and place it behind him or her. Have the children say, "Doggie, Doggie, where's your bone?". The doggie gets three guesses to determine who has the bone. Continue to play, letting the children take turns being the doggie.

Sing: "C Is for Clifford" to the tune of "C is for Cookie."

Read the Bible verse.

Say: Clifford and Emily Elizabeth are good friends. We can be good friends to each other here too. The Bible tells us that friends always love one another.

Pray: Thank you, God, for good friends. Amen.

C Is for Clifford

C is for Clifford, that's good
enough for me.
C is for Clifford, that's good
enough for me.
C is for Clifford, that's good
enough for me.
Clifford, Clifford, Clifford.

Group Fun

Resources

large sheet of paper, posterboard, or chalkboard; markers or chalk

Make a dog comparison chart. After reading the story, review with the children the things Clifford does in the book. List the things Clifford does. Then for each item on the list, ask the children how Clifford is different from most dogs.

Example:

Clifford	Most Dogs
brings back a stick and a police officer	only bring back a stick

Goodbye Circle

Let the children talk about the things they enjoyed doing today. Point out the letters of the day, "A, B, C, D, E" and encourage each child to name a letter and a word that starts with that letter.

Pray: Thank you, God, for letters, words, and friends like Clifford. Amen.

Evaluation

Was each child able to name the letters of the day? Was each child able to make the letter sound? Was each child able to name an object that began with a letter of the day? Make note of the children's abilities and find ways to help them meet the goals and objectives.

Lesson 12

Little Red Riding Hood

Goals:

To help the children learn letter names.

To help the children learn letter sounds.

To help children learn that letters are put together to make words.

To expose the children to a variety of children's literature.

Objectives: By the end of this session the children will:

Listen to the "Book of the Day."

Write or trace a "letter of the day."

Name an object that begins with a "letter of the day."

Faith Connections

Bible verse: God is my helper.

(Psalm 54:4)

In the story of Little Red Riding Hood, the little girl had a helper. Children need the opportunity to know that they have a helper too—God is always with them and able to help them when they need it.

Teacher's Prayer

Dear God, strengthen me as I try to help each of the children in my class when they struggle. Be with me and give me the words to teach them that you are their best helper—a helper who is always there and loves them. Amen.

Teacher Talk:

When we put letters together, they can make words.

Every letter has a special sound.

The letter __ sounds like ___ .

The Bible uses letters and words to tell stories that teach us about God.

Center Time

Continue the centers from Lesson 11.
For this lesson add or change the following:

Cooking Center

Teacher Talk

The letter __ sounds like __ .

Resources

resealable sandwich bags, toasted "O" cereal, chocolate chips, raisins, measuring cups

Set out the bags. Place each food in a separate bowl with a small measuring cup. Let the children place a scoop of each food into the bag to make a "Little Red Riding Hood trail mix." The trail mix can be placed in the Art Center.

Art Center

Teacher Talk

Every letter has a special sound.

Resources

paper plates, staplers, markers and crayons, paper cut in two- by twelve-inch strips

Have the children make Little Red Riding Hood baskets. Let each child use markers and crayons to decorate the back of a paper plate. Help the children fold the plate in half and staple the rim together, leaving the top open. Let each child staple a strip to the top of the plate to make a handle for the basket. If the children made the trail mix (see Cooking Center), let them place the bags of trail mix inside their baskets.

Building Center

Teacher Talk

When we put letters together, they can make words.

Resources

craft sticks, paper, marker, glue

Use the marker to write the letter "H" on a piece of paper. Encourage the children to use the craft sticks to make the letter. Then let the children glue the craft sticks together however they wish.

Tell the children that in the story of Little Red Riding Hood, the woodcutter helped Little Red Riding Hood. *Helped* and *Hood* start with the letter "H."

As children arrive, have a recording of "Peter and the Wolf" playing.

Letters Center

Teacher Talk

The letter __ sounds like __ .

Resources

paper, markers, table, objects from home (or collected by teacher) that start with today's letters

Write "F, G, H, I, J," one letter per sheet of paper. Hang the letters over the table. Encourage the children to name the objects and tell what letter they start with. The children can move each object near the letter it starts with.

Writing Center

Teacher Talk

When we put letters together, they can make words.

Resources

index cards, markers, paper, pencils, tracing paper

Write "Little Red Riding Hood" on index cards, one word per card. Underline the "H." Let the children trace the letters or words, or they can write letters to Little Red Riding Hood, the grandmother, the woodcutter, or even the wolf.

Worship Center

Teacher Talk

The Bible uses letters and words to tell stories that teach us about God.

Resources

children's Bible, picture of Jesus with children

Set out the Bible. Hang the picture of Jesus nearby. Let the children look through the Bible.

Say: Sometimes I wish I had a helper. Maybe you do too. I always feel better when I remember that God is my helper and yours. God gave us a special person to love us and help us—Jesus.

Pray: Thank you, God, for helping us and for giving us Jesus to help us too. Amen.

Wonder Time

Call the children together for wonder time.

Wonder Question: I wonder who can help us if we have a big problem?

Say: In today's story Little Red Riding Hood has a big problem, and a helper comes just when she needs it.

Sing: "Little Red Riding Hood" to the tune of "Twinkle, Twinkle, Little Star." Have index cards, one per child, with the letter "H" written on them. Give each child a card with an "H." Name the letter and practice its sound. Tell the children that they are going to sing about Little Red Riding Hood. When they say "Hood" or "helper," they are to emphasize the "H" sound and hold up the letter.

Little Red Riding Hood

Little Red Riding Hood
Took a basket in the woods,
Visited Grandma, saw a
wolf.
A helper scared off that
bad wolf.
Little Red Riding Hood
Took a basket in the woods.

Read the Bible verse.

Say: Little Red Riding Hood's helper was a woodcutter. We have an even better helper who is always there when we need help: God.

Pray: Thank you, God, for being our helper. Amen.

Open the Bible to Psalm 54:4.

Say: "God is my helper" (Psalm 54:4).

Have the children repeat the Bible verse.

Group Fun

Resources

cardboard boxes (cereal, cake mix, and others of similar sizes), construction paper (green and brown), scissors, tape, glue, cassette/CD player, cassette/CD, red scarfs or red streamers

Help the children build a forest. Encourage the children to cut or tear the construction paper and tape or glue the pieces to the boxes to make trees. Set the trees on the floor and on chairs around the room to make a forest.

When the forest is built, play music from the cassette/CD and encourage the children to use the scarfs or streamers to dance through the forest like Little Red Riding Hood.

Goodbye Circle

Let the children talk about the things they enjoyed doing today. Point out the letters "F, G, H, I, J" and encourage each child to name a letter and a word that starts with the letter.

Pray: Thank you, God, for letters, words, and special helpers. Amen.

Evaluation

Was each child able to name the letters of the day and make the letter sounds? Was each child able to name an object of the letter of the day? Make plans to help those children who are having difficulties.

Lesson 13

Miss Mary Mack

Teacher Talk:

When we put letters together, they can make words.

Every letter has a special sound.

The letter __ sounds like ___ .

The Bible uses letters and words to tell stories that teach us about God.

Goals:

To help the children learn letter names.

To help the children learn letter sounds.

To help children learn that letters are put together to make words.

To expose the children to a variety of children's literature.

Objectives: By the end of this session the children will:

Listen to the "Book of the Day."

Write or trace a "letter of the day."

Name an object that begins with a "letter of the day."

Faith Connections

Bible verse: Worship the LORD with joy.

(Psalm 100:2, *Good News Bible*)

Preschool children need the opportunity to know that God loves them and wants them to enjoy life. The book of the day is filled with joy and enthusiasm, just as the worship of God should be.

Teacher's Prayer

Dear God, thank you for another opportunity to share joy and love with the children in my care. Be with each one of us as we strive to worship you with all the joy in our hearts. Amen.

Center Time

Continue the centers from Lessons 11 and 12. For this lesson add the following centers:

As children arrive, say: "Pretend you are an elephant, and swing your trunk as you walk to a center."

Art Center

Teacher Talk

Every letter has a special sound.

Resources

black and purple construction paper; scraps of black, silver, and purple collage materials; silver glitter, glue, scissors

Encourage the children to use the materials to make a collage of Miss Mary Mack colors.

Cooking Center

Teacher Talk

The letter __ sounds like __ .

Resources

table, chairs, paper plates, napkins, plastic knives, peanut butter, crackers

Let the children use knives to spread peanut butter on the crackers and enjoy their snacks—something an elephant might like to snack on.

Letters Center

Teacher Talk

The letter __ sounds like __ .

Resources

paper, markers, table, objects from home (or collected by teacher) that start with today's letter

Write "K, L, M, N, O" on paper, one letter per sheet of paper. Hang the letters. Encourage the children to name the objects and tell what letter they start with. The children can set the objects under the letter they start with.

Writing Center

Teacher Talk

When we put letters together, they can make words.

Resources

index cards, paper, pencils

Write the words *elephant* and *zoo* on index cards. Hang them where the children can see them. Let the children write the words or write letters to Miss Mary Mack.

Science Center

Teacher Talk

When we put letters together, they can make words.

Resources

books about elephants, "Ranger Rick" magazines, "ZooBooks" (or any type of magazine and book about animals and elephants)

Let the children look at the books and magazines.

Water Table Center

Teacher Talk

The letter __ sounds like __ .

Resources

water table with water (or several dishpans with water), plastic zoo-type animals, towels, washcloths

Encourage the children to wash the animals, like Miss Mary Mack washed the elephant.

Worship Center

Teacher Talk

The Bible uses letters and words to tell stories that teach us about God.

Resources

children's Bible, cassette/CD player, cassette/CD of children's Bible songs, rhythm instruments

Set out the Bible. Play the cassette/CD. Set out the rhythm instruments. Let the children play the rhythm instruments with the music.

Say: God loves when we worship with joy. One way to do that is by playing music and singing.

Pray: Thank you, God, for loving happy sounds and loving me. Amen.

Open the Bible to Psalm 100:2.

Say: "Worship the LORD with joy" (Psalm 100:2, *Good News Bible*).

Have the children repeat the Bible verse.

Wonder Time

Call the children together for wonder time.

Wonder Question: I wonder how high an elephant can jump?

Say: In today's story Miss Mary Mack goes to the zoo to watch the elephants jump. She and the elephant have a wonderful day together, and finally the elephant comes to live with her!

Play: "Elephant Jump."

Read the Bible verse.

Say: Miss Mary Mack and her elephant friend had a very happy day together. They were so happy they jumped with joy. We can be very happy too—we have good friends here, and we have fun together. We know God loves us. The Bible tells us to worship God with joy.

Pray: Thank you, God, for wanting us to be happy. Amen.

Elephant Jump

Have the children stand in a line.

Say: We are going to try jumping, like Miss Mary Mack and the elephant did. I will tell you how to jump, and then we will all try it.

Have the children jump in the following manner: short jump, high jump, soft jump, loud jump, silly jump.

Group Fun

Resources

alphabet letters, copies of Braille pages (available from Braille Institute, Federation for the Blind), American Sign Language alphabet *(see page 224)*

Help the children learn about different kinds of alphabets. Before class begins, photocopy the sign language for the letters (see page 224). Point out the alphabet letters that the children have been learning. Focus on the letters of the day. Pass the Braille pages for the children to touch. Explain their use. Talk about how the children would learn the alphabet if they could not hear. Teach sign language for letters of the day: "K, L, M, N, O."

Goodbye Circle

Let the children talk about the things they enjoyed doing today. Point out the letters of the day: "K, L, M, N, O." Encourage each child to name a letter and a word that starts with the letter.

Pray: Thank you, God, for friends. Thank you for the different kinds of alphabet and for days filled with joy and your love. Amen.

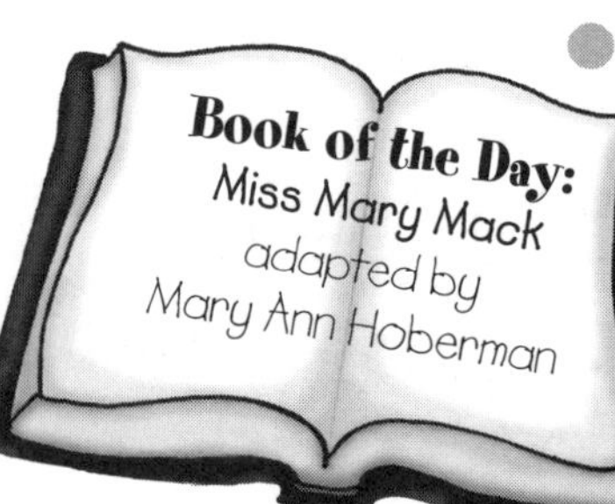

Evaluation

Was each child able to name the letters of the day and make the letter sounds? Was each child able to name an object of the letter of the day? Make note of those children who may still be having difficulties, and make plans to help them reach the objectives.

Lesson 14

The Little Engine That Could

Goals:

To help the children learn letter names.

To help the children learn letter sounds.

To help children learn that letters are put together to make words.

To expose the children to a variety of children's literature.

Objectives:

By the end of this session the children will:

Listen to the "Book of the Day."

Write or trace a "letter of the day."

Name an object that begins with a "letter of the day."

Faith Connections

Bible verse: I can do all things through Christ who strengthens me.

(Philippians 4:13, adapted)

Preschool children encounter new experiences and new opportunities on a daily basis. The book of the day and this verse are an opportunity for them to learn that even if something is difficult, they can do it if they try—and God and God's Son, Jesus, will help them.

Teacher's Prayer

Dear God, be with me when things are difficult. Help me to remember to keep trying, and with your help I can do anything. Amen.

Teacher Talk:

When we put letters together, they can make words.

Every letter has a special sound.

The letter __ sounds like ___ .

The Bible uses letters and words to tell stories that teach us about God.

Center Time

Continue the centers from Lessons 11-13. For this lesson add or change the following:

As children arrive, say: "You are special. You can do many things."

Writing Center

Teacher Talk

When we put letters together, they can make words.

Resources

stencils or outlines of alphabet letters, paper, pencils

Let the children trace or outline the alphabet letters. Help the children find today's letters.

Dramatic Play Center

Teacher Talk

Every letter has a special sound.

Resources

tickets, luggage, hats, old jackets, chairs, paper and pencils

Let the children play "train station." They can make tickets or use those provided. They can make "signs" for the station.

Letters Center

Teacher Talk

The letter __ sounds like __ .

Resources

paper, markers, table, objects from home (or collected by teacher) that start with today's letters

Write "P, Q, R, S, T" on paper, one letter per sheet of paper. Hang the letters over the table. Let the children name the objects and tell what letter they start with. Children can set the objects under the letter they start with.

Art Center

Teacher Talk

Every letter has a special sound.

Resources

paper, black and gray paint, paintbrushes, paint smocks

Let the children create "smokestack" designs or "smoky pictures" with the materials.

Math Center

Teacher Talk

Every letter has a special sound.

Resources

craft sticks, black spray paint or permanent black marker

Before class, spray paint craft sticks black or color the craft sticks with a black permanent marker. Encourage the children to make train tracks or other patterns with the craft sticks.

Building Center

Teacher Talk

When we put letters together, they can make words.

Resources

blocks, empty shoeboxes, plastic or small stuffed animals

Let the children use the blocks and boxes to make train tracks, train stations, and trains for the animals to ride in.

Worship Center

Teacher Talk

The Bible uses letters and words to tell stories that teach us about God.

Resources

children's Bible, train engine and cars

Let the children look at the Bible and pictures. The children can play with the train and cars.

Say: This train has to pull all these cars up and down mountains and for long distances. It needs special fuel to help it do such a hard job. We need help on hard jobs too. We need the Bible and God. No matter what we have to do, God is with us.

Pray: Thank you, God, for helping us whenever we need you. Amen.

Wonder Time

Call the children together for wonder time.

Wonder Question: I wonder how a very little train could make it up a very big hill?

Say: In today's story, **The Little Engine That Could**, a little blue engine pulls a great big train all the way up and over a great big hill. The engine could pull the train because it tried very hard.

Sing: "I'm a Train" to the tune of "Head, Shoulders, Knees and Toes." Have the children walk around in a circle with arms bent and pumping.

I'm a Train

I'm a choo-choo train.
I'm a train.
I'm a choo-choo train.
I'm a train.
I ride in the sun.
I ride in the rain.
I'm a choo-choo train.
I'm a train!
(Have the children continue walking, saying: "Chugga chugga chugga chugga choo choo!")

Read the Bible verse.

Say: Sometimes we have to do very hard things, too, just like the little blue engine in the story. But we have God and Jesus to help us when we need help.

Pray: Thank you, God, for helping us when we have something very hard to do. Thank you for Jesus. Amen.

Open the Bible to Philippians 4:13.

Say: "I can do all things through Christ who strengthens me" (Philippians 4:13, adapted).

Have the children repeat the Bible verse.

Group Fun

Resources

egg cartons, colored construction paper, buttons, beads, chenille stems, scissors, yarn, crayons, glue

Help the children make egg carton trains. Before class, cut the egg cartons lengthwise to create six-section pieces. Set out the egg carton sections and other materials. Help the children as needed to create "trains" with the materials provided.

Goodbye Circle

Let the children talk about the things they enjoyed doing today. Point out the letters of the day, "P, Q, R, S, T" and encourage each child to name a letter and a word that starts with the letter.

Pray: Thank you, God, for helpers, and for being with us whenever we need you. Amen.

Book of the Day:
The Little Engine That Could
by Watty Piper

Evaluation

Was each child able to name the letters of the day and make the letter sounds? Make plans to help any child who was not able to meet the day's objectives.

Lesson 15

Chicka Chicka Boom Boom

Teacher Talk:

When we put letters together, they can make words.

Every letter has a special sound.

The letter __ sounds like ___ .

The Bible uses letters and words to tell stories that teach us about God.

Goals:

To help the children learn letter names.

To help the children learn letter sounds.

To help children learn that letters are put together to make words.

To expose the children to a variety of children's literature.

Objectives: By the end of this session the children will:

Listen to the "Book of the Day."

Write or trace a "letter of the day."

Name an object that begins with a "letter of the day."

Faith Connections

Bible verse: Sing a new song to the LORD.

(Psalm 98:1, *Good News Bible*)

Learning new things and having new experiences can be fun. Making new friends and playing with friends can be exciting. Preschool children live in a world where everything is new and exciting. They need to know that new things can be good, and that God is with them in every new adventure.

Teacher's Prayer

Dear God, be with me as I embark on this new day and this new adventure with the children in my class. Help me to sing "a new song" with them, as we learn together and come closer to you. Amen.

Center Time

Continue the centers from Lessons 11-14. For this lesson add or change the following:

Art Center

Teacher Talk

The letter __ sounds like __ .

Resources

paper, tempera paint, paint smocks, palm leaves or paper cut in the shape of palm leaves

Let the children use the palm leaf brushes to paint or make designs on the paper.

Cooking Center

Teacher Talk

Every letter has a special sound.

Resources

paper plates, pieces of coconut cut from a whole coconut, small pitcher of coconut milk, paper cups, whole coconut cut open

Encourage the children to look at the inside of the coconut and taste the coconut and milk.

Writing Center

Teacher Talk:

The letter __ sounds like __ .

Resources

variety of alphabet letters cut from sandpaper, paper, pencils, tape

Tape the sandpaper letters to the table. Have the children lay the paper on top of a letter and rub over the letter with the pencil to make a letter rubbing. Have the children name the letters that they use. The children can also write letters on the paper.

Science Center

Teacher Talk

Every letter has a special sound.

Resources

whole coconut, magnifying glass, balance scale with selection of weights

Encourage the children to explore the coconut by touching it, shaking it, looking at it up close, and by weighing it.

As children arrive, help each child identify the first letter of her or his name.

Letters Center

Teacher Talk

The letter __ sounds like __ .

Resources

paper, markers, table, objects from home (or collected by teacher) that start with today's letters

Hang the letters from the previous days. Add "U, V, W, X, Y, Z." Have the children name the objects and tell what letter they start with. The children can set the objects under the letter they start with.

Alphabet Clothesline Center

Teacher Talk

Every letter has a special sound.

Resources

clothesline (or heavy string) strung across room, clothespins, index cards, paper, markers, crayons

Write the letters of the alphabet on the cards, one letter per card. Hang the cards. Encourage the children to hang the alphabet cards in order on the line.

Worship Center

Teacher Talk:

The Bible uses letters and words to tell stories that teach us about God.

Resources:

children's Bible, whole coconut, apple, orange, banana

Encourage the children to look through the Bible and examine the fruits.

Say: Some of these fruits are things you know and eat often. Some of them may be new. God made many different kinds of fruits and many other things in the world that are new to us. God made all things because God loves you and me.

Pray: Thank you, God, for making new things for us and for the old things we already know. Amen.

Open the Bible to Psalm 98:1.

Say: "Sing a new song to the LORD" (Psalm 98:1, *Good News Bible*).

Have the children repeat the Bible verse.

Wonder Time

Alphabet Prayer Song

Thank you, God, for a, b, c,
And all the letters up to z.
For apples, balls, and
cookies too.
Thanks for friends like you
and you. (*Point to others in the room.*)
Thank you, God, for a, b, c,
And all the letters up to z.

Call the children together for wonder time.

Wonder Question: I wonder why God created so many fun new things to do in the world?

Say: In today's book, Chicka Chicka Boom Boom, the alphabet letters all get together to play and climb trees. It's a silly, fun book to read, and it's a fun way to learn our alphabet.

Play: "Letter Match" with the children. Before class begins, write uppercase and lowercase letters on index cards, one letter per card. Use markers in a variety of colors, but use the same color for the uppercase and lowercase of each letter. Have the children sit in a circle, and set the cards on the floor in front of you. Encourage the children to find the "match" for a card you hold up. Make sure each child has a chance to play.

Read the Bible verse.

Say: We can learn to sing new songs, learn new games to play, and lots of other new things. We can pray to God with words, or pray by singing to God. Let's pray with music now. Listen to what I sing, and then repeat each line after me.

Sing a prayer: Alphabet Prayer Song to the tune of "Twinkle, Twinkle, Little Star."

Group Fun

Resources

index cards, marker, paper punch, yarn, scissors

Play Chicka, Chicka, Boom, Boom with the children. Before class, write a letter of the alphabet on each card. Give each child a card and have him or her punch a hole on top of the card. The children can then string yarn through the hole to make an alphabet letter necklace to wear. Encourage the children to wear their letter cards as you read (or reread) the story.

Goodbye Circle

Let the children talk about the things they enjoyed doing today. Point out the letters of the day, "U, V, W, X, Y, Z" and encourage each child to name a letter and make its sound.

Pray: Thank you, God, for new songs and for learning new things. Amen.

Evaluation

Was each child able to name each of the alphabet letters this week? Did each child meet the objectives? Make plans to help those children who are having difficulty learning the alphabet or the letter sounds.

NUMBERS

Preschool children need the opportunity to develop problem-solving skills. They are developmentally ready to learn counting, matching, patterning, and other number-related skills. During this week's activities the children will participate in a variety of number activities through learning center activities, games, songs, and books.

This lesson is intended to reinforce number skills that are an ongoing part of your classroom program, as well as to introduce some new number-related activities.

Lesson 16

Counting Fun

Goals:

To help the children discover problem-solving skills.

To develop number ideas, including one-to-one correspondence, classification, comparison, patterns, and sequences.

To count to ten and understand number concepts.

Objectives: By the end of this session the children will:

Find examples of numerals in magazines.

Correctly count assorted objects aloud.

Correctly use the terms: fast, faster, fastest.

Faith Connections

Bible verse: Jesus grew both in body and in wisdom.

(Luke 2:52, *Good News Bible*)

Preschool children may have difficulty connecting the baby Jesus at Christmas with the grown man in the New Testament. They need to know that Jesus was once a child and learned many new things—just like them.

Teacher's Prayer

Oh, God, be with me as I help the young children in my class grow in body, wisdom, and knowledge about you. Amen.

Teacher Talk:

We use numbers every day for many things.

We can learn new things.

What do you think we should do next?

If you think of the biggest number in the world, God loves you even more than that.

Center Time

Set up your centers as described on pages 6–9. For this lesson add the following:

As children arrive, play "Ten in a Bed" from **Wee Sing Silly Songs** (Price Stern Sloan, 1986).

Calendar Center

Teacher Talk

We use numbers every day for many things.

Resources

large calendar with days marked and empty spaces for dates, set of numbers for dates, tape; or laminated calendar, dry erase markers

Display the calendar. Circle the day's date on the calendar. Let the children attach the day's date or write it on the class calendar. Use this each day this week.

Art Center

Teacher Talk

We use numbers every day for many things.

Resources

paper, magazines, scissors, glue

Have the children find numerals in the magazines, cut or tear them out, and glue them on paper as a collage. Precut the numbers for younger children.

Writing Center

Teacher Talk

We can learn lots of new things.

Resources

index cards, pencils, paper, envelopes

Write each child's name and address on an index card. Help the children find their own address cards. They can copy the card, write their address on the envelope, and write a letter.

Building Center

Teacher Talk

What do you think we should do next?

Resources

collection of assorted sizes of blocks

Let the children build anything they wish, but have them count each block as they use it. Have the children see how many blocks they can count and use to build something.

Math Center

Teacher Talk

We use numbers every day for many things.

Resources

collection of interesting objects to count, such as feathers, rubber fishing worms (without hooks), shells, pebbles; containers

Let the children count each group of objects and mix or sort the objects into the containers.

Cooking Center

Teacher Talk

We can learn lots of new things.

Resources

paper plates, marker, toasted "O" cereal, raisins, chocolate chips, pretzels

Before class, use a marker to divide each plate into four sections. Number each section one through four. The children can choose from the foods, and they can count out the correct number for each section and place them on the plate—then eat their snack.

Worship Center

Teacher Talk

If you think of the biggest number in the world, God loves you even more than that.

Resources

children's Bible, large jar filled with some type of small object (popcorn kernels or dried beans, for example)

Let the children look through the Bible and move the jar to look at the contents.

Say: That jar is full of ____. If we counted the ___, how many do you think there would be? There sure would be a lot! Well, no matter how many ___ are in that jar, that number is much smaller than how much God loves you.

Pray: Thank you, God, for loving us so much. Amen.

Wonder Time

Call the children together for wonder time.

Wonder Question: I wonder why God wants us to grow big and learn new things?

Say: When we were born, we were just little babies, like Jesus was. We couldn't walk or talk. Now we are bigger, and we can do lots more things. It's fun to learn new things and to grow bigger and bigger.

Encourage the children to talk about the different kinds of things they have learned.

Play: "Roll Over."

Read the Bible verse.

Say: Each of you is growing too, just like Jesus did. You are getting bigger and learning new things. This week we are going to learn lots of new things about numbers.

Pray: Thank you, God, for helping us grow and learn new things. Amen.

Roll Over

Set out an area rug or a large piece of paper from a roll of paper. Tell the children that it is the "bed." Have the children lie on the bed and practice rolling, like in the song and story. Sing the song while rolling, if desired.

Open the Bible to Luke 2:52.

Say: "Jesus grew both in body and in wisdom" (Luke 2:52, *Good News Bible*).

Have the children repeat the Bible verse.

Group Fun

Resources

empty coffee cans with lids, sand, aquarium gravel, washers, tape, paper, markers, one- by four-inch boards

Let the children play rollover races. Before class, cut paper to fit the outside of the cans. Give each child a can, lid, and paper. The children can use the markers to decorate the paper, then tape the paper on the can. Allow the children to choose which material (sand, gravel, washers) they wish to put inside their can. Tape the lid on the can. Set the boards with one end elevated to make inclined planes. The children can place their cans at the top of the boards and allow them to roll down the boards. Have rolling races. Discuss which cans are faster. Be sure to use the terms *fast*, *faster*, and *fastest*.

Goodbye Circle

Let the children talk about the things they enjoyed doing today. Have the children crouch down, count backwards from ten to one, and yell "Blast off!" as they jump in the air.

Pray: Thank you, God, for helping us learn new things today. Amen.

Evaluation

Was each child able to meet the day's objectives? Make plans to help those children who were not able to meet the objectives.

Lesson 17

Patterns All Around Us

Teacher Talk:

We use numbers every day for many things.

We can learn lots of new things.

What do you think we should do next?

God provides for all of our needs.

Goals:

To help the children discover problem-solving skills.

To develop number ideas, including one-to-one correspondence, classification, comparison, patterns, and sequences.

To count to ten and understand number concepts.

Objectives: By the end of this session the children will:

Recognize and copy a simple pattern.

Practice counting.

Faith Connections

Bible verse: Jesus took the seven loaves and the fish, gave thanks to God, gave them to the disciples; and the disciples gave them to the people.

(Matthew 15:36, *Good News Bible*, adapted)

Numbers are everywhere. Preschool children need to see numbers as figures that represent real objects, and they need the opportunity to manipulate objects to learn number skills. This verse also shows that Jesus recognized and modeled the importance of prayer. Children need to learn that prayer is a way to talk to God and to thank God for what we have been given.

Teacher's Prayer

Thank you, God, for the blessings you have given me in the shape of the children in my class. Help me to see each child as a blessing, and give me the skills I need to bring each one closer to you. Amen.

Center Time

Continue the centers from Lesson 16.
For this lesson add or change the following:

As children arrive, point out any patterns that the children may have on their clothing.

Math Center

Teacher Talk

We can learn lots of new things.

Resources

beads, strings, parquetry blocks, pegboards and pegs

Before class, make several patterns with the objects listed above. You may string beads on several strings in different patterns, or set out the blocks or pegboards with sample patterns for the children to copy. Encourage the children to use the materials to copy the sample patterns, then to try to create patterns of their own.

Cooking Center

Teacher Talk

What do you think we should do next?

Resources

paper plates, plastic knives, crackers, peanut butter or soft cream cheese, raisins

Set out the plates and knives and foods. Encourage the children to spread peanut butter or cream cheese on their crackers, then to make patterns on the spread with the raisins. Let the children eat the patterns they created.

Writing Center

Teacher Talk

We can learn lots of new things.

Resources

paper, marker, pencils

Before class, create several patterns on pieces of paper for the children to copy. This will help the children learn prewriting skills.

' / ' / ' / ' / ' / '
o O o O o O o O o
- / - / - / - / - / -

Encourage the children to use the paper and pencils to copy the patterns, and then to create patterns and/or letters of their own.

Art Center

Teacher Talk

We use numbers every day for many things.

Resources

paper, variety of stamps, smocks, tempera paint, paper towels, shallow tray; or nonpermanent stamp pad

Provide nonpermanent ink pads or make paint pads. Fold paper towels and place them in the bottom of a shallow tray. Pour tempera paint on the paper towels. Encourage the children to use the stamps and paint or ink to create patterns on their paper.

Manipulatives Center

Teacher Talk

We can learn lots of new things.

Resources

variety of different shapes of blocks, index cards, marker

Before class, trace each shape of block on an index card, making several copies of each shape. If desired, laminate the cards to make them more durable. Encourage the children to make a pattern with the cards, then to copy the pattern using the blocks.

Worship Center

Teacher Talk

God provides for all of our needs.

Resources

loaf of bread uncut on plate

Set the bread on a plate on a table.

Say: When we are tired, we need to sleep. When we are thirsty, we need to drink. When we are hungry, we need to eat. God provided nighttime for sleep, water to drink, and foods to eat. Let's thank God for everything God has given us.

Pray: Thank you, God, for taking care of us. Amen.

Open the Bible to Matthew 15:36.

Say: "Jesus took the seven loaves and the fish, gave thanks to God, gave them to the disciples, and the disciples gave them to the people" (Matthew 15:36, *Good News Bible*, adapted).

Have the children repeat the Bible verse.

Wonder Time

Call the children together for wonder time.

Wonder Question: I wonder how much food it would take to feed four thousand people?

Say: Four thousand is a very big number. It would take a lot of food to feed them all. But Jesus fed all of them with seven loaves of bread and a few fish.

Read the Bible verse.

Say: Jesus could feed that many people with just a little food because Jesus is God's Son. Before Jesus and everyone ate, Jesus said a prayer to God. That's what we do too.

Pray: Thank you, God, for food and friends, and for helping us learn new things. Amen.

Say: It makes me happy to know that God loves us and takes care of us. We are going to sing a special song now to show how happy we are. We'll make music too, while we sing.

Sing: "If You're Happy and You Know It" (with word changes).

If You're Happy and You Know It

Give each child a rhythm instrument. Tell the children to play their instruments each time they count to ten.

If you're happy and you know it,
count to ten.
1-2-3-4-5-6-7-8-9-10.
(Play instruments.)
If you're happy and you know it,
count to ten.
1-2-3-4-5-6-7-8-9-10.
(Play instruments.)
If you're happy and you know it,
And you really want to show it;
If you're happy and you know it,
count to ten.
1-2-3-4-5-6-7-8-9-10.
(Play instruments.)

Group Fun

Resources

none

Explain to the children that they will copy each movement you make seven times. Ask the children to take turns choosing an action they would like to do. Continue the activity until all the children have had a turn naming a movement. Count aloud as you do each movement. Suggestions for movements include clapping, touching your nose, sitting down, and jumping up and down.

Goodbye Circle

Let the children talk about the things they enjoyed doing today. Ask each child to clap seven times.

Pray: Thank you, God, for school and for learning new things. Amen.

Evaluation

Was each child able to count and clap to seven? Was each child able to recognize and repeat a pattern? Make plans to help those children who are having difficulty meeting the day's objectives.

Lesson 18

Counting: Time and Money

Goals:

To help the children discover problem-solving skills.

To develop number ideas, including one-to-one correspondence, classification, comparison, patterns, and sequences.

To count to ten and understand number concepts.

Objectives: By the end of this session the children will:

Name three different coins.

Count aloud to twelve.

Faith Connections

Bible verse: God called the light Day, and the darkness God called Night.

(Genesis 1:4-5, adapted)

Preschool children know the difference between night and day, and they know what clocks are. They know that clocks tell time, and they frequently ask what time it is. They know that money is used to buy things. They need the opportunity to begin to learn about telling time and to learn about the different types of coins. They also need to know that God created time, day, and night, and that all things are gifts from God.

Teacher's Prayer

Dear God, it never feels as if there is enough time in the day. Be with me as I spend time with the children in my class. Help me as I try to teach them that time is a gift from you to be enjoyed and used to its fullest. Amen.

Teacher Talk:

We use numbers every day for many things.

We can learn lots of new things.

What do you think we should do next?

God loves us and is with us every minute of the day.

Center Time

Continue the centers from Lessons 16-17.
For this lesson add or change the following:

As children arrive, ask, "Is it day or night?"

Math Center

Teacher Talk

We use numbers every day for many things.

Resources

collection of coins: quarters, dimes, nickels, and pennies; four different containers

Set out the coins in a pile with the empty containers nearby. Have the children sort the coins. Talk about the names of the different coins.

Art Center

Teacher Talk

We can learn lots of new things.

Resources

coins, index cards, paper, crayons, double-sided tape

Tape coins to index cards, one coin per card, or tape the coins to the table (to prevent them from moving). Tape at least two sets of each coin, so the children can rub the front and back of each coin. Have the children place the paper over the coins and use the side of the crayons to make rubbings. The children can make a collage of rubbings on one piece of paper if they choose.

Dramatic Play Center

Teacher Talk

We use numbers every day for many things.

Resources

play money, cash register, empty containers and boxes of food, stickers for pricing, pencils, old coupons, old purses and wallets

Let the children play "Grocery Store." They can mark prices on the foods with the stickers and pencils and use the money and coupons to shop.

Clock Center

Teacher Talk

We can learn lots of new things.

Resources

selection of different kinds of clocks that work, broken clock

Display the working clocks so the children can see them move. Let the children explore the inside workings of the broken clock.

Writing Center

Teacher Talk

We use numbers every day for many things.

Resources

old clock, crayons, paper plate or paper circle

Display a clock at the writing table at the children's eye level. Provide a paper plate or paper circle for each child. Have the children use the crayons to write the numbers 1 through 12 on the plates or circles to make clock faces.

Worship Center

Teacher Talk

God loves us and is with us every minute of the day.

Resources

clock with second hand

Set the clock on a table so the children can see the second hand move.

Say: Every time the little hand moves, some time has passed. All day long, time passes as we do different things. Sometimes we eat, sometimes we sleep, sometimes we learn, and sometimes we play. No matter where we are or what we are doing, God loves us all the time.

Pray: Thank you, God, for loving us every second, minute, and hour of the day. Amen.

Wonder Time

Call the children together for wonder time.

Wonder Question: I wonder what it would be like if we didn't have night and day?

Say: There are things that we can do at daytime, and things that we only do at night. One thing we can only do at night is see the stars.

Sing: "Twinkle, Twinkle, Little Star"

Read the Bible verse.

Say: God provided day and night because God loves us and knows what we need.

Pray: Thank you, God, for loving us and for giving us the things we need—like day and night and stars and time.

Twinkle, Twinkle, Little Star

Twinkle, twinkle, little star,
How I wonder what you are.
Up above the world so high;
Like a diamond in the sky.
Twinkle, twinkle, little star,
How I wonder what you are.

Open the Bible to Genesis 1:4-5.

Say: "God called the light Day, and the darkness God called Night" (Genesis 1:4-5, adapted)

Have the children repeat the Bible verse.

Group Fun

Resources

rhythm instruments (with at least one triangle), low chair (or stool)

Say the rhyme "Hickory, Dickory Dock." Tell the children they are going to take turns acting out the rhyme and playing instruments. Let one child be a clock and one be a mouse. Give each remaining child a rhythm instrument. The child who is the clock stands on the floor, while the rest stand in a circle around him or her. The mouse stands next to the chair (which is next to the "clock"). Help the children repeat the rhyme (adapted). When the children say "tick-tock," they should play their instruments. The mouse stands on the chair to go "up the clock" and gets off the chair to "run down." When the clock strikes one, only the children with a triangle play—striking the instrument one time. Practice the actions, then do the rhyme with the actions.

Hickory, dickory dock, tick-tock
The mouse ran up the clock, tick-tock.
The clock struck one.
The mouse ran down.
Hickory, dickory dock, tick-tock.

Repeat the activity, giving the children a chance to play different parts and different instruments.

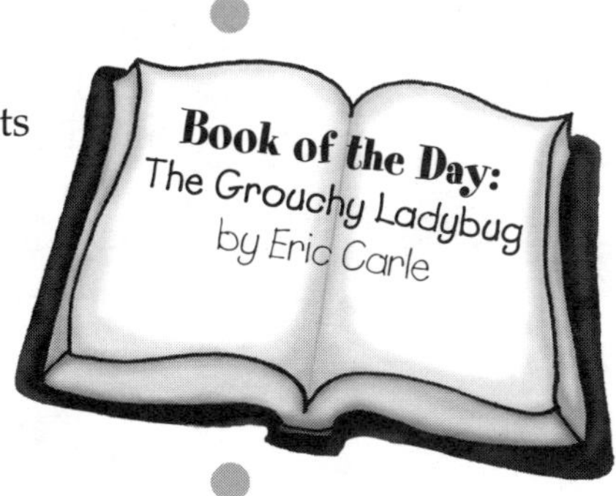

Goodbye Circle

Let the children talk about what they enjoyed. Have them count to twelve. Hold up coins. Let each child name the coin you are holding.

Pray: Thank you, God, for daytime with friends here at school, and nighttime to sleep. Amen.

Evaluation

Was each child able to meet the day's objectives? Are there children who have difficulty sitting still? Make note of each child's abilities, and make plans to help those children who are having trouble meeting the day's objectives.

Lesson 19

Measurements

Teacher Talk:

We use numbers every day for many things.

We can learn lots of new things.

What do you think we should do next?

God loves each one of us, no matter what size we are.

Goals:

To help the children discover problem-solving skills.

To develop number ideas, including one-to-one correspondence, classification, comparison, patterns, and sequences.

To count to ten and understand number concepts.

Objectives:

By the end of this session the children will:

Use a measuring device to measure an object provided.

Put a set of objects in order, based on size.

Faith Connections

Bible verse: God said to Noah, "Build a boat and make it 450 feet long, 75 feet wide, and 45 feet high." Noah did everything that God commanded.

(Genesis 6:15, 22; *Good News Bible*, adapted)

Preschool children are learning the concept of size and measurement. They need the opportunity to explore these concepts through concrete use of measuring tools and different sizes of objects. Preschool children need to know that measurements are important—Noah had to use the specific measurements that God gave him to make the ark.

Teacher's Prayer

Dear God, the children in my class are growing and learning. Help me as I teach them the things they need to know to be strong followers of Christ. Amen.

Center Time

Continue the centers from Lessons 16-18. For this lesson add or change the following:

Math Center

Teacher Talk

What do you think we should do next?

Resources

construction paper in a variety of colors, scissors

Before class, cut paper into a variety of basic shapes of different sizes. The children can sort the shapes and place them in order according to size.

Art Center

Teacher Talk

We can learn lots of new things.

Resources

rolls of adding machine tape, heavy yarn, scissors, markers, crayons, stickers

Hang rolls of adding machine tape from the ceiling using heavy yarn, or lay the rolls on the floor. When the children visit the center, pull the tape down to the child's feet and cut the paper to match the child's height (or roll the tape along the child as the child lies on the floor). Let the children decorate their body tape.

Writing Center

Teacher Talk

We can learn lots of new things.

Resources

straws, paper, pencils, alphabet printed on paper

Before class, cut several straws into one-inch pieces. Let the children look at the letters on the paper and write one or more letters on their paper, then use the "inch straws" to measure their letters.

Cooking Center

Teacher Talk

We use numbers every day for many things.

Resources

licorice "whips," ruler, napkins

Set licorice on the table next to a ruler. Have the children measure a piece of licorice, then eat it.

As children arrive, encourage each child to say his or her age and to show how many that is by holding up the correct number of fingers.

Building Center

Teacher Talk

We use numbers every day for many things.

Resources

variety of blocks

Let each child take a turn lying on the floor while another child sets blocks to measure the child's length. The children can work together to build block "towers" to specific heights: belly button height, knee height, shoulder height (no higher than a child's shoulder).

Measuring Center

Teacher Talk

We use numbers every day for many things.

Resources

craft sticks, bathroom scale

Have the children use craft sticks to measure objects in the room. The children can take turns standing on the scale to be weighed.

Worship Center

Teacher Talk

God loves each one of us, no matter what size we are.

Resources

children's book about Noah's ark (suggestion: *Noah's Ark*, by Peter Spier), yardstick

Set out the book opened to the picture of the ark. Set the yardstick nearby.

Say: When God told Noah to build a boat, God told Noah exactly how big to make it. Noah had to measure the wood and follow the directions that God gave him. The size of the ark was important. But God loves each one of us, no matter what size we are. The size of a person isn't important to God. Each person is special.

Pray: Thank you, God, for sizes that are important and sizes that aren't. Amen.

Open the Bible to Genesis 6:15, 22.

Say: "God said to Noah, 'Build a boat and make it 450 feet long, 75 feet wide, and 45 feet high.' Noah did everything that God commanded" (Genesis 6:15, 22; *Good News Bible*, adapted).

Have the children repeat the Bible verse.

Wonder Time

Call the children together for wonder time.

Wonder Question: I wonder why God made so many different sizes of people and things?

Say: Each one of you is different and special. Some of us are tall, and some are not—just like some of us have brown hair, and some do not.

Play: "Growing Up."

Read the Bible verse.

Say: Sometimes size is important. God wanted Noah to build the ark a very special size, so God told him exactly how big to build it. Sometimes size isn't important—God loves each one of us, no matter what size we are.

Pray: Thank you, God, for all different kinds of sizes. Amen.

Growing Up

Have the children repeat the words and do the actions with you.

Crouch down small.
(Start from standing position; crouch as small as possible.)
Stand up tall.
(Jump up and stretch arms high over head.)
Spread your arms out wide,
(Extend arms straight out to the sides.)
Now bring them to your side.
(Press arms tight to your side).
Take one step, two steps, three steps, four.
(March in place with hands on hips.)
If we're not tall yet, we'll grow some more!
(Place hands on top of head, then jump high.)

Group Fun

Resources

none

Lead the children in a scavenger hunt. Tell the children they are going to search the room for things that are special sizes. Give the directions one at a time. Have the children look for:

- Something as long as their finger.
- Something they can hug with both arms.
- Something as tall as they are.
- Something as long as their foot.

Have the children bring each object back to the circle or name the object and demonstrate its size.

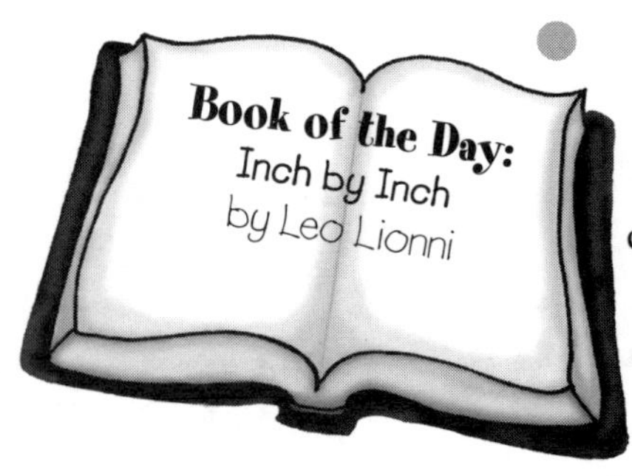

Goodbye Circle

Let the children talk about the things they enjoyed. Ask them to jump up as high as they can and then crouch as small as they can.

Pray: Thank you, God, for the special size you made each one of us. Amen.

Evaluation

Were the children able to discuss and use the terms small and smaller, or big and bigger? Was each child able to correctly demonstrate his or her age by holding up fingers? Make plans to help any children who did not meet the day's objectives.

Lesson 20

More Number Fun

Goals:

To help the children discover problem-solving skills.

To develop number ideas, including one-to-one correspondence, classification, comparison, patterns, and sequences.

To count to ten and to understand number concepts.

Objectives: By the end of this session the children will:

Sort objects provided.

Make number books.

Faith Connections

Bible verse: Jesus said, "Even the hairs of your head are all counted."

(Matthew 10:30, adapted)

Every preschool child is different. They come in all shapes, sizes, colors, and abilities. You probably have a variety of different types in your classroom. As their teacher, the preschool children in your class expect you to spend time with them, help them, and love them just the way they are. They need to know that they are special to you. They especially need to know that each one of them is special to God, who knows everything there is to know about them—even the number of hairs on their heads.

Teacher's Prayer

Dearest Lord, you know me and my needs, and you love me. You have created so many different special people—some of whom are in my care today. Help me to love them and get to know them even better. Amen.

We use numbers every day for many things.

We can learn lots of new things.

What do you think we should do next?

God knows you and loves you.

Center Time

Continue the centers from Lessons 16-19. For this lesson add the following:

Estimation Station

Teacher Talk

We use numbers every day for many things.

Resources

clear glass jar with marbles inside (between ten and thirty), paper, pencil

Set the jar with the marbles inside on a table. Encourage the children to look at the jar and to guess how many marbles are in the jar. Write each child's guess on a piece of paper.

Math Center

Teacher Talk

We use numbers every day for many things.

Resources

empty muffin tins; variety of objects to sort, such as buttons, beads, or golf tees

Encourage the children to sort the objects into piles in the muffin tins.

Art Center

Teacher Talk

We use numbers every day for many things.

Resources

paper, marker, small pieces of yarn, cotton balls, glue

Before class, draw large outlines of the numbers 1 through 5. Photocopy the numbers to provide copies for each child. Set out the yarn and cotton balls. Encourage the children to glue the materials inside the numeral outlines.

Building Center

Teacher Talk

We can learn lots of new things.

Resources

a variety of different shaped blocks

Have the children sort the blocks according to shapes, then use just one shape to build structures.

Writing Center

Teacher Talk

We use numbers every day for many things.

Resources

index cards, paper, pencils

Before class, write each child's phone number on an index card labeled with the child's name. Set the cards on the table. Have the children copy their phone numbers on the paper.

Home Living Center

Teacher Talk

We can learn lots of new things.

Resources

silverware tray, assorted flatware

Set out the tray and flatware. Encourage the children to sort the flatware into the silverware tray.

Worship Center

Teacher Talk

God knows you and loves you.

Resources

hanging or hand mirror

Display the mirror. Encourage the children to look at themselves in the mirror and to describe themselves.

Say: How many eyes do you have? How many ears? Noses? Hands and feet? How many hairs do you have on your head? Some of those things were easy to count, but it would take a very long time to count the hairs on your head. We don't have to, though. God knows you and how many hairs are on your head. God loves you very much.

Pray: Thank you, God, for loving and knowing (*name of child*). Amen.

Wonder Time

Call the children together for wonder time.

Wonder Question: I wonder how we can find out how many marbles are in this jar? (Hold up jar from "Estimation Station.")

Say: We can count the marbles in the jar. Let's count together. (Count the marbles and compare the guesses to the actual number.)

Sing: "If You're Happy and You Know It."

Read the Bible verse.

Say: It would be very hard to count all the hairs on our heads. But God already knows what the number is. God knows everything about each one of us and loves each of us very much.

Pray: Thank you, God, for knowing and loving each one of us. Amen.

If You're Happy and You Know It

If you're happy and you know it,
count to ten.
1-2-3-4-5-6-7-8-9-10.
(Play instruments.)
If you're happy and you know it,
count to ten.
1-2-3-4-5-6-7-8-9-10.
(Play instruments.)
If you're happy and you know it,
And you really want to show it;
If you're happy and you know it,
count to ten.
1-2-3-4-5-6-7-8-9-10.
(Play instruments.)

Open the Bible to Matthew 10:30.

Say: "Jesus said, 'Even the hairs of your head are all counted'" (Matthew 10:30, adapted).

Have the children repeat the Bible verse.

Group Fun

Resources

paper, markers, pencils, stapler, numbers 1 through 5 written on paper, variety of collage materials, scissors, glue

Help each child make a number book. Display the written numbers at the children's eye level. Give each child five sheets of paper. Help the children as needed to write a number on each page, using the numbers 1 through 5. Set out the collage materials. Have the children glue on the number of objects represented by the numeral printed on each page. When the pages are completed, help the children staple the edges together to make a book.

Goodbye Circle

Let the children talk about the things they enjoyed doing today. Call out a number between one and ten to each child, and have the child jump the number of times you directed.

Pray: Thank you, God, for knowing us, caring for us, and loving us. Amen.

Evaluation

Was each child able to meet the day's objectives? If any child has had difficulty with the number concepts during the week, make plans to help him or her meet the objectives.

Unit 2

The Earth Is Growing

Goals:

1. The children will learn that plants grow from seeds.

2. The children will participate in a variety of activities that will help them learn what seeds need in order to grow.

3. The children will explore fruits, vegetables, flowers, and trees.

4. The children will to use different senses to explore plant life.

5. The child will learn the importance of taking of the world.

This month the children will have the opportunity to explore how things grow. Spring is filled with new life and growth. These lessons help the children understand that the new life we see in the spring comes from God.

God cares for the earth and for the things that grow on the earth. Use these lessons as an opportunity to help your children learn how they can work with God to take care of the earth.

The Bible tells us that God cares for each one of us even more than God cares for the flowers. Constantly tell your children that God loves them and takes care of them. Model God's love for your children each day.

Bible Stories for This Unit:

Genesis 1 (The Creation)
Genesis 2 (The Garden of Eden)
Matthew 6: 25-34 (The Lilies of the Field)
Matthew 13:31-32 (The Mustard Seed)
Mark 4: 1-9 (The Parable of the Sower)

SEEDS

Most children know that plants grow from seeds, but they probably do not know what a seed is. The purpose of this week's unit is to help children learn more about seeds and planting seeds. The children will participate in a variety of activities that help them learn what seeds need in order to grow, that we eat some types of seeds, and that some seeds travel before they find a place to grow.

Lesson 21

Sprouting Seeds

Goals:

To help children learn what a seed is.

To help children learn what seeds need to grow.

To show that people eat some types of seeds.

To help children learn that there are many different kinds of seeds.

Objectives: By the end of this session the children will:

Plant seeds so they will sprout.

Eat sprouts and recognize that they are eating seeds.

Faith Connections

Bible verse: God commanded, "Let the earth produce all kinds of plants." **(Genesis 1:11, *Good News Bible*, adapted)**

Spring is filled with growing things, new life, and longer days. All new life is a gift of God. Preschool children need the opportunity to learn that all growing things were created by God and that all things start out small and grow larger, just as they are.

Teacher's Prayer

Dear God, thank you for the beauty of this world and for all the growing things in it—especially the children who have been entrusted to my care. Amen.

Teacher Talk:

God made seeds.

Plants grow from seeds.

We can plant seeds and help them grow.

There are some seeds that we eat.

We thank God for seeds.

Center Time

Set up your centers as described on pages 6–9.
To use all week:

As children arrive, have a variety of plants for the children to touch and to care for.

Writing Center

Teacher Talk

Plants grow from seeds.

Resources

paper, pencils

Write the word "Seeds" on a piece of paper. Let the children practice writing the word or the letter "S."

Art Center

Teacher Talk

God made seeds.

Resources

birdseed, paper plates, bottles of glue, shallow container

Place birdseed in a large shallow container. Give each child a paper plate. Let the children make designs on the plates with the glue. Have the children sprinkle birdseed over the plate and shake any loose birdseed back into the container. Let the plates dry. Punch holes in the tops of the plates and tie yarn through the holes to make hangers.

Estimation Station

Teacher Talk

How many seeds do you think are inside this?

Resources

plate with dry bean seeds and a fresh bean pod, paper and pencil

Let the children look at the bean seeds and bean pod. Have them guess how many seeds are inside the pod. Record each child's guess.

Cooking Center

Teacher Talk

There are some seeds that we eat.

Resources

paper plates, well-washed sprouts, tongs

Let the children use tongs to pick up the sprouts to put on their plate and taste.

Math Center

Teacher Talk

Plants grow from seeds.

Resources

four or five small plastic pots, dried beans, tweezers, paper, marker, tape

Mark each pot with a number from one to ten. Set the empty pots on a table. Place beans in a shallow container. Let the children use fingers or tweezers to place the correct number of beans in each pot.

Science Center

Teacher Talk

Plants grow from seeds.

Resources

bag of dried beans, plastic knives, paper plates

The night before class, soak enough beans so each child will have two or three to examine. Set the beans on the children's plates. Let the children peel the seed coats or use plastic knives to examine inside the beans. Let the children eat the beans after they examine them.

Worship Center

Teacher Talk

God made seeds.

Resources

variety of bean seeds (do not use treated seeds—buy dried beans from a food store), pictures of a variety of bean plants (from seed catalogs or seed packages)

Display each bean seed next to a picture of the plant. Let the children examine the seeds and plants.

Say: There are many types of plants in the world. On the table are a few examples. Every plant in the world was created by God. When God created the world, God made plants so people would have food and beautiful things.

Pray: Thank you, God, for creating so many wonderful plants for us to use and enjoy. Amen.

Wonder Time

Call the children together for wonder time.

Wonder Question: I wonder what a seed is?
Say: A seed is a little plant that has not started to grow yet. God created seeds so that all kinds of different plants could grow.
Sing: "Do You Know" to the tune of "Do You Know the Muffin Man?"
Read the Bible verse.
Say: When God created the world, God created plants. God made seeds so the plants could grow.
Pray: Thank you, God, for plants and seeds. Amen.

Do You Know

Do you know
that God made seeds,
God made seeds,
God made seeds?
Do you know
that God made seeds
so all kinds of plants
could grow?

Open the Bible to Genesis 1:11.

Say: "God commanded, 'Let the earth produce all kinds of plants'" (Genesis 1:11, *Good News Bible*, adapted).

Have the children repeat the Bible verse.

Group Fun

Resources

resealable plastic bags, dried beans, open container, paper towels, water, marker

Help the children plant sprouting bags. Place beans in an open container. Give each child a plastic bag and a paper towel. Label each child's bag. Help each child dampen the paper towel and fold it to fit inside the plastic bag. Have the children lay their bags with the paper towel inside flat on a table or on the floor. Each child can then take three or four dried beans and set them on top of the paper towel. Help the children squeeze the air out of the bags and seal the bags tightly shut. Bags can be set on a windowsill or taped to a window with the seeds in view. The children can watch the seeds through the plastic bags.

Teacher Tip: When the seeds have sprouted, the children can eat the sprouts or plant the sprouted seeds in a container of dirt (or outside in a garden).

Or make a class sprout jar. Place about one tablespoon of seeds in a glass quart canning jar. Add enough water to completely cover the seeds. Cover the opening of the jar with cheesecloth and secure with a rubber band. Soak overnight at room temperature. The next day, pour off excess water through the mesh and add fresh water to thoroughly rinse the seeds. Drain the water. Rinse and drain the sprouts twice a day. In between rinsings, set them in a moderately warm area. The sprouts will be ready in a few days.

Goodbye Circle

Let the children talk about the things they enjoyed today. Open the bean pod and count the seeds together, then compare the number with the children's guesses. Ask each child to name something that grows from a seed. Repeat the Bible verse.

Pray: Thank you, God, for all the seeds that you created. Amen.

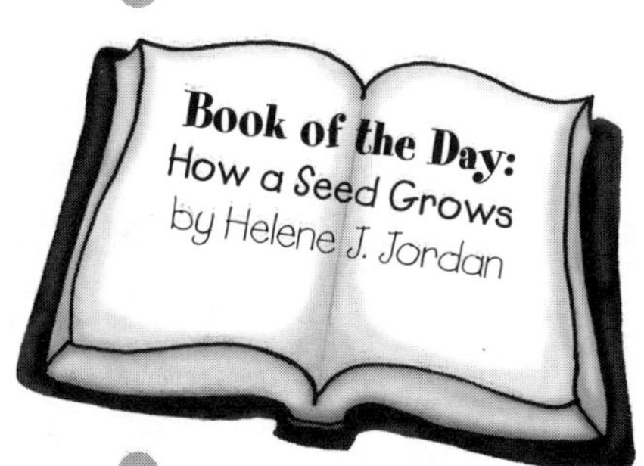

Evaluation

Was each child able to follow directions to create his or her "sprout bag"? Were children able to sit and listen to the story? Make plans to help those children who did not meet the day's objectives.

Lesson 22

Growing Seeds; Exploring Dirt

Teacher Talk:

God made seeds.

Plants grow from seeds.

We can plant seeds and help them grow.

Seeds need good dirt to grow.

We thank God for seeds.

Goals:

To help children learn what a seed is.

To help children learn what seeds need to grow.

To show that people eat some types of seeds.

To help children learn that there are many different kinds of seeds.

Objectives:

By the end of this session the children will:

Plant seeds so they will grow.

Say things seeds need so they can grow.

Faith Connections

Bible verse: Some seeds fell in good soil, and the plants sprouted and grew.

(Mark 4:8, *Good News Bible*, adapted)

Seeds need some sort of medium to grow in, and they need very specific mediums to grow well. Just as seeds need good soil to grow, preschool children need "good soil" also. As their teacher, you need to provide a place for the children in your care to learn and to grow. As you teach your class about growing seeds, you will also be modeling God's love for each of them.

Teacher's Prayer

Dear God, help me to provide the "good soil" that the children in my care need to grow and flourish as strong members of your world. Amen.

Center Time

Set up your centers as described in Lesson 21. Add or change the following:

Art Center

Teacher Talk

God made seeds.

Resources

seed packets, construction paper, paste or glue, crayons or markers

Give each child a piece of construction paper. Have the children draw grass at the bottom of their papers. Then have the children draw stems growing out of the grass. Let the children glue the seed packets at the tops of the stems to make blossoms.

Estimation Station

Teacher Talk

How many seeds do you think are inside this?

Resources

apple, apple seeds, paper and pencil

Let the children look at apple seeds and the apple. Have them guess how many seeds are in the apple. Record each guess.

Cooking Center

Teacher Talk

Seeds need good dirt to grow.

Resources

container of chocolate pudding, chocolate sandwich cookies, paper plate, small cups, serving spoon, plastic spoons

Let the children spoon a small amount of pudding into a cup, then use their hands to break a chocolate cookie into small pieces over the paper plate and stir the pieces into their pudding. Let them eat their "dirt cups."

Science Center

Teacher Talk

Plants grow from seeds.

Resources

three plastic dishpans, shovels, potting soil or topsoil, sand, "poor soil" or gravel

Fill each dishpan partly full with the soil, one type per container. Let the children explore the soils.

As children arrive, place a flower sticker on each child's clothing or on the back of each child's hand.

Seed Display

Teacher Talk

Plants grow from seeds.

Resources

variety of flower seeds, picture of each type of flower you have seeds for (from catalogs or seed packages)

Display each seed next to a picture of the plant. Let the children examine the seeds and plants.

Math Center

Teacher Talk

Plants grow from seeds.

Resources

craft sticks, dried beans, glue

Make a set of seed-counting sticks by gluing beans on craft sticks to represent the numbers 1 to 12. Let the children arrange the sticks in numerical order. Ask the children to name each number as he or she moves a stick.

Worship Center

Teacher Talk

God made seeds.

Resources

table or altar, seeds in a shallow bowl, container of "good soil," watering can with water, children's Bible

Set the items on the table with the soil and water next to the plant and the Bible nearby.

Say: Which things on the table do the seeds need to grow? Seeds need dirt, sunshine, and water so they can grow. We need sunshine and water too, but we need something else that seeds don't need: We need the Bible so we can learn about God and grow to be the kind of people God wants you and me to become.

Pray: Thank you, God, for creating dirt for seeds to grow and for giving us the Bible so we can grow too. Amen.

Open the Bible to Mark 4:8.

Say: "Some seeds fell in good soil, and the plants sprouted and grew" (Mark 4:8, *Good News Bible*, adapted).

Have the children repeat the Bible verse.

Wonder Time

Call the children together for wonder time.

Wonder Question: I wonder why seeds grow in dirt?

Say: Seeds need dirt to grow in because there is a special kind of food in dirt that is just for seeds. They need water and sunshine too. We're going to sing a song that will help us remember what seeds need so they can grow.

Sing: "What Seeds Need" to the tune of "Twinkle, Twinkle, Little Star."

Read the Bible verse.

Say: God provided everything we need so we can help seeds grow. We just need to remember to take care of the seeds and plants that God gave us.

Pray: Thank you, God, for giving us what we need so we can help seeds grow. Amen.

What Seeds Need

Seeds need dirt; seeds need light.
Seeds need water so they'll grow right.
If you want your seeds to grow,
This is what you need to know.
Seeds need dirt; seeds need light.
Seeds need water so they'll grow right.

Group Fun

Resources

paper or plastic foam cups or small pots (one per child), potting soil, water, marigold seeds, pencil, crayons, permanent markers, newspaper, smocks

Help the children plant flower seeds. Use the pencil to poke several holes in the bottom of the cups if using paper or plastic foam cups. Cover the table or floor with newspaper and have the children wear smocks. Allow the children to decorate their pots or cups with the markers. Watch the children so they do not stain their clothing because the markers are permanent. (Washable markers will run when containers become damp.)

Help the children fill their containers with soil, working over the newspaper-covered area. Let the children sprinkle marigold seeds over the soil, then cover the seeds lightly with soil. The children can then lightly water their plants and place their pots in a sunny area. Have the children check their plants daily to care for them.

Goodbye Circle

Let the children talk about the things they enjoyed doing today. Cut open the apple and count the seeds together, then compare the number with the children's guesses. Ask each child to name one thing seeds need to grow. Repeat the Bible verse.

Pray: Dear God, help our plants grow, and help us grow too. Amen.

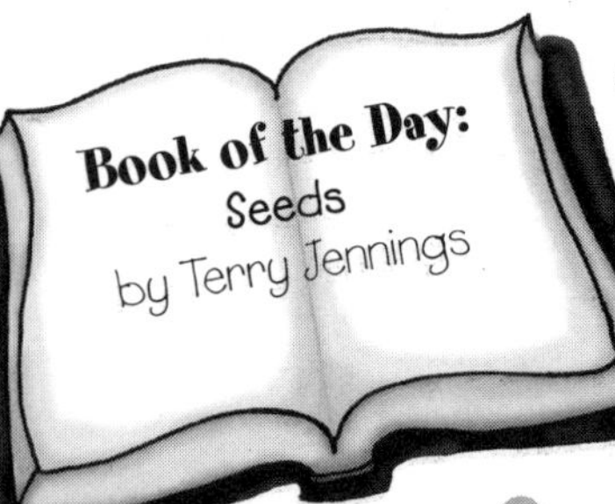

Evaluation

Was each child able to follow directions to plant his or her seed? Was each child able to name one thing seeds need in order to grow? Make note of children who did not achieve the day's objectives, and plan how to help them.

Lesson 23

Seeds You Can Eat

Goals:

To help children learn what a seed is.

To help children learn what seeds need to grow.

To show that people eat some types of seeds.

Objectives: By the end of this session the children will:

Help plant mustard seeds.

Eat several different foods and recognize that they are seeds.

Faith Connections

Bible verse: The mustard seed is the smallest of all seeds, but when it grows up, it is the biggest of all plants.

(Matthew 13:32, *Good News Bible*, adapted)

The children in your class are growing, but not every child is growing at the same rate. Each child is different, and you may have children who have physical limitations. It is important to emphasize that God has a special plan for each person. God plans for the mustard seed to grow very large, and God has plans for each child in your class—and for you.

Teacher's Prayer

Dearest Lord, help me to listen to your voice and your word, so I will know the plans you have for me. Help me to teach each of the children in my care that you have a plan for him or her, and that your plan is as special as each one of them. Amen.

Teacher Talk:

God made seeds.

Plants grow from seeds.

We can plant seeds and help them grow.

There are some seeds that we eat.

We thank God for seeds.

Center Time

Set up your centers as described in Lessons 21-22.
Add or change the following:

As children arrive, tape mustard seeds to small squares of construction paper. Then tape a square to each child's clothing.

Art Center

Teacher Talk

God made seeds.

Resources

birdseed, paper cups, wide masking tape, markers, stickers

Have each child decorate two cups with markers and stickers. Let the children place a small amount of birdseed inside each cup. Help each child tape the cups together to make a "seed shaker." (Be sure the cups are thoroughly taped.)

Estimation Station

Teacher Talk

How many seeds do you think are inside this?

Resources

baby food jar with ten to twenty sunflower seeds inside, picture of sunflower, paper, pencil

Show the children the jar with the seeds and the sunflower picture. Let the children guess how many seeds are in the jar. Record each guess.

Cooking Center

Teacher Talk

There are some seeds that we eat.

Resources

paper plates, edible seeds (cooked peas and beans, roasted sunflower and pumpkin seeds), mustard seeds in a sealed bag and mustard in a bowl with plastic spoons nearby

Set edible seeds on a plate. Let the children taste each variety of seed. Talk about what plants the seeds came from.

Let the children use the spoons to taste a small amount of mustard. Tell the children that the mustard in the dish is made from ground mustard seeds with other seasonings added.

Science Center

Teacher Talk

Plants grow from seeds.

Resources

variety of seeds, magnifying glass

Set seeds in a shallow container. Place a magnifying glass nearby. Let the children touch the seeds and look at them with the magnifying glass. Be careful to only use seeds that can be eaten.

Seed Display

Teacher Talk

Plants grow from seeds.

Resources

mustard seeds (available from gardening stores or health food stores), pumpkin and sunflower seeds, pictures of plants (mustard plant, pumpkin, and sunflower)

Place each seed next to a picture of the plant. Let the children examine the seeds and plants.

Worship Center

Teacher Talk

God made seeds.

Resources

table or altar, pot filled with potting soil, mustard seeds in a shallow bowl, masking tape

Set the pot with soil and the mustard seeds on the table. Place the masking tape nearby.

Say: Jesus talked about the mustard seed in the Bible because it is the smallest seed and grows into the biggest plant. We are going to plant mustard seeds, and you are going to get a "mustard seed bracelet" to help you remember that God loves you and will help you grow.

Have each child place one or two seeds in the pot. Wrap a piece of masking tape, sticky side out, around each child's wrist and have each child place several seeds on the "bracelet."

Pray: Thank you, God, for helping me grow, just like you help the mustard seed grow. Amen.

Wonder Time

Call the children together for wonder time.

Wonder Question: I wonder how a very tiny seed can grow into a very big plant?

Say: God created many kinds of seeds, just like God created many kinds of people. Every single seed and every single person is important.

Sing: "Do You Know" to the tune of "Do You Know the Muffin Man?" Let the children use their seed shakers as they sing the song they learned on Monday. (The last line is changed.)

Do You Know

Do you know that God made seeds,
God made seeds, God made seeds?
Do you know that God made seeds?
Some little and some big.

Read the Bible verse.

Say: God has a special plan for everything God made. God planned for the mustard seed to grow big, and God has special plans for you too.

Pray: Thank you, God, for the special plans you have for me. Amen.

Open the Bible to Matthew 13:32.

Say: "The mustard seed is the smallest of all seeds, but when it grows up, it is the biggest of all plants" (Matthew 13:32, *Good News Bible*, adapted).

Have the children repeat the Bible verse.

Group Fun

Resources

carpet barrel or other large cylinder (or box) large enough for a child to climb into, two-foot-square piece of brown felt, large watering can

Let the children pretend to be seeds. Choose one child to be the "seed" and another to be the "waterer." The "seed" climbs inside the "flowerpot" (cylinder or box), with the felt over the top of the container. The rest of the class stands in a circle around the "flowerpot" and sings the song below to the tune of "Pop Goes the Weasel":

We plant the seed down into the ground.
(*Sing slowly; pretend to pat down seed.*)
Now it needs some water.
(*Child with watering can waters the seed.*)
The sun shines down, the seed starts to grow.
(*Children in circle wave hands in air to act as sunshine; seed stretches arms above head.*)
Pop goes the flower!
(*Seed jumps up high.*)

Repeat several times as time allows, allowing children to play different parts.

Goodbye Circle

Let the children talk about the things they enjoyed doing today. Open the jar and count the seeds inside, then compare the number with the children's guesses. Ask each child to name a seed he or she can eat. Repeat the Bible verse.

Pray: Thank you, God, for all the special kinds of seeds you have made. Amen.

Evaluation

Was each child able to follow directions in order to play the game at the Group Activity? Did each child meet the day's objectives? Make plans to help those children who did not meet the objectives.

Lesson 24

Seeds Can Travel

Teacher Talk:

God made seeds.

Plants grow from seeds.

We can plant seeds and help them grow.

There are some seeds that we eat.

We thank God for seeds.

Goals:

To help children learn what a seed is.

To help children learn what seeds need to grow.

To demonstrate that some seeds travel before they start to grow.

To show that people eat some types of seeds.

Objectives:

By the end of this session the children will:

Name two ways for seeds to grow.

Make blow-paint pictures.

Faith Connections

Bible verse: The LORD will send rain to make your seeds grow.

(Isaiah 30:23, *Good News Bible*, adapted)

Every plant has a special kind of seed or a way to grow. Some seeds are planted on purpose, others travel in unique ways that God has planned. God knows each seed's and each plant's needs and provides for them—through sunlight during the day and rain that falls from the sky. Preschool children need to know that God knows each of their needs and cares for them too. God will provide what they need to grow.

Teacher's Prayer

Thank you, God, for knowing me and my needs. Help me recognize what each of the children in my care needs, and give me the strength and wisdom to meet those needs. Amen.

Center Time

Set up your centers as described in Lessons 21-23. Add or change the following:

As children arrive, have each child blow like the wind. Say, "Some seeds are blown by the wind before they begin to grow."

Science Center

Teacher Talk

Plants grow from seeds.

Resources

several pine cones with seeds, container of water

Set out pine cones. Show the children the winged seeds on each scale of the cone. Let the children sprinkle the open cones with water—after about ten minutes the cones begin to close up. Within an hour the cone will be shut tight.

Dramatic Play Station

Teacher Talk

Plants grow from seeds.

Resources

play gardening tools, plastic or silk flowers, empty seed packets, empty flowerpots, watering can, toy wheelbarrow or wagon

Let the children pretend to plant and care for a garden.

Estimation Station

Teacher Talk

How many seeds do you think are inside this?

Resources

coconut, picture of coconut tree

Let the children look at and shake the coconut. Have them guess how many seeds are in the coconut. Record each child's guess.

Math Center

Teacher Talk

Plants grow from seeds.

Resources

selection of several kinds of seeds in shallow container, egg carton, tweezers

Have the children sort the seeds by shape, color, or size and place each group into a cup in the egg carton.

Art Center

Teacher Talk

God made seeds.

Resources

straws (cut in half), paper, thinned tempera paint, glue, shallow container, plastic spoons, birdseed, table covering, smocks

Cover the table and have the children wear smocks. Have each child drop a small amount of paint on his or her paper. Show the children how to blow through a straw to make colorful designs. Let the children glue seeds to their papers.

Tell the children that God plans for some seeds to be blown by the wind.

Seed Display

Teacher Talk

Plants grow from seeds.

Resources

selection of seeds that "travel": maple seeds (blow in air), coconut (float in water), pine cone and dandelions (seeds blow in the wind), acorn (squirrels carry away), and pictures of each seed when it is grown into a plant

Display each type of seed next to a picture of the plant. Encourage the children to examine the seeds. Discuss how each seed can "travel."

Worship Center

Teacher Talk

God made seeds.

Resources

table or altar, plant, seeds

Set the plant and seeds on the table.

Say: God provided for plants to grow, and God takes care of those plants. Somebody planted seeds to grow this plant, but God made some seeds that can travel on the wind or in the water to get to a place where they can grow. God takes care of each little seed, and God takes care of you.

Pray: Thank you, God, for taking care of each one of us. Amen.

Open the Bible to Isaiah 30:23.

Say: "The Lord will send rain to make your seeds grow" (Isaiah 30:23, *Good News Bible*, adapted).

Have the children repeat the Bible verse.

Wonder Time

> **"Do You Know"**
>
> Do you know that seeds need rain,
> Seeds need rain, seeds need rain?
> Do you know that seeds need rain—
> And God helps them to grow?

Call the children together for wonder time.

Wonder Question: I wonder if seeds can grow without anyone planting them?

Say: God created a wonderful and exciting world with all different kinds of plants and seeds. We can plant seeds and help them grow. But some seeds can travel and be planted without our help. Some blow in the wind, some float on the water, and some are carried by animals. God made them all, and God made sure to provide rain so each seed could grow.

Sing: "Do You Know" to the tune of "Do You Know the Muffin Man"? (This is a new verse to song sung earlier this week.)

Read the Bible verse.

Say: No matter how the seeds travel to where they are planted, they need sun, and they need to be watered. God made sure to take care of the seeds—and God takes care of us.

Pray: Thank you, God, for caring for seeds and especially for caring for us. Amen.

Group Fun

Resources

three or four flowerpots, large spoons, plastic bags, rubber bands

Take the class on a nature walk. Divide the class into three or four small groups. Give each group a plastic bag. Take a walk around your building, and collect soil in the bags from four different areas. (Or bring four different soil samples to class and describe where each sample was found.) Have each group pour its soil sample into a flowerpot, using spoons to transfer the dirt. Label the pots to show where the soil came from. Have the children lightly moisten soil in each pot, then cover each pot with a plastic bag (to hold in the moisture). Hold the bag in place with a rubber band. Ask the children if they think anything will grow. Place the pots in a light place and have the children check the plants each day to watch for growth. You should see results within a week.

Goodbye Circle

Let the children talk about the things they enjoyed today. Ask each child to name a seed he or she learned about today. Hold up the coconut and read the children's guesses: The coconut is a seed, so the correct guess is "one." Repeat the Bible verse.

Pray: Thank you, God, for so many wonderful ways seeds get planted. Amen.

Evaluation

Was each child able to meet the day's objectives? Were children able to use the tweezers (fine motor skill) to manipulate the seeds in the Math Center? Make plans to help those children who are having difficulties.

Lesson 25

All Kinds of Seeds

Goals:

To help children learn what a seed is.

To help children learn what seeds need to grow.

To demonstrate that some seeds travel before they start to grow.

To show that people eat some types of seeds.

To demonstrate that there are many different kinds of seeds.

To understand that God created all things—including them.

Objectives: By the end of this session the children will:

Name different plants that have seeds.

Make seed paperweights.

Faith Connections

Bible verse: God looked at everything God had made, and God was very pleased.

(Genesis 1:31, *Good News Bible*, adapted)

When God began creation, there was nothing. Out of that nothing God created this wonderful world we live in, filled with all kinds of living things. As God created each part of the universe, God looked at what was made and was pleased. At the end of the six days of labor, God looked at everything and was very pleased. Preschool children need to learn that God created the universe and all living things—including them. They need to know that God is pleased with each part of God's creation—and God is pleased with them and loves them very much.

Teacher's Prayer

Dear God, thank you for this wonderful world you created, filled with marvelous sights, sounds, and people. Help me to show each child in my care that he or she is loved and valued by you. Amen.

Teacher Talk:

God made seeds.

Plants grow from seeds.

We can plant seeds and help them grow.

There are some seeds that we eat.

We thank God for seeds.

Center Time

Set up your centers as described in Lessons 21-24. Add or change the following:

As children arrive, ask, "Name one thing that we eat that grows from a seed."

Art Center

Teacher Talk

God made seeds.

Resources

seeds, play clay (a type that hardens)

Have the children mold clay into a shape that can be used as a paperweight, whatever shape they choose. Let the children press seeds into the top of the paperweight.

Estimation Station

Teacher Talk

How many seeds do you think are inside this?

Resources

orange, orange seeds, paper and pencil

Let the children look at the orange and orange seeds. Have them guess how many seeds are in the orange. Record their guesses.

Cooking Center

Teacher Talk

There are some seeds that we eat.

Resources

paper plates, slices of cucumber, bananas, plastic knives

Set out bananas, knives, and cucumber slices. Let the children slice the bananas and take cucumber slices to eat. Help the children find seeds in each food (small black dots in the banana).

Math Center

Teacher Talk

Plants grow from seeds.

Resources

break-apart plastic eggs, marker, dry beans or seeds

Mark each egg with a different number from one to ten. Place beans or seeds in a shallow container. Have the children look in each cup and place the correct number of beans or seeds in the cup.

Science Center

Teacher Talk

Plants grow from seeds.

Resources

three pots (one with a newly planted seed, one with a seedling, and one with a large plant), paper, pencils

Let the children look at each pot and discuss what is happening. Have them draw the three stages of the plant's growth.

Seed Display

Teacher Talk

Plants grow from seeds.

Resources

packet of vegetable seeds, packet of flower seeds; acorn, pine cone, and seeds from a maple tree; pictures of each plant you have seeds for

Set each type of seed next to the picture of what it will grow to be. Let the children discuss each seed and what it will be when it is grown.

Worship Center

Teacher Talk

God made seeds.

Resources

variety of healthy plants, selection of seeds

Set the plants on the table. Encourage the children to look at, smell, and touch the plants.

Say: Every plant here is one of God's creations. Each of these seeds has a tiny plant inside, ready to grow. They are God's creations. You were created by God too. God loves everything that God created—and God loves you.

Pray: Thank you, God, for creating plants, seeds, and (*name each child*). Amen.

Wonder Time

Call the children together for wonder time.

Wonder Question: I wonder how many different kinds of seeds there are?

Say: When we look out the window, we can see all kinds of growing things. They all started as seeds. All the plants in this room started as seeds. Let's pretend to be seeds.

Play: "I Am A Seed." Play soft music while the children do the motions.

Read the Bible verse.

Say: God created all the seeds and plants and everything in the world. God made them, and God loves them. God made us, and God loves us too.

Pray: Thank you, God, for making plants and seeds and me. Amen.

I Am a Seed

Have the children stand in a circle and repeat what you say and do.

I am a seed.
(Sit down and curl into a ball.)
When I am planted, my roots begin to grow.
(Straighten out one leg.)
My roots try to drink up water so I can grow.
(Make slurping sounds.)
Pretty soon more roots grow.
(Straighten out the other leg.)
The sun shines on me, and I grow a little bit more.
(Wiggle fingers in air.)
I push up out of the ground.
(Lift head and slowly stand.)
Soon I am a great big plant.
(Spread arms out wide.)

Open the Bible to Genesis 1:31.

Say: "God looked at everything God had made, and God was very pleased" (Genesis 1:31, *Good News Bible,* adapted).

Have the children repeat the Bible verse.

Group Fun

Resources

heavy cardboard or posterboard, construction paper, craft glue, cotton swabs, pencils, variety of seeds

Have the children make seed mosaics. Before class, cut cardboard or posterboard the size of the construction paper. Give each child a piece of construction paper and cardboard. Have the children use glue to cover the cardboard with the paper (or do this ahead of time so the glue can dry). When the glue is dry, have the children draw a shape or picture on the paper. The children can then use the seeds to fill in the shapes or picture by spreading glue over the area and sprinkling seeds over the glue. Have the children spread the glue with the cotton swabs. Encourage the children to use different varieties of seed for different parts of the picture. Be sure to let the "mosaic" dry before moving it.

Goodbye Circle

Let the children talk about things they enjoyed today. Slice open the orange and count the seeds. Compare the number with the estimations. Ask each child to name two things that grow from seeds. Repeat the Bible verse.

Pray: Thank you, God, for loving me and caring for me. Amen.

Evaluation

Was each child able to follow directions to create a seed mosaic? Was each child able to name two things that grow from seeds? Make plans to help those children who were unable to meet the day's objectives.

VEGETABLES AND FRUITS

This week's activities build on the seed study from last week. Children will participate in a variety of activities that allow them to explore and taste an assortment of fruits and vegetables. The activities encourage cooperation and classroom interaction as they expand the children's knowledge about growing things.

On Wednesday you and your children will explore the book **Stone Soup**. That day each child will need to bring in a vegetable, either fresh or canned depending on which option you choose, to be used in making the soup. On Friday you and your children will make a class fruit cup. Each child will need to bring in a piece of fruit that day. See page 223 for notes to photocopy.

Lesson 26

Farms and Farmers

Teacher Talk:

Farmers grow all kinds of food.

Farmers plant seeds and help them grow.

There are many kinds of fruits and vegetables.

God created many different kinds of plants.

Goals:

To help children learn about people who help us have food to eat.

To learn that God created many different kinds of fruits and vegetables.

To help children appreciate a variety of different fruits and vegetables.

Objectives:

By the end of this session the children will:

Name things a farmer does.

Work together to create a garden mural.

Faith Connections

Bible verse: God commanded, "Let the earth produce all kinds of plants." (Genesis 1:11, *Good News Bible*, adapted)

Some children will have never seen or worked in a garden. They may not realize that fruits and vegetables come from farms, not just the grocery store. Preschool children need to have the opportunity to learn about farms and farmers. They need to know that God created plants so people would have food.

Teacher's Prayer

O God, creator of all things, thank you for the food you provide for our bodies. Help me to feed the minds and spirits of the children in my care. Amen.

Center Time

Set up your centers as described on pages 6-9. For this lesson add the following:

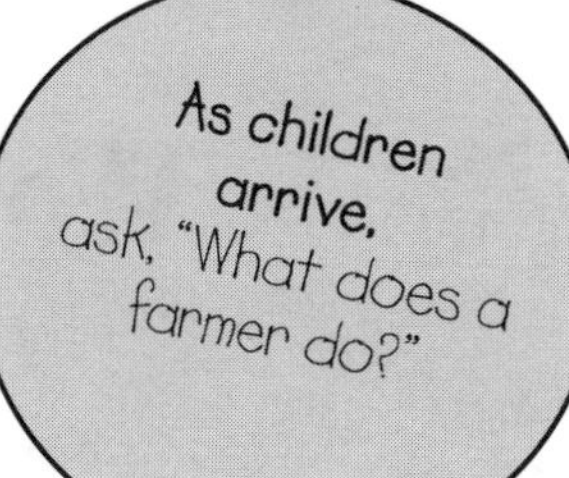

Building Center

Teacher Talk

Farmers grow all kinds of food.

Resources

play barn and animals, assorted blocks, trucks, tractors

Encourage the children to use the materials to create a farm. The children can be as creative as they wish and play "farm" with the materials.

Manipulatives Center

Teacher Talk

Farmers plant seeds and help them grow.

Resources

old shirt and jeans, newspapers

Let the children stuff newspapers into the shirt and pants to create a scarecrow. Tell the children that scarecrows keep birds from eating the seeds the farmer planted.

Dramatic Play Center

Teacher Talk

Farmers grow all kinds of food.

Resources

overalls, jeans, jackets, gloves, boots, old hats

Let the children pretend to be farmers.

Writing Center

Teacher Talk

Farmers grow all kinds of food.

Resources

index cards, marker, paper, pencils, envelopes

Write the word *farm* on a card and place it on the table. The children can copy the word.

Home Living Center

Teacher Talk

Farmers grow all kinds of food.

Resources

table, chairs, play sink and stove, pots and pans

Encourage children to use the materials provided to play "farm kitchen." Children can pretend to cook and eat foods they might find on a farm.

Art Center

Teacher Talk

Farmers grow all kinds of food.

Resources

brown tempera paint, sponges, brown paper bags, smocks, shallow trays, table covering, scissors

Cover the table and have the children wear smocks. Cut large potato shapes out of brown paper bags. Pour brown tempera paint into shallow trays. Give each child a paper potato. Let the children use the sponges to paint their potatoes. Tell the children that potatoes grow underground in the dirt.

Sand and Water Table

Teacher Talk

Farmers plant seeds and help them grow.

Resources

sand table with sand, digging tools, toy tractors, small rakes

Place the digging tools and other materials in the sand table. The children can use the materials to pretend to plant and grow seeds. They can pretend to "farm" and make patterns in the sand.

Worship Center

Teacher Talk

God created many different kinds of plants.

Resources

children's Bible, variety of fruits and vegetables

Set the Bible and produce on the table. Encourage the children to look through the Bible and touch and smell the produce items.

Say: All of the fruits and vegetables that are on that table were created by God. When God created the world, God created all different kinds of plants so people would have food.

Pray: Thank you, God, for providing fruits and vegetables for us to eat. Amen.

Open the Bible to Genesis 1:11.

Say: "God commanded, 'Let the earth produce all kinds of plants'" (Genesis 1:11, *Good News Bible*, adapted).

Have the children repeat the Bible verse.

Wonder Time

Call the children together for wonder time.

Wonder Question: I wonder what kinds of things farmers grow?

Say: When God created the world, God created many different kinds of plants so people would have food to eat. Some people have gardens in their yards, but most people buy their food from grocery stores. Farmers are the people who grow the food we buy.

Sing: "The Farmer in the Dell" (adapted) to the traditional tune.

Read the Bible verse.

Say: God created all the different plants so we would have food. Farmers grow all kinds of food so we can buy the food at the grocery store.

Pray: Thank you, God, for providing food and farmers to grow food. Amen.

"The Farmer in the Dell"

(Verse 1) The farmer in the dell,
the farmer in the dell, Hi-ho the
derry-o, the farmer in the dell.

(Verse 2) The farmer plants a seed,
the farmer plants a seed …
(pretend to plant)

(Verse 3) The farmer pulls the weeds,
the farmer pulls the weeds …
(pretend to weed)

(Verse 4) The farmer picks the corn,
the farmer picks the corn …
(pretend to pick)

(Verse 5) The farmer goes to bed,
the farmer goes to bed …
(pretend to go to sleep)

Group Fun

Resources

large piece of paper, crayons and markers, pictures of fruits and vegetables (from magazines and catalogs) or copies of pictures of a variety of fruits and vegetables that children can color, scissors, glue

Help the children make a garden mural. Lay the paper on the floor or a table. Have the children color the bottom half of the paper brown to represent dirt. When the children have finished coloring, they can glue on the pictures of the fruits and vegetables. Help the children decide if the pictures should go under or over the dirt. Label the mural: Things That Grow on a Farm.

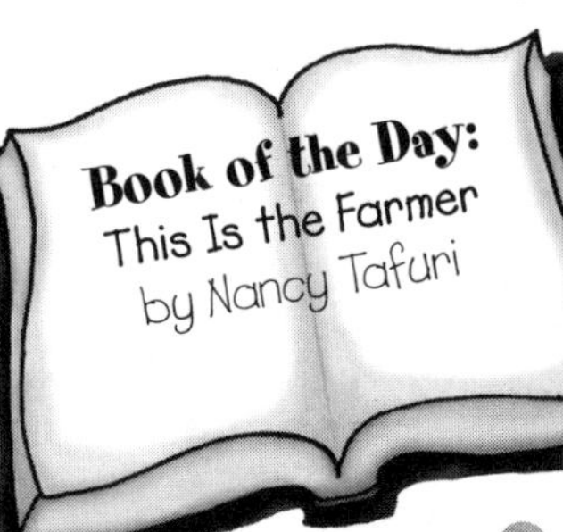

Goodbye Circle

Let the children talk about the things they enjoyed doing today. Ask each child to name two things a farmer does. Repeat the Bible verse.

Pray: Thank you, God, for farmers and the things they grow. Amen.

Evaluation

Was each child able to name two things farmers do? Is each child comfortable speaking out loud at circle time? Were children able to work together during Group Fun to create the project? Make notes of any children who had difficulties and plan ways to help them.

Lesson 27

Vegetables

Goals:

To learn that God created many different kinds of fruits and vegetables.

To help children appreciate a variety of different fruits and vegetables.

Objectives: By the end of this session the children will:

Taste at least two different vegetables.

Name vegetables.

Faith Connections

Bible verse: Daniel said, "Give us vegetables to eat and water to drink."

(Daniel 1:12, *Good News Bible*, adapted)

Vegetables are an important part of a daily diet, but they tend to be foods that children are reluctant to eat. Preschool children need to know that God created vegetables for people to eat because God cares about us, and that vegetables not only are good for us but taste good.

Teacher's Prayer

Dear God, you know there are times when I am reluctant to do something that I know I should do. Help me to be patient with the children in my care when they don't want to do something they should. Be with me and the children as we try to be the people you want us to be. Amen.

Teacher Talk:

There are many different kinds of vegetables.

God created many different kinds of plants.

It's fun to taste new foods.

Vegetables come in many different colors.

We can help plants grow.

Center Time

Set up your centers as described in Lesson 26. For this lesson add the following:

Art Center

Teacher Talk

Vegetables come in many different colors.

Resources

different varieties of vegetables—each a different color, markers or paints the color of the vegetables, paintbrushes (if using paints), smocks, paper

Set out the vegetables, with the art materials nearby. Encourage each child to look at the different colors of the vegetables and to create a picture using those colors. If desired, the children can draw and color a picture of the vegetables.

Cooking Center

Teacher Talk

It's fun to taste new foods.

Resources

paper plates and napkins, tongs, slices of raw vegetables such as celery, broccoli, carrots

Set out the plates, napkins, and vegetable platter. Let the children use tongs to serve themselves. Encourage them to taste each vegetable.

Math Center

Teacher Talk

There are many different kinds of vegetables.

Resources

variety of vegetables of different sizes and colors

Encourage the children to sort the vegetables by size, by color, and by type.

Science Center

Teacher Talk

We can help plants grow.

Resources

sweet potatoes (3 or 4), glass jars, toothpicks, water

Help the children place toothpicks horizontally around the middle of the sweet potatoes and balance each potato on the rim of a jar. The children can add water until the bottom of the potato is covered. Set the potato jars in a sunny space, and have the children check the water level daily. The vines will sprout in about two weeks.

Vegetable Center

Teacher Talk

There are many different kinds of vegetables.

Resources

variety of fresh vegetables, variety of canned vegetables (with pictures on cans)

Set out vegetables, both fresh and canned. Let the children examine and compare the vegetables. Help the children learn the names of the vegetables.

Writing Center

Teacher Talk

There are many different types of vegetables.

Resources

three or four different vegetables, index cards, paper, pencils

Write the name of each vegetable on an index card, and set the card next to the vegetable. Encourage the children to copy the words on the paper.

Worship Center

Teacher Talk

God created many different kinds of plants.

Resources

children's Bible, several plants, several different vegetables

Set the Bible, plants, and vegetables on a table. Encourage the children to look at the Bible, plants, and vegetables.

Say: God created many different kinds of plants when God created the world. Some plants grow vegetables, like the ones on this table. God created vegetables so people just like you would have healthy food to eat. God did that because God loves you.

Pray: Thank you, God, for all the different plants and vegetables you made for us. Amen.

Wonder Time

Call the children together with a song.

Eat Your Beans

Eat, eat, eat your beans,
Corn and broccoli too.
Vegetables, vegetables,
Vegetables, vegetables.
They are good for you.

Wonder Question: I wonder why God made so many different kinds of vegetables?

Say: We saw a lot of different kinds of vegetables on the tables in the learning centers, but there are many more kinds than we saw today.

Ask each child to name a favorite vegetable.

Sing: "Eat Your Beans" to the tune of "Row, Row, Row Your Boat."

Read the Bible verse.

Say: Daniel lived a long, long time ago. Daniel knew that God created vegetables because God loves us and wants us to grow healthy and strong.

Pray: Thank you, God, for giving us healthy food to eat. Amen.

Open the Bible to Daniel 1:12.

Say: "Daniel said, 'Give us vegetables to eat and water to drink'" (Daniel 1:12, *Good News Bible*, adapted).

Have the children repeat the Bible verse.

Group Fun

Resources

large sheet of paper or posterboard, washable markers, tape

Make a class chart of likes and dislikes. Hang the paper horizontally at children's eye level. Tell the children they are going to make a list of vegetables. Ask children to name some vegetables. Draw a picture of each vegetable across the top of the chart. Draw a horizontal line under the pictures, and make vertical lines between the vegetable pictures. Give each child a marker. Say the name of the first vegetable on the chart. Have children take turns going up to the chart and making a happy or unhappy face under the vegetable, to indicate whether he or she likes that particular vegetable. Do the same with each vegetable on the chart.

After the chart has been filled in, have children help you read the information on it. Ask questions such as: "How many people in this class like corn? How many like beans?" Count the faces on the chart to find the answers.

Goodbye Circle

Let the children talk about the things they enjoyed doing today. Ask each child to name two vegetables. Repeat the Bible verse.

Pray: Thank you, God, for healthy and delicious vegetables. Amen.

Evaluation

Was each child able to meet the day's objectives? Did each child participate in the group project? Make plans to help any children who had difficulties.

Note: Send reminders home to parents to send in canned vegetables (or fresh vegetables, if you choose) with their children tomorrow (see page 223).

Lesson 28

Stone Soup Day

Teacher Talk:

There are many different kinds of vegetables.

It's fun to taste new foods.

God created the world and everything in it.

Goals:

To learn that God created many different kinds of fruits and vegetables.

To help children appreciate a variety of different fruits and vegetables.

Objectives: By the end of this session the children will:

Use the vegetables provided to make vegetable soup.

Separate plants (vegetables) from non-plants (stones).

Faith Connections

Bible verse: God looked at everything God had made, and God was very pleased.

(Genesis 1:31, *Good News Bible*, adapted)

Preschool children are just beginning to learn about a small portion of God's creation. Everything is new and exciting, but they are old enough to already be developing likes and dislikes. They are young enough, however, to be able to try new things and new experiences. As the children create their "stone soup," they have the opportunity to create and try something new — a delicious vegetable soup. You can help them to try this new food experience and help them to enjoy it!

Teacher's Prayer

Thank you, God, for this opportunity to help the children in my care try and explore new parts of your creation. Amen.

Center Time

Set up your centers as described in Lessons 26-27. For this lesson add the following:

Art Center

Teacher Talk

God created the world and everything in it.

Resources

assortment of stones, washable markers and crayons, vegetable stickers

Let each child choose a stone and color it with crayons or markers. When the children have colored their stones, they can choose vegetable stickers to attach to their "stone soup stones."

Home Living Center

Teacher Talk

It's fun to taste new foods.

Resources

play stove and refrigerator; table and chairs; play dishes, pots and pans, food items; aprons

Encourage the children to "cook" a meal using the materials provided.

Math Center

Teacher Talk

There are many different kinds of vegetables.

Resources

unpopped popcorn, egg carton, marker, shallow bowl

Place the popcorn in a shallow bowl. Mark each cup of the carton with a number from one to twelve. Have the children count out the correct amount of popcorn and place it in each cup.

Sand Table

Teacher Talk

God created the world and everything in it.

Resources

Sand table with sand, assortment of small stones, digging tools and buckets

Allow the children to dig and play in the sand and manipulate the rocks as they choose.

As children arrive, have a basket or box where the children can place any vegetables they brought from home.

Puzzle Center

Teacher Talk

There are many different kinds of vegetables.

Resources

several vegetable puzzles (purchased or teacher-made)

Tip: To create a puzzle, glue a picture of a vegetable (from a catalog or enlarged from a coloring book) to a piece of poster board. Laminate the puzzle if desired. Cut it into four or five pieces for the children to put together.

Encourage the children to put together puzzles that show different vegetables.

Science Center

Teacher Talk

God created the world and everything in it.

Resources

four or five different vegetables, four or five assorted stones, magnifying glass

Have the children sort the food items from the non-food items. Let them examine the vegetables and stones with the magnifying glass.

Worship Center

Teacher Talk

God created the world and everything in it.

Resources

several different plants and vegetables, two or three stones

Set the materials on the table for the children to look at and explore.

Say: When God created the world, God made many different things. Each thing God made is special and important — plants, stones, vegetables, and especially people. God loves each thing God created, and God loves *(name each child)*.

Pray: Thank you, God, for all the wonderful things you created. Amen.

Open the Bible to Genesis 1:31.

Say: "God looked at everything God had made, and God was very pleased" (Genesis 1:31, *Good News Bible*, adapted).

Have the children repeat the Bible verse.

Wonder Time

Call the children together for wonder time.

Wonder Question: I wonder how we can make soup out of a stone?

Say: In our story today, we will learn about how some people made soup together. Then we are going to make our own special "stone soup" with the vegetables each of you brought.

Sing: "Stone Soup Song" to the tune of "Do You Know the Muffin Man?"

Read the Bible verse.

Say: God created this wonderful world and was pleased with everything that was made. We are so lucky that God made such wonderful things for us to use and enjoy.

Pray: Thank you, God, for this beautiful world and for all the foods you made for us to eat. Amen.

Stone Soup Song

Do you know how to make stone soup,
Make stone soup, make stone soup?
Do you know how to make stone soup?
We're making it today.

Put corn and beans inside the pot,
In the pot, in the pot.
Put lots of vegetables in the pot —
(Say or sing loudly and shake finger)
BUT NO STONES, PLEASE!

Group Fun

Resources

cans of vegetables brought from home, one large can of chicken broth, seasonings as desired, large pot, can opener, bowls, ladle, spoons

Help the children make stone soup. Open each child's can and help the child drain off the liquid in the can. Have the children pour their cans of vegetables into the pot. Add the can of chicken broth and any seasonings you choose. Heat the soup to boiling, stirring often, as you read the story. When the soup has come to a boil, allow it to simmer for a short time. Ladle the soup and enjoy.

Teacher Tip: If preferred, children can bring fresh vegetables, but the soup will take longer to cook and you will need to plan for chopping the vegetables. Determine which method you prefer in advance so you can direct parents what to supply.

Goodbye Circle

Let the children talk about the things they enjoyed doing today. Ask each child to name one ingredient of their stone soup. Repeat the Bible verse.

Pray: Thank you, God, for good food to eat and the whole world you created. Amen.

Evaluation

Was each child able to meet the day's objectives? Was each child able to participate in the group activity? Make plans to help children who are having difficulties meeting the objectives set this week.

Lesson 29

All Kinds of Fruit

Goals:

To learn that God created many different kinds of fruits and vegetables.

To help children appreciate a variety of different fruits and vegetables.

Objectives: By the end of this session the children will:

Name two different fruits.

Taste two different fruits.

Make paper plate apples.

Faith Connections

Bible verse: God said, "I have provided all kinds of fruit for you to eat."

(Genesis 1:29, *Good News Bible*, adapted)

Most children enjoy eating fruit but may not have tried a wide variety. Preschool children need the opportunity to learn that God created many different kinds of fruit, and that fruits are a food that is good for us to eat.

Teacher's Prayer

O God, you have created so many wonderful foods to nourish our bodies. Help me to nourish the minds of the young children in my care, as well as their bodies. Amen.

Teacher Talk:

There are many different kinds of fruits.

It's fun to taste new foods.

Fruits come in many different colors.

God created many different kinds of plants.

Fruits and vegetables grow from seeds.

It's important to eat foods that are good for us.

Center Time

Set up your centers as described in Lessons 26-28. For this lesson add the following:

As children arrive, ask, "What color is an apple?"

Art Center

Teacher Talk

There are many different kinds of fruits.

Resources

play dough or other modeling clay that comes in colors

Encourage the children to create different kinds of fruits with the clay.

Fruit Center

Teacher Talk

There are many different kinds of fruits.

Resources

variety of fresh fruits, variety of canned fruits (with pictures on cans)

Set out fresh and canned fruits. Let the children examine the fruits and compare them. Help the children learn the names of the fruits.

Cooking Center

Teacher Talk

It's fun to taste new foods.

Resources

table, chairs, paper plates, napkins, dried apples and bananas, fresh bananas, plastic knives

Encourage the children to try the dried fruits and to peel, slice, and eat pieces of fresh banana. Talk about the differences.

Math Center

Teacher Talk

Fruits come in many different colors.

Resources

variety of different apples (several of each kind) or apple shapes cut from red, green, and yellow construction paper.

Set out the apples. Or cut apple shapes in different sizes and colors from construction paper. Encourage the children to sort the apples by type, size, and color.

Science Center

Teacher Talk

Fruits and vegetables grow from seeds.

Resources

pot of dirt, apples, knife, water

Place the apples next to the pot of dirt. Slice the apple and have the children look at the seed pattern. (If you slice the apple in half horizontally, you see a star pattern.) Slice the apple and let the children eat the slices. After the children have tasted the apple, they can each place a seed in the pot. When the seeds are planted, cover them lightly with soil and water the seeds. The children can care for the plant and track its growth.

Note: Keep the knife away from the children.

Writing Center

Teacher Talk

There are many different kinds of fruit.

Resources

three or four different fruits, index cards, paper, pencil

Write the name of each fruit on an index card, and set the card next to the fruit. Encourage the children to copy the words.

Worship Center

Teacher Talk

God created many different kinds of plants.

Resources

Children's Bible, several plants, different fruits

Set the Bible, plants, and fruits on the table. Encourage the children to look at the materials.

Say: God created many kinds of living things when God created the world. Some plants grow fruits like the ones on this table. God created these fruits and many other kinds so all people could have healthy and delicious food to eat. God did that because God loves you.

Pray: Thank you, God, for all the wonderful fruits and vegetables you created for us. Amen.

Wonder Time

Call the children together for wonder time.

> **"Eat Your Fruit"**
> Eat, eat, eat your fruit.
> Eat fruit every day.
> Apples, pears, bananas too.
> Eat fruit every day.

Wonder Question: I wonder why God made so many different kinds of fruit?

Say: Fruits come in all shapes and colors.

God made them all. We saw some different kinds of fruit today, but there are many other kinds of fruit.

Ask each child to name their favorite fruit.

Sing: "Eat Your Fruit" to the tune of "Row, Row, Row Your Boat."

Play a game. Let the children play "Duck, Duck, Goose" using the words "Apple, Apple, Orange." Have the children sit in a circle on the floor. Choose one child to be the farmer. Have the farmer go around the circle, tapping each child on the head and saying, "Apple." Then have the farmer tap one child on the head and say, "orange." The "orange" jumps up and chases the farmer around the circle until the farmer sits down in the vacant space. The runner becomes the new farmer.

Read the Bible verse.

Say: We already learned that God created seeds, plants, and vegetables. God created fruit, too.

Pray: Thank you, God, for all the wonderful foods you created for us to eat. Amen.

Open the Bible to: Genesis 1:29.

Say: "God said, 'I have provided all kinds of fruit for you to eat' " (Genesis 1:29, *Good News Bible*, adapted).

Have the children repeat the Bible verse.

Group Fun

Resources

small paper plates; red, green, and yellow construction paper or tissue paper; glue

Give each child a small paper plate to make an apple. Let each child decide if she or he wants to make a red, green, or yellow apples. Give each child construction or tissue paper in the color of his or her choice. Let the children tear the paper into small pieces. Then have the children glue the pieces onto their paper plates. Encourage the children to completely cover the plates. Let the children add pieces of green paper at the top of their plates to make stems.

Goodbye Circle

Let the children talk about the things they enjoyed doing today. Ask each child to name two fruits. Repeat the Bible verse.

Pray: Thank you, God, for healthy foods to eat, like fruits and vegetables. Amen.

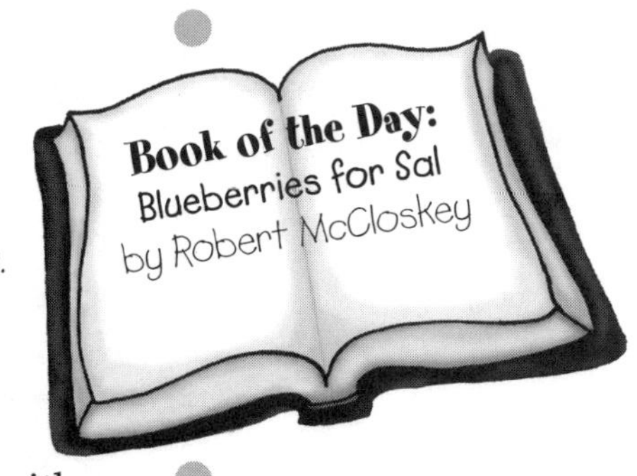

Evaluation

Was each child able to meet the day's objectives? Make plans to work with any children who are having difficulties.

Note: Remind parents to send fresh fruit with their children tomorrow so the class can make a fruit salad (see page 223).

Lesson 30

Eating the Alphabet

Teacher Talk:

It is important to eat foods that are good for us.

There are many different kinds of fruits.

It's fun to taste new foods.

God created many different kinds of plants.

Goals:

To learn that God created many different kinds of fruits and vegetables.

To help children appreciate a variety of different fruits and vegetables.

To help children know a plant's life cycle.

To learn about healthy foods.

Objectives:

By the end of this session the children will:

Help make a fruit salad.

Taste and classify a sweet fruit and a sour fruit.

Faith Connections

Bible verse: A healthy tree has good fruit.

(Matthew 7:17, *Good News Bible*, adapted)

Trees need certain things in order to grow and produce fruit. That is God's plan. Children also need certain things in order to grow strong and healthy. During the week the children have had the opportunity to try a variety of fruits and vegetables, as well as creating and eating vegetable soup. It is important to reinforce with the children in your class that they need to eat healthy foods and try new things, and that God has provided the foods we need.

Teacher's Prayer

Dearest Lord, give me the words I need to help the children in my care grow strong and healthy in body, mind, and spirit. Amen.

Center Time

Set up your centers as described in Lessons 26-29. For this lesson add the following:

As children **arrive,** let the children place any fruit they brought for the fruit salad in a basket or box.

Science Center

Teacher Talk

It's fun to taste new foods.

Resources

melon slices, lemon or grapefruit slices, dishes

Place each fruit on a dish. Let each child try a piece of fruit and see which is sweet and which is sour.

Dramatic Play Center

Teacher Talk

God created many different kinds of plants.

Resources

bushel baskets, berry baskets, small paper sacks, plastic fruits and vegetables, play money, cash register

Let the children use the materials to set up a fruit and vegetable stand.

Writing Center

Teacher Talk

God created many different kinds of plants.

Resources

variety of fruits and vegetables, index cards, paper, pencils

Set fruits and vegetables on a table. Write the letter of the alphabet that each item starts with on an index card, and put the card next to the produce item. The children can copy the letters.

Math Center

Teacher Talk

God created many different kinds of plants.

Resources

plastic or real fruits and vegetables (or pictures)

Have the children sort fruits and vegetables by color, size, or type.

Manipulatives Center

Teacher Talk

There are many different kinds of fruits.

Resources

lemons and limes, basket, two bowls, tongs

Place lemons and limes in a basket. Let the children use tongs to move the fruit and sort it by color.

Art Center

Teacher Talk

There are many different kinds of fruits.

Resources

plastic berry baskets, tempera paint, shallow containers, paper, fruit stickers, smocks, table covering

Cover the table and have the children wear smocks. Pour paint into shallow containers, providing two or three colors. Place a berry basket next to each container. Let the children dip the baskets into the paint, then stamp the design on paper. They can then add fruit stickers to their pictures.

Worship Center

Teacher Talk

It is important to eat foods that are good for us.

Resources

seeds, plants, fruits and vegetables, picture of tree

Arrange the items in the order listed above. Encourage the children to look at the items.

Say: Many different kinds of things grow from seeds: plants, fruits and vegetables, and trees. Seeds need dirt, sun, and rain so they can grow into healthy plants and trees. People need good food and exercise so they can grow too. God provides everything seeds and people need to grow.

Pray: Thank you, God, for helping (*name each child*) grow. Amen.

Open the Bible to Matthew 7:17.

Say: "A healthy tree has good fruit" (Matthew 7:17, *Good News Bible*, adapted).

Have the children repeat the Bible verse.

Wonder Time

Call the children together with a song.

A, B, C Song

A, B, C, D, E, F, G,
Fruits and vegetables are good for me.
I will eat them every day.
I'll be strong for work and play.
A, B, C, D, E, F, G,
Fruits and vegetables are good for me.

Wonder Question: I wonder why God made so many different kinds of foods?

Say: We need all different kinds of foods so we can grow. Fruits and vegetables are two kinds of plants that God made for us to eat.

Sing: "A, B, C Song" to the tune of "The A, B, C's."

Read the Bible verse.

Say: You are not trees; you are boys and girls. But you need to grow just like the trees. God provides the things you need to grow, just like God takes care of the trees.

Pray: Thank you, God, for taking care of me and providing good food for me to eat. Amen.

Group Fun

Resources

fruit children brought from home, plastic knives, large bowl, orange juice, large serving spoon, paper cups, spoons

Let the children make fruit cups. Have each child wash the fruit he or she brought from home. The children can then cut their own fruit, using the plastic knives (with adult supervision). Have each child place the cut pieces of fruit in the large bowl. Have children take turns stirring the fruits together. Pour a small amount of orange juice over the fruit to keep the fruit from turning brown. Children can serve themselves from the bowl by using a large serving spoon to put fruit salad into their cups. Eat and enjoy! Discuss the colors and tastes of the different fruits in the salad.

Goodbye Circle

Let the children talk about the things they enjoyed doing today. Ask each child to name two healthy foods. Repeat the Bible verse.

Pray: Thank you, God, for giving us so many good healthy foods to eat. Amen.

Book of the Day: Eating the Alphabet: Fruits and Vegetables From A to Z by Lois Ehlert

Evaluation

Did each child have the fine motor skills to cut the fruit provided? Was each child able to meet the day's objectives? Make note of any children having difficulties, and plan ways to help them meet the objectives.

FLOWERS

The month's study of growing things continues this week with an emphasis on flowers. During the week the children will have the opportunity to study different kinds of flowers. They will also use flowers to reinforce math and science skills and knowledge of colors.

Each day the children will create a different type of flower in the "Flower Creation Center." Have children create extras each day, and make a "flower garden" in the room that grows during the week.

Lesson 31

Flower Fun

Goals:

To help reinforce color identification skills.

To learn that God created many different types of flowers.

To give children the opportunity to use different senses to explore plant life.

To help children know a plant's life cycle.

Objectives: By the end of this session the children will:

Examine flowers with a magnifying glass.

Name two flowers.

Faith Connections

Bible verse: God commanded, "Let the earth produce all kinds of plants." (Genesis 1:11, *Good News Bible*, adapted)

Your children have already had the opportunity to learn about vegetables and fruits, which provide nourishment for our bodies. Flowers nourish our senses with their beauty and scent. Children need the opportunity to appreciate the beauty of God's creation.

Teacher's Prayer

Thank you, God, for the beauty of the world you created for us. Help me to show that beauty to the children in my care. Amen.

Teacher Talk:

God created many different kinds of plants.

Flowers come in many different colors.

Flowers grow from seeds.

There are many different kinds of flowers.

Center Time

Set up your centers as described on pages 6-9. For this lesson add the following:

Art Center

Teacher Talk

Flowers come in many different colors.

Resources

several pink flowers (real or artificial) in a container; variety of pink art materials: construction paper, ribbon, markers and crayons, stickers, paint; paintbrushes; smocks

Place the flower container and art materials on the art table. Encourage each child to name the color of the flowers, and create a "pink collage" with the materials provided.

Flower Creation Center

Teacher Talk

Flowers come in many different colors.

Resources

various colors of tissue paper, green chenille stems, scissors

Before class cut tissue paper into large squares. Each child can take three to five tissue paper squares, placing each square on top of the others. Show the children how to fold them like a fan. When folded, help the children twist a chenille stem around the center of the flower, then fan open the paper to separate the layers.

Math Center

Teacher Talk

Flowers grow from seeds.

Resources

construction paper, marker, scissors, large seeds (sunflower or similar), flower pattern (see page 212), shallow container

Before class, photocopy the flower pattern (see page 212). Use the pattern to cut flower shapes from the construction paper. Write a number on each flower (one to ten). Set the flowers on the math table, with the seeds in a shallow container. The children can count out seeds and place the correct number on each flower.

As children arrive, place a flower sticker on the back of each child's hand or on the child's clothing.

Science Center

Teacher Talk

Flowers grow from seeds.

Resources

several real flowers (either on a plant or in a vase), magnifying glass

Encourage the children to examine the flowers, using their eyes with the magnifying glass, their fingers (touch), and their noses (smell).

Writing Center

Teacher Talk

There are many different kinds of flowers.

Resources

index card, marker, paper and pencils, flower (real or artificial)

Write the word *flower* on the index card. Place the flower next to the card. Have the children copy the word.

Worship Center

Teacher Talk

God created many different kinds of plants.

Resources

several of each: vegetables, fruits, flowers (plant or in a vase)

Set the fruit, vegetables, and flowers on a table. Encourage the children to examine each of the objects provided.

Say: God made fruits and vegetables so we can eat them and be healthy. Some flowers grow on plants in order to help the vegetables and fruit grow. The best parts of flowers, though, are their colors and smells. They are a beautiful part of God's creation that we can all enjoy.

Pray: Thank you, God, for creating flowers for us to enjoy. Amen.

Wonder Time

Call the children together with a song or with fingerplays.

Wonder Question: I wonder why God made flowers?

Say: Many different plants have flowers. They are a special part of plants. They grow from seeds just like all the other plants we have been learning about this month.

Sing: "Plant Your Seeds" to the tune of "Row, Row, Row Your Boat."

Read the Bible verse.

Say: Flowers are part of the plants that God created. They are a beautiful part of this wonderful world God made.

Pray: Thank you, God, for flowers, fruits, and vegetables. Amen.

Plant Your Seeds

Plant, plant, plant your seeds,
In the flower bed.
Pansies, tulips, marigolds -
Raise your pretty heads.

Water, water, water your seeds,
In the flower bed.
Pansies, tulip, marigolds -
Raise your pretty heads.

Additional verses: Weed your seeds / Watch your seeds

Teacher Tip: If desired, have children act out the words to the song.

Open the Bible to Genesis 1:11.

Say: "God commanded, 'Let the earth produce all kinds of plants'" (Genesis 1:11, *Good News Bible*, adapted).

Have the children repeat the Bible verse.

Group Fun

Resources

artificial or construction paper flowers (one for every two or three children), tape player, tape

Let the children play "Pass the Flower." Have the children sit in a circle and distribute the flowers around the circle.

Say: When you hear the music start, pass the flowers around the circle. When the music stops, if you are holding a flower you must turn around and face the other direction.

Begin the game. Each time the music stops, children must turn around. Eventually everyone will have moved several different times. The game is challenging, but fun — and no one loses.

Goodbye Circle

Let the children talk about the things they enjoyed doing today. Ask each child to name two flowers. Repeat the Bible verse.

Pray: Thank you, God, for all the different plants you created. Amen.

Evaluation

Was each child able to listen to and follow the directions of the group activity? Was each child able to name two flowers? Make notes of those children who had difficulties.

Lesson 32

Flower Power

Teacher Talk:

God created many different kinds of plants.

Flowers come in many different colors.

Flowers grow from seeds.

Flowers can grow in a garden.

Goals:

To help reinforce color identification skills.

To learn that God created many different types of flowers.

To strengthen children's self-esteem.

To encourage language skills.

Objectives:

By the end of this session children will:

Sort a selection of flowers by color.

Name five things that they can do.

Faith Connections

Bible verse: The LORD God planted a garden in Eden.

(Genesis 2:8)

A garden is a special place, created for special plants to grow. God created this special garden in Eden when the world was first made. Flowers were a part of this garden. Your class is a garden where some very special plants that God created are getting ready to flower. The children in your class need your love and nurturing, and they need to know that they are all important parts of God's garden of people.

Teacher's Prayer

Dear God, you are the ultimate gardener, the creator of all growing things. Help me to take care of the young children growing in my class, and give me the wisdom to help them become the best flowers of humanity they can be. Amen.

Center Time

Set up your centers as described in Lesson 31. For this lesson add or change the following:

Art Center

Teacher Talk

Flowers come in many different colors.

Resources

fingerpaint paper, fingerpaints in various colors (no dark colors)

Have the children cover their papers with a variety of colors. Have the children name the colors they choose. Allow the pictures to dry flat. They will be used as part of the group project. (Be sure each child's name is on his or her paper.)

Dramatic Play Center

Teacher Talk

God created many different kinds of plants.

Resources

gardening gloves, artificial plants and flowers, hats, gardening tools, plastic pots, foam

Let the children pretend to garden and create pots of flowers with the objects provided.

Flower Creation Center

Teacher Talk

Flowers come in many different colors.

Resources

paper, cupcake liners, markers, glue

Encourage the children to glue cupcake liners to paper to create flowers. The children can use the markers to decorate the flowers and add stems, leaves, and other items.

Puzzle Center

Teacher Talk

Flowers grow from seeds.

Resources

flower seed packets (2 of each kind)

Use the seed packets to play a concentration game. Turn all the packets face down. Have a child turn over one picture. Then have the child try to turn over the matching packet. If the packet matches, leave both packets face up. If the packet does not match, turn the picture face down again. Continue until all the matches are found.

Math Center

Teacher Talk

Flowers come in many different colors.

Resources

selection of artificial flowers in a variety of colors

Have the children sort the flowers by color, and help them name the colors as they sort. Ask the children to describe other ways the flowers could be sorted, such as by size, shape, or type.

Writing Center

Teacher Talk

Flowers can grow in a garden.

Resources

index card, marker, paper and pencils, pictures of flower gardens

Write the word *garden* on the index card. Place the pictures of the flower gardens next to the card. Have the children copy the word.

Worship Center

Teacher Talk

God created many different kinds of plants.

Resources

construction paper flowers, chenille sticks, pot filled with plastic foam (or other similar material), glue, scissors, pictures of children in your class (or pictures of children from a magazine)

Attach the paper flowers to the chenille sticks. Place a picture of a child in the center of each flower, then "plant" the flowers in the pot. Set the pot of "children flowers" on the table. Encourage the children to look at the "children flowers."

Say: We have a special kind of flower here today. They are "children flowers." Each one of you is a special part of God's world. You grow and grow just like the flowers we have been studying.

Pray: Thank you, God, for (*name each child*), a special "children flower" in God's garden. Amen.

Open the Bible to: Genesis 2:8.

Say: "The LORD God planted a garden in Eden" (Genesis2:8).

Have the children repeat the Bible verse.

Wonder Time

Call the children together.

Wonder Question: I wonder how seeds turn into flowers?

Say: We're going to sing a song together that will help us remember what seeds need so they can grow.

Sing: "Will My Flowers Grow?" to the tune of "The Wheels on the Bus."

Read the Bible verse.

Say: God planted a special garden when God made the world. God made all kinds of plants, and God has made many kinds of people. Everything God made is special and growing.

Pray: Thank you, God, for making me a part of your special garden. Amen.

Will My Flowers Grow?

The seeds in the pack go in the ground,
(Pretend to plant.)
In the ground, in the ground.
The seeds in the pack go in the ground.
Will my flowers grow?

The rain from the sky falls drip, drop, plop,
(Wiggle fingers downward.)
Drip, drop, plop, drip, drop, plop.
The rain from the sky falls drip, drop, plop.
Will my flowers grow?

The sun in the sky is yellow and bright,
(Look up and shade eyes with hand.)
Yellow and bright, yellow and bright.
The sun in the sky is yellow and bright.
Will my flowers grow?

The seeds in my garden grow up, up, up,
(Bend down; slowly stand up.)
Up, up, up; up, up, up.
The seeds in my garden grow up, up, up.
(Slowly wiggle fingers up.)
Look! See my flowers grow!
(Point with finger.)

Group Fun

Resources

scissors, markers, crayons, tape, fingerpaint pictures (from Art Center), templates for flower petals and circular flower centers (see page 211), glue, construction paper, tempera paint, paint brushes

Say: People grow, just like flowers do.

Have the children name some things they can do, using the words "I can" in their sentences, such as: "I can ride my bike." Photocopy the flower pattern to make templates (see page 211). Give children the petal and flower center templates. They can trace the pieces on their fingerpaint pictures and cut them out. Have children tape the petals to the back of the flower centers. On each child's flower, write the word *can* in the center. Have each child dictate five things he or she can do. Write the phrases on the petals. If desired, have children glue the "flower power" flower to a large piece of construction paper, and add stems and leaves with construction paper, paint, or markers.

Goodbye Circle

Let the children talk about the things they enjoyed doing today. Ask each child to name something he or she can do. Repeat the Bible verse.

Pray: Thank you, God, for all the wonderful things the children can do. Amen.

Evaluation

Was each child able to trace and cut out the flower part templates? Was each child able to name five things he or she could do? Help anyone who had difficulties.

Lesson 33

Planting a Rainbow

Goals:

To help reinforce color identification skills.

To learn that God created many different types of flowers.

To help children appreciate a variety of plant life.

To give children the opportunity to use different senses to explore plant life.

To help children know a plant's life cycle.

Objectives: By the end of this session children will:

Examine bulbs and seeds with a magnifying glass.

Name a color that is in a rainbow.

Faith Connections

Bible verse: In the countryside the flowers are in bloom. This is the time for singing.

(Song of Songs 2:12, *Good News Bible*)

When we plant flowers or other growing things, we wait and wait for them to grow. When they finally grow and bloom, we rejoice! Our world blossoms in springtime. In many parts of the world there are changes in the spring: animals, plants, insects, and people all recognize the change. Preschool children need to know that flower time is a time for rejoicing, a time for thanking God for God's many gifts.

Teacher's Prayer

Dearest Lord, thank you for this wonderful world. Help me to rejoice and sing with the children in my care as we celebrate the time of flowers. Amen.

Teacher Talk:

God created many different kinds of plants.

Flowers come in many different colors.

Flowers grow from seeds.

Music and flowers can make us happy.

Center Time

Set up your centers as described in Lessons 31-32. For this lesson add or change the following:

> As children arrive, play "The Waltz of the Flowers" from "The Nutcracker Suite."

Dramatic Play Center

Teacher Talk

God created many different kinds of plants.

Resources

toy cash register, play money, garden supplies, variety of plants (real or artificial), seed and bulb packages

Let the children play garden store. They can set up their store and "sell" the items using the play money and cash register.

Flower Creation Center

Teacher Talk

Flowers come in many different colors.

Resources

coffee filters, watercolors, paintbrushes, green chenille stems

Let the children paint coffee filters with watercolors. Discuss how the colors blend. When the filters are dry, help the children gather the center of their flowers and wrap chenille stems around the centers to create stems.

Writing Center

Teacher Talk

Flowers come in many different colors.

Resources

index cards, markers, paper, pencils, tape

Write the word *rainbow*, one letter per card, using a different color for each letter. Hang the cards in order. Have the children copy the word.

Math Center

Teacher Talk

Flowers come in many different colors.

Resources

28 craft sticks (or tongue depressors), tempera paint in rainbow colors, egg cartons

Before class, paint the ends of craft sticks in rainbow colors, four in each color. The sticks can be painted by dipping the ends in paint, then poking the stick into an upside down egg carton to dry. Create a pattern with four or five of the sticks. Let the children copy the pattern. Let them create new patterns for other children to copy.

Science Center

Teacher Talk

Flowers grow from seeds.

Resources

different bulbs and flower seeds, magnifying glass, picture of the flower each bulb or seed will grow into

Set each bulb and seed group next to the picture of the grown plant. Let the children explore the bulbs and seeds with the magnifying glass. Discuss how the bulbs and seeds change to become the plant.

Music Center

Teacher Talk

Music and flowers can make us happy.

Resources

cassette/CD player, cassette/CD of happy music, flower stickers, long strips of crepe paper in rainbow colors

Play the cassette/CD. Let the children place flower stickers on the crepe paper strips. Encourage the children to dance and move to the music while waving the rainbow streamers.

Worship Center

Teacher Talk

God created many different kinds of plants.

Resources

seed packet, pot of blossoming flowers (real)

Place the seeds and flowerpot on the table.

Say: It takes a long time for a seed to grow into a flower. But God has a plan, and the flowers grow when God's plan says it's time. When we see all the flowers that God created grow , we can sing and be happy—and say thank you to God.

Pray: Thank you, God, for flowers. Amen.

Wonder Time

Call the children together with a song.

Wonder Question: I wonder how many different colors of flowers there are?

Say: God created many different kinds of flowers—all sizes, all shapes, and all colors.

Sing: "Flowers Can Be" to the tune of "The Farmer in the Dell."

Read the Bible verse.

Say: We know that God loves us very much because God provides us with food and beautiful flowers. God takes care of everything we need.

Pray: Thank you, God, for flowers and the things we need. Amen.

Flowers Can Be

Have children take turns naming a color. As each child names a color, sing the following words: *(Example: child named "red")*

Flowers can be *(red)*,
Flowers can be *(red)*,
God made them all you know,
Flowers can be *(red)*.

Repeat until each child has had a turn.

Open the Bible to Song of Songs 2:12.

Say: "In the countryside the flowers are in bloom. This is the time for singing" (Song of Songs 2:12, *Good News Bible*).

Have the children repeat the Bible verse.

Group Fun

Resources

large piece of paper, green yarn, stapler, colored construction paper, scissors, glue, markers, fabric scraps and wallpaper samples, paper clips, cardboard tubes, empty thread spools, flower stamps, washable tempera paint, shallow containers

Help the children make a garden mural. Before class, lay strips of green yarn vertically on the paper and staple in place. These will be the "stems" for the children's flower creations. Write "Rainbow Garden" on a piece of construction paper and fasten it to the top of the mural.

Encourage the children to use the materials provided to make flowers for the mural. Children can cut and color flowers from the paper, fabric, and wallpaper. The flowers can be fastened to the stems using paper clips. If desired, children can also create flowers directly on the paper using the stamps provided: crease cardboard tubes vertically to use as flower petal stamps, use thread spools as flower stamps, or use commercial flower stamps. Encourage the children to be as creative as possible and to use a variety of rainbow colors.

Goodbye Circle

Let the children talk about the things they enjoyed doing today. Ask each child to name a color that is in a rainbow. Repeat the Bible verse.

Pray: Thank you, God, for rainbow-colored flowers that you created for us. Amen.

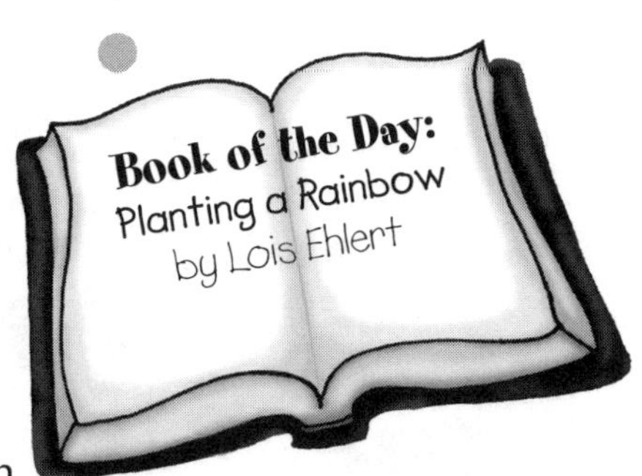

Evaluation

Was each child able to listen and follow directions to help create the garden mural? Was each child able to name a rainbow color? Make plans to help those children who are having difficulties.

Lesson 34

A Garden in Bloom

Teacher Talk:

God created many different kinds of flowers.

Flowers come in many different colors.

Flowers grow from seeds.

Flowers can be short or tall.

Flowers need water to grow.

Goals:

To help reinforce color identification skills.

To learn that God created many different types of flowers.

To help children appreciate a variety of plant life.

To give children the opportunity to use different senses to explore plant life.

To help children know a plant's life cycle.

To help children know that they are an important part of God's creation.

Objectives: By the end of this session children will:

Demonstrate that flowers drink water.

Sort flowers by size.

Listen and follow directions to create flower puppets.

Faith Connections

Bible verse: Not even King Solomon with all his wealth had clothes as beautiful as one of these flowers.

(Matthew 6:29, *Good News Bible*)

All week long the children have been exploring and experimenting with flowers. They have named their colors, explored their scents, and learned their names. Children need to know that no matter how beautiful the flowers are, in God's eyes they are each the most beautiful creation there is.

Teacher's Prayer

Loving God, help me to see each child as one of your beautiful creations, and help me show them how beautiful and important they are to you. Amen.

Center Time

Set up your centers as described in Lessons 31-33. For this lesson add or change the following:

Art Center

Teacher Talk

Flowers come in many different colors.

Resources

green construction paper, green paint, green markers, silver glitter

Let the children use green paint, markers, and glitter to decorate their papers.

Dramatic Play Center

Teacher Talk

Flowers come in many different colors.

Resources

bright dress-up clothing, jewelry, mirror

Let the children dress up in the clothing and admire themselves in the mirror.

Flower Creation Center

Teacher Talk

Flowers come in many different colors.

Resources

small white paper "nut cups," cotton swabs, craft glue, silver glitter, shells, green construction paper, construction paper, markers, scissors

Let the children create "silver bells and cockle shell flowers" by gluing nut cups to paper, then using cotton swabs to apply glue to the cups. Help the children sprinkle glitter on the glue. They can cut construction paper and glue it on to create stems and leaves, or they can use markers. Have each child glue shells onto the flower.

Math Center

Teacher Talk

Flowers can be short or tall.

Resources

assortment of artificial flowers

Choose flowers that are different sizes and lengths, or cut the stems in different lengths. Have the children arrange the flowers by size.

Sand Table

Teacher Talk

Flowers can be short or tall.

Resources

sand table with sand, small plastic shovels, empty plastic containers, artificial flowers in a variety of heights and colors.

Have the children plant pots and rows of flowers. Discuss sizes, using words such as *short*, *tall*, *shorter*, and *tallest*.

Science Center

Teacher Talk

Flowers need water to grow.

Resources

white carnations (1 per child), paper cups (1 per child), food coloring, water

Cut flowers so they stand upright in the cups. Have each child fill a cup ¾ full with water and place a flower in the cup. Each child can put several drops of food coloring in his or her cup. The carnations will take on the color of the food coloring. (The process takes time; have the children check after an hour, at the end of class, and again the next day.)

Worship Center

Teacher Talk

God created many different kinds of flowers.

Resources

vase or pot of real flowers, mirror, construction paper, tape, scissors

Before class, cut a large number of flower petals from paper. Tape them to the mirror, leaving a large opening in the center so when the children look in the mirror, they will see their faces in the center of the flower petals. Set the flowers near the mirror.

Say: All week we have been learning about the beautiful flowers that God created. You are a beautiful creation of God's also, and God loves you.

Pray: Thank you, God, for *(name each child)*, a beautiful creation in your world. Amen.

Open the Bible to Matthew 6:29.

Say: "Not even King Solomon with all his wealth had clothes as beautiful as one of these flowers" (Matthew 6:29, *Good News Bible*).

Have the children repeat the Bible verse.

Wonder Time

Call the children together with a song.

Flowers Grow

Flowers grow, flowers grow.
That's part of God's plan.
Red and yellow, pink and blue
God makes the flowers grow.

Wonder Question: I wonder which flowers God loves the most?

Say: God made many, many different kinds of flowers. Some are small and some are tall. Some smell good and some smell very bad. They come in all kinds of sizes and shapes.

Sing: "Flowers Grow" to the tune of "Jingle Bells."

Read the Bible verse.

Say: This week we've been making all kinds of beautiful, special flowers. In the Bible verse I just read, it said that flowers were very, very beautiful. God loves the flowers, but God thinks that each one of you is even more beautiful and more special than any of the flowers in the world.

Pray: Thank you, God, for making me more special than the beautiful flowers. Amen.

Group Fun

Resources

paper lunch bags, plastic foam balls, knife, construction paper, markers, wiggle eyes, glue

Help the children make a flower puppet. Before class cut each of the foam balls in half. Give each child a paper bag and a ball half. Have the child glue the ball half to the front of the bag. The children can then use the materials provided to complete their flowers by making stems, leaves, and petals. When the flowers are completed, the children can glue two wiggle eyes to each ball to create "flower faces." Encourage the children to place their hands inside the bag and move their puppets.

Say: We're going to learn a poem about a flower garden. Say what I say and do what I do.

Say the poem "Mary, Mary, Quite Contrary" (see page 219) for the children.

Goodbye Circle

Let the children talk about the things they enjoyed doing today. Ask each child to name something flowers need to grow. Repeat the Bible verse.

Pray: Thank you, God, for special flowers and special people. Amen.

Evaluation

Was each child able to meet the day's objectives? Make note of those children having difficulties, and plan how to help them learn those skills they need.

Lesson 35

Our Beautiful World

Goals:

To help reinforce color identification skills.

To learn that God wants us to take care of the world and the things on it.

To help children appreciate the beauty of God's world.

To give children the opportunity to use different senses to explore plant life.

To help children know a plant's life cycle.

Objectives:

By the end of this session the children will:

Take a nature hike.

Name two things that God made.

Faith Connections

Bible verse: God looked at everything God had made, and God was very pleased.

(Genesis 1:31, *Good News Bible*, adapted)

God created a perfect world filled with all kinds of living things. We were given those things to use, enjoy, and protect. Earth Day is April 22, and serves as a reminder to us that we are responsible for the health and well-being of the earth and everything on it. Preschool children are able to learn that they can help take care of God's world too.

Teacher's Prayer

Dear God, you created a perfect world and gave it to me and the children in my care to protect. Be with us as we try to care for that very special gift. Amen.

Teacher Talk:

God created many different kinds of plants.

Flowers come in many different colors.

We can help take care of the world that God made.

Flowers grow from seeds.

Center Time

Set up your centers as described in Lessons 31-34. For this lesson add or change the following:

> As children arrive, say, "God made the world, and God made you."

Puzzle Center

Teacher Talk

God created many different kinds of plants.

Resources

several purchased puzzles of flowers, gardens, or the world

Have the children put the puzzles together and talk about what pictures are on the puzzles.

Teacher Tip: Cut pictures from a magazine, glue them to posterboard, and have them laminated. Cut them into pieces for the children to put together.

Math Center

Teacher Talk

Flowers grow from seeds.

Resources

sequence pictures of a plant's growth cycle (see page 213)

Photocopy and cut apart the pictures of a plant's growth cycle (see page 213). Let the children place the pictures in the correct sequence.

Flower Creation Center

Teacher Talk

Flowers come in many different colors.

Resources

plastic soft drink bottles, scissors, tissue paper, glue (thinned with water and placed in a shallow container), paintbrushes, magnetic tape strips, green construction paper

Let the children use the bottoms of plastic soft drink bottles to make flower magnets. Before class cut the bottoms off soft drink bottles about one inch from the bottom.

Give each child a plastic bottom. Let the child paint thinned glue inside the bottom. Have the children then tear or cut tissue paper into small pieces and press the pieces onto the glue. Attach a piece of magnetic tape to the back of each plastic flower. Have each child cut a thin strip of green construction paper and glue it to the back to make a stem.

Science Center

Teacher Talk

Flowers grow from seeds.

Resources

pictures of lupines (see page 214) or real lupines

Photocopy the lupine picture (page 214) or provide real lupines. Let the children look at the lupines and compare them to other flowers they studied this week. How are they the same? How are they different?

Art Center

Teacher Talk

We can help take care of the world God made.

Resources

paper lunch bag, markers and crayons, flower stickers

Have the children decorate the bags to take home and use as litter bags.

Writing Center

Teacher Talk

Flowers grow from seeds.

Resources

seed packets, garden catalog, paper, pencils

Set out seed packets and a garden catalog, with the paper and pencils nearby. Let the children copy letters or words from the printed material.

Worship Center

Teacher Talk

We can help take care of the world God made.

Resources

inflatable globe, plants, vase or pot of flowers

Set the plants and flowers on the table. Encourage the children to explore the globe.

Say: God created all kinds of plants and beautiful flowers. God created the whole world for us to use and enjoy, but we have to take care of the gift God gave us. Each of us can do something to help take care of the world.

Pray: Thank you, God, for giving us the whole world to enjoy and take care of. Amen.

Wonder Time

Call the children for wonder time. Before class place an earth ball or inflated globe inside a box. Wrap the box in gift paper.

Wonder Question: I wonder what's inside this box? *(Let each child hold the box. Open the box and show the contents.)*
Say: God made the whole world and everything in it. It's a wonderful gift.
Sing: "God Made the Flowers" to the tune of "The Farmer in the Dell."
Read the Bible verse.
Say: When someone gives us a present, we have to take care of it. The world is God's present to us, so we have to help take care of the world and everything in it.
Pray: Dear God, we will try to take care of the present you gave us—the world. Amen.

God Made the Flowers

God made the flowers;
God made the trees.
God made the whole wide world,
And God made me.

Thank you for the flowers;
Thank you for the trees.
Thank you, God, for all you made:
The plants, the world, and me.

Open the Bible to Genesis 1:31.

Say: "God looked at everything God had made, and God was very pleased" (Genesis 1:31, Good News Bible, adapted).

Have the children repeat the Bible verse.

Group Fun

Resources

plastic bags (for trash), paper, markers, crayons; or T-shirts (brought from home), leaves, flowers, cardboard, paintbrushes, fabric paint

If the weather allows, take a nature hike. Encourage the children to look for flowers and other natural things that God made. Use all your senses as you explore your environment: Look for as many plants as you can find; smell any growing things (especially flowers); touch the things (but don't pick) and describe how they feel; listen for and describe the sounds you hear. Talk about how each person can take care of the world. Pick up any trash you find as you walk. When you return from the hike, have each child draw a picture of something he or she saw.

If you need an alternative to this activity, help the children make flower print T-shirts. Have each child bring a T-shirt from home. Provide leaves and flowers that tend to be flat, such as daisies, pansies, and violets. Help each child place a piece of cardboard inside his or her shirt before painting. Let the child pick a flower, then "paint" the flower carefully with a paintbrush and fabric paint. Have the child place the flower, paint side down, somewhere on the front of the T-shirt. Tell her or him to press lightly, then lift the flower off. Repeat the process with other flowers and leaves.

Goodbye Circle

Let the children talk about the things they enjoyed doing. Ask each child to name two things that God made. Repeat the Bible verse.

Pray: Thank you, God, for this beautiful world that you made. Amen.

Evaluation

Was each child able to sit and listen to the story? Were children able to meet the day's objectives? Make plans to help those children who are having difficulties.

TREES

This week's study concludes the "Growing Things" month. During the coming week the children will learn the parts of a tree, names of trees, tree products, and other interesting tree facts as they participate in a variety of learning center and group activities. Each day the children will work to create a classroom forest by creating trees in a variety of different art media.

Ask parents to participate in these lessons by helping their children collect leaves to bring to class to study. The suggested culminating project for the week is to plant a small tree on the grounds of your building. You will need to get permission to do so in advance, and then determine some means to raise the funds. One inexpensive source of seedlings is the National Arbor Day Foundation, but they would need to be contacted well in advance of the project in order to allow time for the order to arrive.

Lesson 36

What Is a Tree?

Teacher Talk:

God created many different kinds of plants.

A tree is a plant with a stem made of wood.

Trees grow from seeds.

Bananas are a fruit that grows on trees.

Goals:

To learn that God created many different types of trees.

To help children learn about how trees grow.

Objectives:

By the end of this session the children will:

Taste a fruit that grows on a tree.

Use three different senses to study a tree.

Faith Connections

Bible verse: God commanded, "Let the earth produce all kinds of plants." (Genesis 1:11, *Good News Bible*, adapted)

Preschool children need the opportunity to learn that trees are one of the plants that God created for people to enjoy and use.

Teacher's Prayer

Dearest Lord, help me to share a love of nature with the children in my care. Let me inspire them to respect and care for the gifts you gave us. Amen.

Center Time

Set up your centers as described on pages 6-9. For this lesson add the following:

Art Center

Teacher Talk

A tree is a plant with a stem made of wood.

Resources

pieces of bark (from dead trees; do not remove bark from live trees), paper, pencils, crayons

Set the bark pieces on a table. Have the children place their papers over the bark and use the pencil or the crayons to create rubbings.

Cooking Center

Teacher Talk

Bananas are a fruit that grows on trees.

Resources

paper plates and napkins, bananas, plastic knives, basket

Place the bananas and knives on a plate or in a basket. Encourage the children to peel and slice pieces of bananas to eat and enjoy.

Math Center

Teacher Talk

God created many different kinds of trees.

Resources

variety of different leaves, baskets

Place leaves in a pile, with baskets nearby. Let the children sort the leaves into the baskets. Ask the children to describe the characteristics they are using to determine where the leaves should go.

Science Center

Teacher Talk

Trees grow from seeds.

Resources

rooted seed (either from outside or one you started indoors), pieces of bark, twigs, leaves, magnifying glass

Place the different tree parts on a table with the magnifying glass nearby. Encourage the children to study the tree parts with the glass.

As children arrive, ask, "What kind of plant grows very, very tall?" (a tree)

Tree Center

Teacher Talk

God created many different kinds of trees.

Resources

paper, sponges cut into small pieces, brown and green tempera paint in shallow containers, smocks, table covering

Cover the table and have the children wear smocks. Let the children use the sponges to paint pictures of a tree.

Writing Center

Teacher Talk

A tree is a plant with a stem made of wood.

Resources

index cards, picture of tree, marker, paper, pencils, tape

Write the following words on the index cards, one word per card: *roots, trunk, branch, leaf*. Hang the picture of the tree. Attach the words to the appropriate parts of the tree. Let the children copy letters or words.

Worship Center

Teacher Talk

God created many different kinds of plants.

Resources

picture of tree, plants

Set the tree picture and plants on a table.

Say: We have been learning about different kinds of plants this week. The plant we're learning about now is one that grows very tall—a tree. God made trees as a special plant that we can learn about, use, and take care of.

Pray: Thank you, God, for all the different kinds of plants you made. Amen.

Open the Bible to Genesis 1:11.

Say: "God commanded, 'Let the earth produce all kinds of plants'" (Genesis 1:11, *Good News Bible,* adapted).

Have the children repeat the Bible verse.

Wonder Time

Call the children together for wonder time.

Wonder Question: I wonder how trees grow?

Say: A tree is a special plant. Its stem is called a trunk and it is made of wood so it can be very strong. That's because trees grow very tall; they need strong stems so they won't fall down. We're going to sing a song that will help us learn the name of four important parts of a tree.

Have the children stand in a circle, with their feet together, their arms up and out wide, and their fingers stretched apart. Each child is now a "tree."

Sing: "Leaves, Branches, Trunk, and Roots" to the tune of "Mary Had a Little Lamb."

Read the Bible verse.

Say: God made trees in a special way, just like God made each one of you special. God loves every tree, and God loves you.

Pray: Thank you, God, for special trees and special people. Amen.

Leaves, Branches, Trunk, and Roots

Leaves *(wiggle fingers)*, branches *(wave arms)*, trunk *(wiggle body)* and roots *(stomp feet)*
Trunk *(wiggle body)* and roots *(stomp feet.)*,
Trunk *(wiggle body)* and roots *(stomp feet.)*.
Leaves, branches, trunk, and roots,
(Repeat actions as above.)
The four parts of a tree.

Group Fun

Resources

paper, crayons

Have each child bring a paper and crayon on a walk outside. Choose a tree to "meet." If possible, choose a place with several trees so each tree has only a small group of children to study it. Look at the trees from far away first, so you can see the whole tree. Talk about the tree's shape and what it looks like. Walk up to the tree and examine it closely. How does it feel? What color is it? What does it smell like? Examine the shape and size of the leaves on the tree. Have each child "hug" his or her tree. Can they get their arms around the trunk? Encourage each child to make a rubbing of the bark on his or her tree. If the weather cooperates, read the book of the day while sitting under a tree.

Goodbye Circle

Let the children talk about the things they enjoyed doing. Ask each child to name a part of a tree. Ask each child to demonstrate how big around his or her tree is. Repeat the Bible verse.

Pray: Thank you, God, for giving us trees to hug and care for. Amen.

Evaluation

Were children able to follow directions and participate in the tree study project during group time? Make plans to help those children who are having difficulties.

Lesson 37

Trees Help Us

Goals:

To learn that God created many different types of trees.

To help children appreciate a variety of plant life.

To help children learn the importance of taking care of the world.

To help children learn about how trees grow.

Objectives: By the end of this session the children will:

Name ways trees help us.

Name different trees.

Faith Connections

Bible verse: God made all kinds of beautiful trees grow there and produce good fruit.

(Genesis 2:9, *Good News Bible, adapted*)

Trees provide shade and beauty, but they are also extremely important to the functioning of our world. They provide shelter and food for many living things. Preschool children need the opportunity to learn that God provided many different kinds of trees to help us and for us to enjoy.

Teacher's Prayer

Thank you, God, for this opportunity to teach the young children in my care about nature and its purpose. Help me show them that we each have a part in caring for this world. Amen.

Teacher Talk:

God created many different kinds of plants.

God created many different kinds of trees.

Trees help us in many different ways.

Plums are a fruit that grows on trees.

Wood comes from trees.

Center Time

Set up your centers as described in Lesson 36. For this lesson add the following:

As children arrive, show something made out of wood. Say, "Wood comes from trees."

Art Center

Teacher Talk
Wood comes from trees.

Resources
paper, craft sticks, glue, markers

Have the children create pictures or designs. Explain that craft sticks are made of wood, a part of a tree. Let the children create trees with their sticks, then use markers to finish the pictures.

Building Center

Teacher Talk
Wood comes from trees.

Resources
variety of wooden blocks

Ask the children to look at the blocks as they build with them and talk about where the wood came from.

Dramatic Play Center

Teacher Talk
Trees help us in many different ways.

Resources
picnic basket, play food, table cloth, play dishes, dress-up clothes

Set out the materials. Encourage the children to pretend to have a picnic under a tree.

Tree Center

Teacher Talk
Trees help us in many different ways.

Resources
pictures of trees, variety of fruit, pieces of wood, small objects made from wood, picture of wooden house

Display the pictures. Set out the "tree objects." Have the children name each object and discuss how each one came from a tree.

Science Center

Teacher Talk
A tree is a plant with a stem made of wood.

Resources
small pieces of a variety of different kinds of wood, magnifying glass

Teacher Tip: Ask a local lumberyard or wood shop for samples. Most places will be glad to give you small blocks of a variety of different woods. (Be sure to label each piece.)

Encourage the children to compare different wood samples, using the magnifying glass as well as noses and fingers.

Cooking Center

Teacher Talk
Plums are a fruit that grows on trees.

Resources
paper plates and napkins, plastic knives, plums

Place plums and plastic knives on a plate. Have the children slice and taste the fruit.

Worship Center

Teacher Talk
God created many different kinds of trees.

Resources
basket of leaves, pictures of several different kinds of trees, bowl of fruit

Place the objects on a table. Have the children look at the objects and discuss them.

Say: All the things here are from trees; the leaves and all the fruit here grew on trees. God made many kinds of trees for us to use and enjoy.

Pray: Thank you, God, for giving us all different kinds of trees. Amen.

Wonder Time

Call the children together with a song.

Wonder Question: I wonder why God made trees?

Say: God made many different kinds of trees for us to use and enjoy. Who can think of a way that trees help us? (*They provide wood, shade, and fruit.*)

Play: "Name Something Wood." Have children sit in a circle and look around the room. Ask children to say with you: "I see something that comes from a tree. I see ___." Give each child a chance to name something in the room that comes from a tree.

Sing: "Trees Give Us" to the tune of "The Farmer in the Dell."

Read the Bible verse.

Say: God made many different trees just like God made many different people.

Pray: Thank you, God, for giving us so many trees to use and enjoy. Amen.

Trees Give Us

God made the trees.
God made the trees.
All kinds of trees all over the
world.
God made the trees.

Trees give us fruit.
Trees give us fruit.
Apples, plums, bananas too.
Trees give us fruit.

Trees give us shade.
Trees give us shade.
Maple, pine, and oak trees too,
Trees give us shade.

Trees give us wood.
Trees give us wood.
Maple, pine, and oak trees too,
Trees give us wood.

Open the Bible to Genesis 2:9.

Say: "God made all kinds of beautiful trees grow there and produce good fruit" (Genesis 2:9, *Good News Bible, adapted*).

Have the children repeat the Bible verse.

Group Fun

Resources

large piece of mat board (32" x 40"), 30 cardboard tubes, washable brown tempera paint, paint brushes, craft glue, tape, clothespins, leaves (1 per child)

Teacher Tip: A low-melt glue gun would work well in attaching the cardboard tubes to the background, but it should ONLY be used by an adult.

Help the children make a tree mural. Give each child several cardboard tubes to paint brown. These will be used to create the trunk and branches. While the tubes dry, talk about the parts of a tree and how trees help us. When the tubes are dry, lay them on the mat board and work together to create a tree trunk and branches. (A triangular "pine tree" shape is easiest). Tell the children that they will be decorating their "tree" during the rest of the week. When the tree is glued in place, give each child a leaf and a clothespin. Have each child glue the leaf to the clothespin, then clip the clothespin to a tree "branch" (it can be clipped to the open ends of a tube branch).

Goodbye Circle

Let the children talk about the things they enjoyed doing. Ask each child to name a tree and a way trees help us. Repeat the Bible verse.

Pray: Thank you, God, for trees that help us. Amen.

Evaluation

Were the children able to work together to create the tree? Was each child able to name something that came from a tree?

Lesson 38

All Kinds of Trees

Teacher Talk:

God created many different kinds of trees.

A tree is a plant with a stem made of wood.

Some trees grow very tall.

Fruit grows on trees.

Trees grow from seeds.

Goals:

To learn that God created many different types of trees.

To help children appreciate a variety of plant life.

To help children learn the importance of taking care of the world.

To help children learn about how trees grow.

Objectives: By the end of this session the children will:

Taste a fruit that grows on a tree.

Name a giant tree.

Faith Connections

Bible verse: Abraham planted a tamarisk tree and worshiped the LORD.

(Genesis 21:33, *Good News Bible*, adapted)

God created many different kinds of plants when the world was made, but trees are the largest and longest living. Trees often serve as memorials and markers because of their long life spans. When Abraham wished to honor God and thank God, he chose to do so by planting a tree. Preschool children can learn that trees are special and important, to us and to God.

Teacher's Prayer

Loving God, you protect us and care for us by giving us a world filled with a variety of plant life. Help me to teach the children in my care to honor your gift by caring for it and appreciating it. Amen.

Center Time

Set up your centers as described in Lessons 36-37. For this lesson add the following:

Art Center

Teacher Talk

Some trees grow very tall.

Resources

pictures of tall trees (such as redwoods), paper, washable tempera paints, paintbrushes, smocks

Display pictures of tall trees. Let each child use paints to make a picture of a very tall tree or any other type of tree she or he chooses.

Cooking Center

Teacher Talk

Fruit grows on trees.

Resources

table, chairs, paper plates and napkins, dates, plastic knives

Place the dates on a plate. Let the children slice and taste the fruit. Tell the children that this is a fruit Jesus might have eaten, and that the trees dates grow on can be almost 60 feet tall.

Math Center

Teacher Talk

Trees grow from seeds.

Resources

acorns, pine cones and other tree seeds; shallow bowls (one for each seed type)

Place tree seeds in a container on the table. Have the children sort the seeds into the bowls.

Science Center

Teacher Talk

Trees grow from seeds.

Resources

acorns, pine cones, and other tree seeds; pictures of each tree represented by a seed; magnifying glass

Place each type of seed next to the picture of the tree. Have the children study the seeds with the magnifying glass. Talk about how seeds get planted and grow to become trees.

As children arrive, say, "Pretend you are a very tall tree. How tall can you grow?"

Tree Center

Teacher Talk

God created many different kinds of trees.

Resources

tree created yesterday from paper tubes, cupcake papers, tissue paper, clothespins, glue, tape

Hang the tree created yesterday. Have the children create spring blossoms from cupcake papers and tissue paper. Let each child tear a small piece of tissue paper and then crumple it into a ball. Have the children glue the paper balls into the center of the cupcake papers to make blossoms. Attach the blossoms to the clothespins using glue or tape. The children can fasten the clothespins to the tree.

Writing Center

Teacher Talk

Trees grow from seeds.

Resources

small bowl of tree seeds, picture of grown tree, index cards, paper and pencil

Write the words *seeds* and *tree* on index cards. Place each card next to the appropriate object. Have the children copy the words.

Worship Center

Teacher Talk

God created many different kinds of trees.

Resources

variety of tree seeds, pot of dirt

Place the seeds next to the pot. Let each child place a seed into the pot and pat it in place.

Say: These seeds may grow into trees if we care for them and water them. Trees are important plants God created, and we can help take care of God's world by planting more trees.

Pray: Dear God, we love you and will try to help this tree grow. Amen.

Open the Bible to Genesis 21:33.

Say: "Abraham planted a tamarisk tree and worshiped the LORD" (Genesis 21:33, *Good News Bible*, adapted).

Have the children repeat the Bible verse.

Wonder Time

Call the children together.

Wonder Question: I wonder how big a tree can get?

Say: There are many different kinds of trees, and they can be short and tall. Some trees can grow taller than our whole building! No matter how big a tree grows, it starts from a seed.

Sing: "I'm an Oak Tree" to the tune of "Twinkle, Twinkle Little Star")

Read the Bible verse.

Say: God gave us special seeds that can grow into giant trees. Only God could make something so big start with something so small.

Pray: Thank you, God, for making giant trees come from tiny seeds. Amen.

I'm an Oak Tree

Have the children stand in a circle as they sing. When they are trees, have the children stand tall with arms up high. When they are small or seeds, have them crouch down low.

I'm an oak tree, big and tall.
Once I was an acorn small.
Oak trees start as little seeds.
Little seeds become oak trees.
I'm an oak tree, big and tall.
Once I was an acorn small.

Group Fun

Resources

80' length of yarn, cassette/CD player, cassette/CD, green crepe paper streamers

Have children help you lay the yarn in a circle around the room. This is the circumference of an average redwood. Have the children stand around the outside edge of the circle. Talk about how big the circle is and how big the tree would be.

Give each child a green crepe paper streamer. Have the children move around the circle as you play the cassette/CD. Encourage the children to bend and move as if they were branches and leaves in the wind. When the children have danced for a short time (or when they are tired of the activity) have the children hold hands and make as big a circle as they can. Can they make a circle as big as the tree? Have the children jump as high as they can. Can they jump as high as a tree? Have the children curl up as tiny as they can. Can they become as small as a seed?

Goodbye Circle

Let the children talk about the things they enjoyed doing today. Ask each child to name a giant tree. Repeat the Bible verse.

Pray: Thank you, God, for giant trees, and small trees, and all kinds of trees in the world. Amen.

Evaluation

Was each child able to listen and follow directions as you did the group activity? Are the children comfortable speaking up and answering questions at group time? Make notes of any children who are having difficulties.

Lesson 39

A Tree Is a House

Goals:

To learn that God created many different types of trees.

To help children appreciate a variety of plant life.

To help children learn the importance of taking care of the world.

To help children learn about how trees grow.

Objectives: By the end of this session the children will:

Name animals that live in trees.

Examine an animal's home that was in a tree.

Faith Connections

Bible verse: In the trees near by,
the birds make their nests and sing.
(Psalm 104:12, *Good News Bible*)

Every living thing is part of God's creation. All things are part of a web of interdependence; we all need each other. Preschool children need to know that trees are more than just very tall plants—trees provide homes for many different kinds of animals. When we plant a tree or help a tree, we help more than just one tree. We help to care for God's creation.

Teacher's Prayer

Creator God, you made a world full of life. Help me to protect those living things that are within my care. Amen.

Teacher Talk:

God created many different kinds of trees.

A tree is a plant with a stem made of wood.

Trees grow from seeds.

Fruit grows on trees.

Many animals live in trees.

Center Time

Set up your centers as described in Lessons 36-38. For this lesson add the following:

As children arrive, say, "Think of an animal that makes its home in a tree."

Science Center

Teacher Talk

Many animals live in trees.

Resources

bird's nest and bee's nest (real if possible, or use books about bees and birds), magnifying glass

If you have the actual nests, let the children examine them with a magnifying glass. If you have books, look through them with the children.

Dramatic Play Center

Teacher Talk

Many animals live in trees.

Resources

large cardboard box such as an appliance box, large pieces of paper, markers, tape

Let the children cover the box with paper to create a house in a tree. The children can decorate the house with markers, then enjoy playing inside.

Writing Center

Teacher Talk

Many animals live in trees.

Resources

index cards; marker; paper; pencils; pictures of birds, bats, bees, and so forth

Write the names of animals who live in trees on index cards (bird, bat, bee). Hang them at the children's eye level. Place the pictures of the animals next to their names on the cards. Write only the names of animals you have pictures of. Let the children copy the words.

Home Living Center

Teacher Talk

Fruit grows on trees.

Resources

table, chairs, paper plates and napkins, orange slices

Place orange slices on a plate. Encourage the children to eat the "fruit from a tree" snacks.

Art Center

Teacher Talk

A tree is a plant with a stem made of wood.

Resources

twigs from trees and small branches from pine trees, tempera paint, paper, smocks, table covering, shallow containers

Cover the table and have the children wear smocks. Pour paint into shallow containers. Give each child a piece of paper. Let the children paint with the twigs and branches.

Tree Center

Teacher Talk

Many animals live in trees.

Resources

magazines and old greeting cards, clothespins, glue, tape, scissors

Have the children find pictures of animals that live in trees in the magazines and cards. Let the children cut out the pictures and glue or tape them to clothespins, then fasten them to the paper tube tree.

Worship Center

Teacher Talk

God created many different kinds of trees.

Resources

tree seeds planted yesterday, bird's nest

Place the pot with planted seeds and the nest on a table for the children to examine.

Say: It takes a long time for a seed to grow into a tree. But if we take care of it, it will grow. That is part of God's plan. When the tree is tall and grown, it might become a home for a bird, squirrel, or even a rabbit. All kinds of animals and insects live in trees. That is also part of God's plan. We can help by planting and taking care of trees.

Pray: Thank you, God, for making me part of your plan. Amen.

Wonder Time

Call the children together.

Wonder Question: I wonder what lives in a tree?

Say: When you go outside and look at a tree, what kinds of animals do you see in the tree? *(birds, squirrels, various insects)* Talk about other animals that live in trees: bats, foxes, rabbits and mice.

Sing: "In a Tree" to the tune of "Head, Shoulders, Knees and Toes."

Read the Bible verse.

Say: Trees are very helpful—they provide wood and food and shade for us. They also provide homes for many different kinds of animals.

Pray: Thank you, God, for making trees to be homes for the animals. Amen.

In a Tree

Birds
(Flap wings.)
And squirrels
(Hold hands like paws on either side of chin.)
Live in trees, live in trees.
(Stand tall with arms in air as branches.),

Birds and squirrels live in trees, live in trees
And bats
(Make wings.)
And rabbits
(Hold hands up to make rabbit ears.)
And caterpillars too.
(Move right hand in undulating motion.)
Birds and squirrels live in trees.

Open the Bible to Psalm 104:12.

Say: "In the trees near by, the birds make their nests and sing" (Psalm 104:12, *Good News Bible*).

Have the children repeat the Bible verse.

Group Fun

Resources

prepared cookie dough, food coloring, tree shaped cookie cutters, cookie sheets, oven, wax paper

Help the children make tree cookies. Lay out wax paper so each child has a surface to work on. Give each child a small handful of dough. Have each child make a thumbprint in her or his dough. Add two or three drops of green food coloring to the dough. Have the children knead the color into the dough. Let the children flatten the dough and cut out tree shapes using the cookie cutters. Bake the cookies as directed on the package, then eat and enjoy. While the cookies are baking, do the "Tree Walk" action poem. Have the children repeat each line and motions.

Tree Walk

We're going on a nature walk *(Walk in place.)*
To see what we can see. *(Place your hand over your eyes.)*
We'll smell some pretty flowers *(Sniff.)*
And find a special tree.
Look, there's a perfect one. *(Point.)*
Come on and follow me.
The sun is getting very hot *(Wipe your brow.)*
And I found a shady tree.
Let's lie down *(Lie down on the floor.)*
And take a rest.
Look up! Look up! I see a small bird's nest. *(Point to sky.)*
A squirrel is walking down the trunk, *(Walk your fingers down your arm.)*
And another one—that's two. *(Hold up two fingers.)*
Some ants are climbing on my hand. *(Walk your fingers down your hand.)*
And look there are some on you! *(Point to others.)*

Goodbye Circle

Let the children talk about the things they enjoyed doing today. Ask each child to name an animal that lives in a tree. Repeat the Bible verse.

Pray: Thank you, God, for trees and animals that live in trees. Amen.

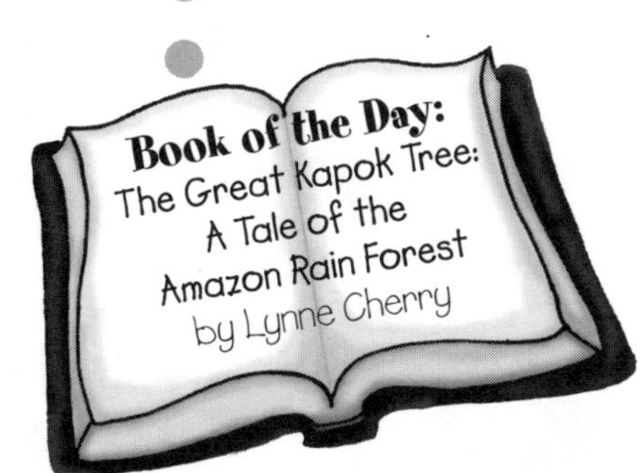

Evaluation

Was each child able to meet the day's objectives? Were children able to listen to and follow the directions for the group activities? Make plans to help any children who are having difficulties.

Lesson 40

A Tree Is Nice

Teacher Talk:

God created many different kinds of plants.

God created many different kinds of trees.

A tree is a plant with a stem made of wood.

Trees grow from seeds.

Maple syrup and nuts come from trees.

Goals:

To learn that God created many different types of trees.

To help children appreciate a variety of plant life.

To help children learn the importance of taking care of the world.

To help children learn about how trees grow.

Objectives: By the end of this session the children will:

Name a food that comes from trees.

Count a tree's rings to determine its age.

Help plant a tree.

Faith Connections

Bible verse: God looked at everything God had made, and God was very pleased.

(Genesis 1:31, *Good News Bible*, adapted)

God created many different kinds of plants, but trees are the giants of the plant world. They are an important part of the ecological balance of our world. Arbor Day is generally celebrated at the end of April, and is a special day dedicated to the planting and caring of trees. God was pleased with all God created, and God expects us to care for each part of that creation.

Teacher's Prayer

Dear God, creator of all things. Thank you for the gift of this beautiful world. Be with me as I try to teach the children in my care the importance of respecting this gift. Amen.

Center Time

Set up your centers as described in Lessons 36-39. For this lesson add the following:

As children **arrive,** say, "God made trees, and God made you!"

Art Center

Teacher Talk

God created many different kinds of trees.

Resources

pine cones, tempera paint, paper, smocks, table covering, shallow containers

Cover the table and have the children wear smocks. Pour paint in to shallow containers. Give each child a piece of paper. Show the children how to dip the pine cones into the paint and then press the cones onto their paper to make prints. Remind the children that pine cones are seeds that grow into pine trees.

Cooking Center

Teacher Talk

Maple syrup and nuts come from trees.

Resources

table, chairs, plate, shallow container, napkins, graham crackers, maple syrup

Place maple syrup in a shallow container. Set graham crackers on a plate. Let each child dip a graham cracker in the maple syrup and enjoy the snack.

Math Center

Teacher Talk

Maple syrup and nuts come from trees.

Resources

different kinds of nuts, baskets, tongs

Place nuts in a large basket. Set empty baskets nearby. Have the children sort the nuts, using tongs to place each type in a basket. Ask the children to describe how the nuts are different.

Dramatic Play Center

Teacher Talk

God created many different kinds of plants.

Resources

gardening gloves and tools, artificial plants

Let the children use the objects to pretend to garden.

Tree Center

Teacher Talk

A tree is a plant with a stem made of wood.

Resources

tree trunk "slices" (cross-cut pieces) showing trees of different ages.

Set out the tree trunk slices. Have the children count the rings to determine each tree's age.

Teacher Tip: Cross-cut trunk pieces may be found by contacting tree-removal services, lumber mills, local park rangers, or local agriculture agents.

Science Center

Teacher Talk

Maple syrup and nuts come from trees.

Resources

several different varieties of nuts, balance scale, magnifying glass, pictures of the trees the nuts came from.

Have the children examine and weigh the nuts. Have the children look at the nuts and the pictures of the trees they came from.

Worship Center

Teacher Talk

God created many different kinds of plants.

Resources

small tree in pot (ready to be planted)

Place the tree and pot on the table or next to the table. Have the children examine it.

Say: This is a small tree that will someday grow to be large enough to make shade for children and homes for animals. We are going to plant it today to help keep God's world beautiful.

Pray: Thank you, God, for giving us trees and this beautiful world. Amen.

Open the Bible to Genesis 1:31.

Say: "God looked at everything God had made, and God was very pleased" (Genesis 1:31, *Good News Bible*, adapted).

Have the children repeat the Bible verse.

Wonder Time

Call the children together with a song or fingerplay.

Wonder Question: I wonder what a tree would say if it could talk?

Say: All week we've been learning about trees. Trees can be big and small. Some have fruits and some have nuts. Some are homes for animals. Trees are nice.

Play: "I'm a Tree." Have the children stand in a circle. Play instrumental music on a cassette/CD player and encourage children to move to the music to act out the following parts of a tree's life: planting the tree, growing, waving in the wind, leaves falling, new leaves growing, becoming very tall.

Read the Bible verse.

Say: Trees are a very special part of the world God made for us.

Pray: Thank you, God, for trees. Amen.

Group Fun

Resources

tree in pot, shovel, watering can with water, several small shovels

Plant a tree with the children. Take the tree outside and set it where it will be planted. (The hole should be dug prior to class.) Allow each child to remove a small amount of dirt from the hole. Place the tree in the hole and plant it according to the directions. Give each child the opportunity to participate by helping to hold the tree and helping replace the dirt in the hole. Each child can then help water the tree.

Sing "If You Like Trees" to the tune of "If You're Happy and You Know It."

If You Like Trees

If you like trees and you know it,
clap your hands.
If you like trees and you know it,
clap your hands.
If you like trees and you know it,
and you really want to show it,
If you like trees and you know it,
clap your hands.

Goodbye Circle

Let the children talk about the things they enjoyed doing today. Ask each child to name one reason he or she thinks a tree is nice. Repeat the Bible verse.

Pray: Thank you, God, for all the many kinds of plants you made for the world. Amen.

Evaluation

Was each child able to achieve the day's objectives? How did the children react to planting a tree? Make note of any children having difficulties.

Unit 3

The Earth Is Alive

Goals:

1. The children will have the opportunity to learn about common types of spring weather.

2. The children will have the opportunity to learn about the water cycle.

3. The children will learn that weather is a natural part of God's plan for the world.

4. The children will have the opportunity to explore bugs, birds, and reptiles and learn that these creatures are an important part of God's creation.

5. The children will have the opportunity to improve their observation skills.

The earth is alive with the many wonderful things God created. In this unit the children will have the opportunity to explore some of those wonderful things. God planned the world with many types of weather conditions including wind, clouds, rain, rainbows, and sunshine. Living things need the water and sunshine and air that weather provides. Weather is an important and natural part of God's creation.

Another important and natural part of God's creation are things that creep and crawl! In this unit your children will have the opportunity to become familiar with bugs, birds, and reptiles. Help your children realize that these creeping and flying creatures have a purpose in God's world.

Bible Stories for This Unit:
Genesis 1 (The Creation)
Genesis 9 (The Rainbow)
Leviticus 26:4 (God Sends the Rain)
Proverbs 6:8 (Ants)
Psalm 145 (All Creatures Praise the Lord)

SPRING WEATHER

This week's unit is designed to help children learn about common types of spring weather. The week is designed to flow in a logical weather sequence: wind, clouds, rain, rainbows, and sunshine. Each day the children will participate in a variety of learning center and group projects which will allow them to learn about the day's weather focus.

If you do not keep a weather calendar as a regular classroom activity, this would be a good time to start one. Use a purchased blank calendar or create a simple one of your own. Each day, as part of group time, ask the children to describe what the weather is like outside, then have a child draw a symbol representing the weather (or use purchased stickers).

Lesson 41

Wind

Teacher Talk:

God planned for the world to have all kinds of weather.

What is the weather like today?

Wind is moving air.

Goals:

To help children learn what weather is.

To provide opportunities for children to learn about various types of spring weather.

To help children learn that God planned the world with many types of weather.

Objectives:

By the end of this session the children will:

Name a way they can tell the wind is blowing.

Do an activity that demonstrates what the wind can do.

Faith Connections

Bible verse: God sends the wind. (Psalm 147:18, *Good News Bible*, adapted)

God planned the world with many types of weather conditions, some that are helpful and some that can be dangerous. The wind can move slowly or very quickly. It can be helpful when it dries clothes on a line or dries the water in a puddle, or it can be dangerous as in a hurricane or tornado. Children need the opportunity to learn what wind is and to know that even though they can't see it, it does exist.

Teacher's Prayer

Dearest Lord, like the wind I know you exist, even though I can't see you. I feel your presence in the world even as I feel the wind on my skin. Help me to teach the children in my care that you exist just as the wind does. Amen.

Center Time

Set up your centers as described on pages 6–9. For this lesson add the following:

As children arrive, have the children blow on a set of wind chimes.

Art Center

Teacher Talk

Wind is moving air.

Resources

paper, washable tempera paint (thinned) (or watercolors and eyedroppers), straws, spoons, table covering, smocks

Cover the table and have the children wear smocks. Spoon a small amount of paint on each child's paper. Show the children how to use straws to blow out and move the paint around the paper.

Building Center

Teacher Talk

Wind is moving air.

Resources

variety of wooden or large cardboard blocks

Encourage the children to use the blocks to build towers (no more than waist high). Have the children try to "blow" the towers over to demonstrate wind power. Can one child blow the tower over? How many children does it take to "blow it down"?

Manipulatives Center

Teacher Talk

Wind is moving air.

Resources

ping pong balls, masking tape, paper towel tube, turkey baster, eye dropper, paper fan, straw, piece of cardboard.

Tape two lines on the floor or table four inches apart. Have the children experiment with moving air. Let the children use the objects provided to move ping pong balls from one line to the other.

Science Center

Teacher Talk

Wind is moving air.

Resources

paper

Help the children fold paper airplanes and fly them. Discuss which planes fly fastest or farthest.

Water Table

Teacher Talk

Wind is moving air.

Resources

water table or dish pan, water, toy sail boats

Let the children play with the sailboats. Discuss how wind makes sail boats move.

Weather Center

Teacher Talk

What is the weather like today?

Resources

weather chart, marker or stickers, fan with streamers attached, newspaper page showing weather

Place a weather chart and the weather section of a newspaper where the children can see them. Turn the fan on so the streamers are blowing.

Writing Center

Teacher Talk

Wind is moving air.

Resources

index card, marker, paper, pencils

Write the word *wind* on an index card. Hang it at the children's eye level. Let the children copy the word.

Worship Center

Teacher Talk

God planned for the world to have all kinds of weather.

Resources

plant

Encourage the children to blow on the plant's leaves to see how they move in the wind.

Say: When you blow on the plant's leaves, they move. You know the wind blows because you can see what it does. We can't see God, but we know God is here because we can see everything God made—the world and everything in it.

Pray: Thank you, God, for things we can see and things we can't see. Amen.

Open the Bible to Psalm 147:18.

Say: "God sends the wind" (Psalm 147:18, *Good News Bible*, adapted).

Have the children repeat the Bible verse.

Wonder Time

Call the children together.

Wonder Question: I wonder what wind is?

Say: Wind is moving air. We can't see it, but we know when it is windy because we can see things move.

Sing: "I'm a Spring Wind" to the tune of "Alouette."

Read the Bible verse.

Say: God planned for the world to have all kinds of weather. Wind is one of the kinds of weather in God's world.

Pray: Thank you, God, for wind and all kinds of weather. Amen.

I'm a Spring Wind

I'm a spring wind,
Just a gentle spring wind.
I'm a spring wind,
Whoo, whoo, whoo, whoo, whoo.
(Cup hands around mouth and blow for each word.)
Do you see the tree leaves blow?
Do you see the sailboats go?
Tree leaves blow, sailboats go. Oh!
I'm a spring wind,
Just a gentle spring wind.
I'm a spring wind,
Whoo, whoo, whoo, whoo, whoo.

Group Fun

Resources

bubble soap (or liquid detergent), water, chenille stick, cups (optional: wind chime; wire coat hangers; yarn, scissors, construction paper, glue; variety of craft materials with holes for easy attachment, such as old keys, buttons, paper clips, old cookie cutters, and old earrings)

Let the children blow bubbles. (This is an outdoor activity.) Give each child a chenille stick, and help the child bend it into a wand by making a circle at one end. Mix detergent and water together, and place a small amount into each cup. Give each child a cup of the mixture. The children can blow bubbles and watch the way the bubbles float. Ask the children questions as they watch the bubbles: Which way are the bubbles floating? Which way is the wind blowing?

As an alternative indoor activity, help the children make wind chimes. Show the children a wind chime and demonstrate its sound. Give each child a hanger and several pieces of yarn. Encourage the children to choose several craft materials, tie them to the yarn (help as needed), and tie the yarn to the hanger. When the wind chime is completed, the children can decorate the hangers with the construction paper by cutting or tearing small pieces and gluing them to the metal.

Teacher Tip: Send a note home the week before the activity asking for parent donations of craft materials.

Goodbye Circle

Let the children talk about the things they enjoyed doing today. Ask each child to name a way they can tell the wind is blowing. Repeat the Bible verse.

Pray: Thank you, God, for the wind that blows. Amen.

Evaluation

Was each child able to listen and follow directions during the group project? Was each child able to meet the day's objectives? Make plans to help those children who are having difficulties.

Lesson 42

Clouds

Goals:

To help children learn what weather is.

To provide opportunities for children to learn about various types of spring weather.

To help children learn that God planned the world with many types of weather.

Objectives: By the end of this session the children will:

Create clouds.

Name the substance that clouds are made of.

Faith Connections

Bible verse: Look at the sky! See how high the clouds are!
(Job 35:5, *Good News Bible*)

Clouds are a majestic part of the sky. We watch them and dream. We look at their shapes and let our imaginations run free. Preschool children need the opportunity to cloud watch and dream. They can also be introduced to the weather function of clouds. They can learn that clouds are a part of God's creation.

Teacher's Prayer

Dear God, clouds let us dream and envision all sorts of wonderful things. Help me unleash the imaginations of the children in my care as we study and enjoy this part of your world. Amen.

Teacher Talk:

God planned for the world to have all kinds of weather.

What is the weather like today?

Clouds are made of tiny drops of water.

Clouds can be different shapes, sizes, and colors.

Center Time

Continue the centers from Lesson 41. For this lesson add or change the following:

As children arrive, say, "Pretend you are a cloud and float into the room."

Art Center

Teacher Talk

Clouds can be different shapes, sizes, and colors.

Resources

blue construction paper, white washable tempera paint, shallow containers, cotton balls, paint smocks, table covering

Cover the table and have the children wear smocks. Pour the paint into shallow containers. Encourage the children to dip the cotton balls into the paint and create cloud pictures on blue construction paper. Throw the cotton balls away as they become soggy.

Cooking Center

Teacher Talk

Clouds can be different shapes, sizes, and colors.

Resources

paper plates and napkins, white bread slices

Place slices of bread on a plate. Encourage the children to eat a slice by biting the edges of the bread to make cloud shapes.

Math Center

Teacher Talk

Clouds can be different shapes, sizes, and colors.

Resources

black and white construction paper, scissors

Before class, cut sets of cloud shapes from white and black paper. Encourage the children to match the clouds and their shadows.

Writing Center

Teacher Talk

Clouds can be different shapes, sizes, and colors.

Resources

index cards, pictures of clouds, marker, paper, pencils

Write cloud names on the index cards (cumulus, cirrus, stratus). Place each card next to the appropriate cloud picture. Encourage the children to copy the cloud names.

Science Center

Teacher Talk

Clouds are made of tiny drops of water.

Resources

glasses of ice water, hand mirror

Set out a mirror and glasses of ice water. Have the children look at the moisture on the outside of the glass (condensation). Have the children hold a hand mirror over the ice water to cool it, then blow across the mirror to create a cloud.

Weather Center

Teacher Talk

Clouds can be different shapes, sizes, and colors.

Resources

weather chart, marker or stickers, cloud pictures

Place a weather chart and a newspaper weather section where the children can easily see them. Hang the pictures of clouds. Encourage the children to look at them and discuss their shapes.

Worship Center

Teacher Talk

God created all kinds of weather.

Resources

window, globe

Place the globe on a table under a window, if possible, or hang a picture of the sky with clouds.

Say: When you look at the sky, what do you see? Everything in the sky was created by God. God put the clouds in the sky, and by looking at the clouds, we can learn to tell what the weather will be. God made the clouds and the sky and this beautiful world because God loves us.

Pray: Thank you, God, for sky, and clouds, and the whole world. Amen.

Wonder Time

Call the children together for wonder time.

I'm a Cloud

Made of water and filled with air,
High up in the sky.
Cumulus, stratus, and cirrus clouds.
I watch you floating by.

Wonder Question: I wonder what clouds are made of?

Say: Clouds are made of many tiny little drops of water that rise into the air. Sometimes they are puffy and white. Sometimes they are dark and gray. They can be high in the sky or low. We can look at them and see all kinds of shapes.

Play: Cloud Jumping. Cut white construction paper into a variety of cloud shapes. Have the children help you tape the clouds to the floor. Play a cassette/CD, and let the children leap from cloud to cloud, moving softly as they think a cloud might.

Sing: "I'm a Cloud" to the tune of "Row, Row, Row Your Boat."

Read the Bible verse.

Say: God made clouds as part of our world. We can look at them and know what kind of weather we are going to have. And we can look at them and pretend they are all kinds of things.

Pray: Thank you, God, for clouds in the sky. Amen.

Open the Bible to Job 35:5.

Say: "Look at the sky! See how high the clouds are!" (Job 35:5, *Good News Bible*).

Have the children repeat the Bible verse.

Group Fun

Resources

none (optional: shaving cream)

If weather allows, go outside and lie down on the ground. Talk about the clouds you see in the sky. What do they look like? What kinds of clouds are they? Have the children describe their color and shape. What direction are they moving?

If weather doesn't allow for cloud watching, make clouds indoors. Spray shaving cream on the classroom tables (you only need a small amount) and let the children create clouds and cloud designs. Be sure the children know this is shaving cream and not a food. When the cloud fun is over, simply wipe the shaving cream off with paper towels and your table will be clean and very fresh smelling!

Goodbye Circle

Let the children talk about the things they enjoyed doing today. Ask each child to tell something they learned about clouds. Repeat the Bible verse.

Pray: Thank you, God, for clouds and all kinds of weather. Amen.

Evaluation

Were the children able to see pictures in the clouds? Was each child able to meet the day's objectives? Make plans to help children who are having difficulties.

Lesson 43

Rain

Teacher Talk:

God planned for the world to have all kinds of weather.

What is the weather like today?

God made rain so plants and animals could grow.

Rain is an important part of our weather.

Goals:

To help children learn what weather is.

To provide opportunities for children to learn about various types of spring weather.

To help children learn that God planned the world with many types of weather.

Objectives: By the end of this session the children will:

Recite the parts of the water cycle.

Name something that rain does.

Faith Connections

Bible verse: I will send you rain at the right time so that the land will produce crops and the trees will bear fruit.

(Leviticus 26:4, *Good News Bible*)

Living things need water to grow—plants, animals, and people. We drink it, we wash in it, we play in it. Rain is part of the cycle that provides our planet's water. Preschool children need to know that rain is an important part of God's plan for the world.

Teacher's Prayer

Dearest Lord, you provided for all of our needs when you created the world. Help me to meet the needs of the children in my care. Amen.

Center Time

Continue the centers from Lessons 41-42. For this lesson add or change the following:

As children arrive, use a mister to spray a small amount of water on each child's hands.

Art Center

Teacher Talk

Rain is an important part of our weather.

Resource

construction paper, watercolor paints, paint-brushes, glue, glitter

Cut paper into large raindrop shapes. Have the children paint the raindrops with water colors. They can decorate the paintings with glitter.

Math Center

Teacher Talk

Rain is an important part of our weather.

Resources

umbrella, paper

Open the umbrella. Place it upside down on the floor. Let the children crunch paper into paper balls and toss them in the umbrella. Encourage the children to count the balls.

Writing Center

Teacher Talk

Rain is an important part of our weather.

Resources

index card, marker, paper, pencils

Write the word *rain* on an index card. Let the children copy the word.

Music Center

Teacher Talk

God planned for the world to have all kinds of weather.

Resources

cassette/CD player, cassette/CD, rain sticks, rhythm instruments

If you do not have access to real rain sticks, make your own. Dip toothpicks in glue, then poke them through wrapping paper tubes. Let dry. Close one end of the tube with a cardboard circle and tape. Pour a half cup of fine gravel inside. Tape the other end closed. Encourage the children to experiment with the sound of the rain stick, and use it to accompany music.

Water Table

Teacher Talk

Rain is an important part of our weather.

Resources

water table, cookie sheet, eyedroppers

Place the cookie sheet in the water table in an inclined position. Let the children drop water on the cookie sheet and "race" the drops down the side. Have the children watch the paths the drops take.

Weather Center

Teacher Talk

What is the weather like today?

Resources

weather chart, weather stickers or markers, pictures of rainy days and lightning

Hang a weather chart. Let the children determine what the weather is like outside today. Have the children look at the rain and storm pictures and talk about what they see.

Worship Center

Teacher Talk

God made rain so plants and animals could grow.

Resources

plant, fruits (2 or 3), vegetables (2 or 3), basket, watering can with water

Place the fruit and vegetables in a basket. Set it on a table next to the plant. Place the watering can next to the plant.

Say: All the fruits and vegetables in this basket came from plants that God made. The plants, like this one, need something special to grow—rain! God made rain so plants and people would have water to drink so they could grow.

Pray: Thank you, God, for making rain so plants can grow and so I can grow too. Amen.

Open the Bible to Leviticus 26:4.

Say: "I will send you rain at the right time so that the land will produce crops and the trees will bear fruit" (Leviticus 26:4, *Good News Bible*).

Have the children repeat the Bible verse.

Wonder Time

Call the children together for wonder time.

Wonder Question: I wonder where rain comes from?

Say: God had a special plan to make rain. It's called the "Water Cycle."

Do: "The Water Cycle Chant" to the tune of "Peanut, Peanut Butter." Have the children repeat the motions after you.

Read the Bible verse.

Say: God created rain so that plants and animals and people would have the water they need so they could grow.

Pray: Thank you, God, for making rain so we would have water. Amen.

The Water Cycle Chant

Chorus
Water, Water Cycle - *(whisper)* Rain!
Water, Water Cycle - *(whisper)* Rain!
Verses:
First God makes a cloud and it rains.
It rains, it really, really rains.
("Rain" fingers downward.)
Chorus
Rain fills up the lakes,
The rivers and the oceans.
It really fills the oceans. *(Make larger and larger circles with your hands.)*
Chorus
The sun comes out and shines.
It shines, it really, really shines.
(Make large circle overhead with arms)
Chorus
The water drops float up.
They float up, they really, really float up. *("Rain" fingers upward.)*
Chorus
The drops form a cloud. A cloud.
They really form a cloud. (*Wiggle fingers in air then bring hands together.*)
Chorus
And then it starts to rain.
It rains, it really, really rains.
("Rain" fingers downward.)
Chorus

Group Fun

Resources

paper plates, construction paper, powdered tempera paint, eye droppers, bowl of water, cookie sheets, box lids, or other large shallow containers, scissors, glue, umbrella pattern (see page 215)

Help the children make rain pictures. Before class, use the pattern (see page 215) to cut the paper plates into umbrella shapes. Give each child an "umbrella." Have each child place the umbrella in a shallow container. Let the child sprinkle powdered tempera paint on the shape. The children can then drop "raindrops" of water on the paint to make "rain designs" using the eyedropper or their fingers (children can place fingers in water then shake their hands over the umbrella). Let the paintings dry. While the paintings are drying, the children can cut handles out of the construction paper. Attach the handles when picture is dry.

Goodbye Circle

Let the children talk about the things they enjoyed doing today. Ask each child to name something that rain does. Repeat the Bible verse.

Pray: Thank you, God, for rain and clouds and all kinds of weather. Amen.

Evaluation

Were children able to listen and follow directions to create the project during group time? Was each child able to meet the day's objectives? Make plans to work with children who need additional help.

Lesson 44

Rainbows

Goals:

To help children learn what weather is.

To provide opportunities for children to learn about various types of spring weather.

To help children learn that God planned the world with many types of weather.

Objectives: By the end of this session the children will:

Name a color that is in a rainbow.

Participate in a rainbow project.

Faith Connections

Bible verse: God said, "When the rainbow appears in the clouds I will remember my promise to you."

(Genesis 9:16, *Good News Bible*, adapted)

In the scripture, God created the first rainbow after a huge rainstorm—a rain storm that flooded the whole earth. That first rainbow was a promise to Noah and his family that God would never destroy the earth with a flood again. Each time we see a rainbow we remember God's promise. Preschool children can learn that rainbows are a part of God's weather, and can be seen after a rain storm. They are a special gift from God.

Teacher's Prayer

Lord of all, thank you for rainbows and sunshine that follow the gray and wet of a stormy day. Help me to remember that there is always good that follows bad, and that you are with me and the children in my care at every moment of every day. Amen.

Teacher Talk:

God planned for the world to have all kinds of weather.

What is the weather like today?

God made rainbows.

Rainbows appear after a rainstorm.

Center Time

Continue the centers from Lessons 41-43. For this lesson add or change the following:

As children arrive, ask, "Have you ever seen a rainbow in the sky?"

Writing Center

Teacher Talk
Rainbows appear after a rain storm.

Resources
index card, marker, paper, pencils

Write the word *rainbow* on a card and hang it at children's eye level. Let the children copy the word.

Art Center

Teacher Talk
Rainbows appear after a rain storm.

Resources
variety of colors of washable tempera paint, paintbrushes, paper, smocks, table covering

Cover the table and have the children wear smocks. Set out the paints and encourage the children to paint using as many colors as possible.

Weather Center

Teacher Talk
What is the weather like today?

Resources
weather chart, weather stickers or markers

Hang the weather chart and encourage the children to determine what the weather is like outside today.

Math Center

Teacher Talk
God made rainbows.

Resources
variety of multi-colored beads, tweezers, containers

Set out the beads in a container. Place tweezers and empty containers nearby. Let the children use the tweezers to sort and pick up the beads by color. (Supervise closely.)

Science Center

Teacher Talk
God made rainbows.

Resources
empty soda bottle, white corn syrup, water, multi-colored crayon shavings

Place crayon shavings in the bottle, then add a half-and-half mixture of corn syrup and water. Cover tightly. Encourage the children to move the bottle up and down to move the rainbow colors. Ask the children to describe what they see.

Cooking Center

Teacher Talk
God made rainbows.

Resources
paper plates and napkins, sugar cookies, canned vanilla frosting, plastic knives, multi-colored sprinkles

Set out the plates, napkins, and knives. Place cookies on a plate with the frosting nearby. Encourage the children to frost a cookie and sprinkle it with "rainbow sprinkles"—then eat and enjoy their rainbow snack.

Worship Center

Teacher Talk
God made rainbows.

Resources
children's Bible, picture of a rainbow

Set the children's Bible on a table. Hang the rainbow picture over the table. Let the children look through the Bible and talk about the picture.

Say: God put the first rainbow in the sky after a huge rainstorm. God made a promise to Noah and all people: Whenever it stops raining, we can look outside and try to find a rainbow. When we see one, we can remember that God loves us.

Pray: Thank you, God, for rainbows that come after rainstorms. Amen.

Wonder Time

Call the children together for wonder time.

Rainbow Colors

Red, orange, yellow, green and blue,
Indigo and violet, too.
All these colors way up high
Make a rainbow in the sky.
Red, orange, yellow, green and blue,
Indigo and violet, too.

Wonder Question: I wonder what makes a rainbow?

Shine a flashlight through a prism to make a rainbow.

Say: Rainbows are made outside when sun shines through raindrops. We can make rainbows by shining a light through special pieces of glass, like this one. Rainbows are always made of seven colors in a special order: red, orange, yellow, green, blue, indigo, and violet. Violet is a purple color, and indigo is a shade of blue.

Sing: "Rainbow Colors" to the tune of "Baa, Baa, Black Sheep."

Read the Bible verse.

Say: Rainbows are a very special part of God's weather plan.

Pray: Thank you, God, for all kinds of weather, and especially for rainbows in the sky. Amen.

Open the Bible to Genesis 9:16.

Say: "God said, 'When the rainbow appears in the clouds I will remember my promise to you'" (Genesis 9:16, *Good News Bible,* adapted).

Have the children repeat the Bible verse.

Group Fun

Resources

large roll of paper, rainbow-colored paint, paintbrushes, paint smocks

Help the children make a rainbow circle. Explain to the children that a rainbow is actually a complete circle—we only see part of it. If we rode in an airplane over a rainstorm we could see a complete rainbow.

Place a large sheet of paper from the roll over a table or on the floor. (You may wish to cover the area with old newspapers first.) Help the children start the mural by painting a large red circle in the center of the paper. Have the children work together to paint circles around the center, in the correct rainbow order. When the painting is done and dry, write each child's name in the center of the rainbow (or have children write their own names in the center). Hang the mural in the classroom.

Goodbye Circle

Let the children talk about the things they enjoyed doing today. Ask each child to name a color of the rainbow. Can anyone name all the rainbow colors? In order? Repeat the Bible verse.

Pray: Thank you, God, for all the rainbow colors. Amen.

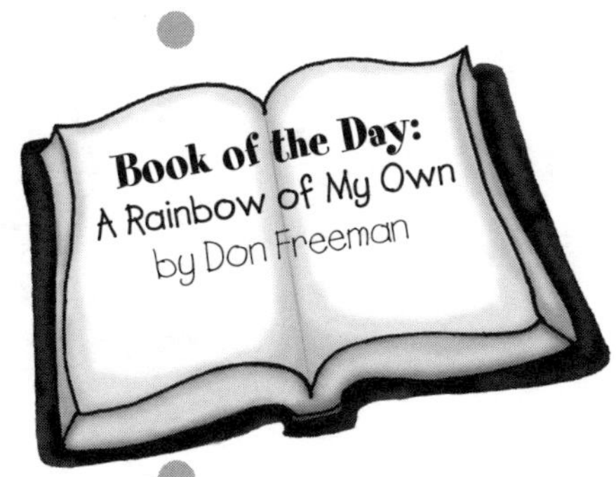

Evaluation

Was each child able to name a rainbow color? Were any children able to name all the colors? Make note of any children who are having difficulty with any of the weather concepts.

Lesson 45

Sunny Days

Teacher Talk:

God planned for the world to have all kinds of weather.

What is the weather like today?

Sunny days make us feel happy and help plants grow.

Goals:

To help children learn what weather is.

To provide opportunities for children to learn about various types of spring weather.

To help children learn that God planned the world with many types of weather.

Objectives: By the end of this session the children will:

Experiment with sun and shadows.

Discover how the sun's warmth affects chocolate.

Faith Connections

Bible verse: God made the sun to rule over the day.

(Genesis 1:16, *Good News Bible*, adapted)

All week the children have been studying different types of weather. They need the opportunity to learn that God created the sun to warm the earth and help things grow, and that sunny days are part of God's weather plan for the earth.

Teacher's Prayer

Dearest Lord, when the sun shines it is so much easier to rejoice in the world. Help me to retain a sunny spirit even when the sun isn't visible. Amen.

Center Time

Continue the centers from Lessons 41-44. For this lesson add or change the following:

Art Center

Teacher Talk

God made the sun to shine during the day.

Resources

paper plates, craft sticks, markers, glitter, glue, tape

Let the children make happy sun faces on their paper plates. Glue or tape a craft stick to the back of each plate to turn it into a puppet.

Building Center

Teacher Talk

God made the sun to shine during the day.

Resources

floor lamp or utility lamp, variety of blocks

Arrange a lamp so it creates shadows. Review safety precautions or supervise if the light is within reach. Let the children build with blocks and experiment with making shadows.

Math Center

Teacher Talk

Sunny days make us happy and help plants grow.

Resources

variety of math counters, masking tape

Make a sun design with masking tape. Have each child use math counters to create a pattern along a sun ray. Ask the children to count the number of counters they used to create the designs.

Science Center

Teacher Talk

Sunny days make us feel happy and help plants grow.

Resources

resealable plastic sandwich bags, plastic spoons, chocolate chips, bowl, sunny window

Have each child place two or three spoonfuls of chocolate chips in a sandwich bag and seal it. Have the children place their bags in a sunny spot. The children can check their bags every 10 minutes. Discuss what happens to the chocolate chips. Plan to use the chips during group fun.

As children arrive, have happy music playing.

Weather Center

Teacher Talk

What is the weather like today?

Resources

weather chart, weather stickers or markers, pictures of sunny days and dark cloudy days, thermometer

Display the weather chart. Encourage the children to determine what the weather is like outside. Talk about the difference between sunny days and cloudy days. Point out the thermometer. Talk about what the temperature is today.

Dramatic Play Center

Teacher Talk

God made the sun to shine during the day.

Resources

hats, sunglasses, sandals, summer-type clothing

Let the children play dressup. Talk about why the clothing is appropriate for a sunny day.

Writing Center

Teacher Talk

God made the sun to shine during the day.

Resources

index card, marker, paper, pencils

Write the word *sunshine* on an index card. Let the children copy the word.

Worship Center

Teacher Talk

God made the sun to shine during the day.

Resources

yellow paper, marker, scissors, tape

Cut a large yellow circle out of paper. Draw on a happy face. Hang the happy face over the table.

Say: Look at the happy sun. God created the sun to shine during the day. It warms us and helps plants grow. It makes us happy.

Pray: Thank you, God, for warm sunny days. Amen.

Open the Bible to Genesis 1:16.

Say: "God made the sun to rule over the day" (Genesis 1:16, *Good News Bible*, adapted).

Have the children repeat the Bible verse.

Wonder Time

Call the children together for wonder time.

Wonder Question: I wonder what the sun does?

Say: When the sun shines during the day it means we are having good weather.

Play: "Shadow Friends."

Sing: "Sunshine" to the tune of "Camptown Races."

Read the Bible verse.

Say: God created the sun to shine during the day. Sunny days are part of God's plan for the world.

Pray: Thank you, God, for sunny days. Amen.

Sunshine

Sunshine makes the plants grow tall.
Sunshine, sunshine.
Sunshine makes the plants grow tall.
Sun, shine today.
God gave us the sun
To shine in the day.
It keeps us warm and makes us smile.
Sun, shine today.

Group Fun

Shadow Friends

Remind the children that when the sun shines, it makes shadows. Tell children they are going to pretend to be shadows. Have each child find a partner. One is the "leader" and the other is the "shadow." The leader does a movement, and the shadow follows the movement. Have partners switch roles.

Resources

posterboard, visor pattern (see page 216), markers, glitter, glue, stickers, hole punch, narrow elastic

Make sun visors. Before class, photocopy the visor pattern (see page 216) for each child. Use the visor to cut the shape out of posterboard for each child. Cut the elastic into 8" lengths (two per child). Give each child a visor to decorate with the materials provided. Have each child glue the photocopied visor onto the posterboard shape. Help each child fold the visor along the dotted line. Punch a hole at each end of the visor and put the elastic pieces through the holes. Tie a knot in each elastic to hold it in place. Tie the visors on the children's heads and knot the elastic ends. The children can then slip their visors on and off.

Teacher tip: Teachers can have elastic already attached to the visors.

Make Peanut Butter Power Bars

Resources:

peanut butter, graham crackers, plastic knives, scissors, bags with melted chips

Give each child a graham cracker and plastic knife. Have the children spread peanut butter on their graham crackers. Help the children cut a corner from the bottom of their bag of melted chips. Children can squeeze the bags of chocolate over the peanut butter, then eat and enjoy.

Book of the Day:
How the Sun Was Brought Back to the Sky
by Mirra Ginsburg

Goodbye Circle

Let the children talk about the things they enjoyed doing today. Ask each child to tell something he or she likes to do on sunny days.

Pray: Thank you, God, for the sun that shines during the day. Amen.

Evaluation

Did each child understand the different weather concepts presented this week? Make plans to help any children having difficulties.

BUGS

This week the children will enjoy learning all about creepy crawly things—bugs! Each day will focus on a different type of bug. The children will also learn the characteristics of insects, as opposed to other types of bugs.

The emphasis this week is that God created bugs as well as all other animal and plant life. Bugs are an important part of God's world, and should be respected and left alone to participate in their part of God's plan.

Ants

Goals:

To help children learn about bugs.

To know that God created bugs.

To learn the characteristics of a variety of different bugs.

Objectives: By the end of this session the children will:

Determine if an ant is an insect.

Sing a song about ants.

Compare their weight-lifting abilities to an ant's.

Faith Connections

Bible verse: Ants store up their food during the summer, getting ready for winter. (Proverbs 6:8, *Good News Bible, adapted*)

This verse focuses on the "wisdom" of ants in storing food, similar to the classic fable, "The Grasshopper and the Ant." God created ants in a specific way, just as each insect has its own plan and purpose. Ants are hard workers and work together—preschool children can learn that lesson from these bugs.

Teacher's Prayer

Lord, please help me to be an "ant"—a person who works hard and works with others to achieve a common good. Amen.

Teacher Talk:

God created ants.

There are many different kinds of bugs.

Insects have three body parts and six legs.

Ants carry things that weigh more then they do.

Ants are very small.

Center Time

Set up your centers as described on pages 6–9. For this lesson add the following:

As children arrive, place a bug sticker on the child's clothing or on the back of the child's hand.

Art Center

Teacher Talk

Ants are very small.

Resources

brown construction paper, glue, sand, shallow tray or box lid, pencils with erasers, small bowl, black tempera paint, cotton swabs, smocks, table covering

Cover the table and have the children wear smocks. Pour sand in a shallow tray or box lid. Pour paint in a bowl. Let the children dip pencil erasers in black paint and stamp them on paper. These are "ants." The children can spread glue on their papers with cotton swabs, hold the paper over the sand container, and sprinkle a small amount of sand over the glue. Shake the paper over the container to remove loose sand.

Cooking Center

Teacher Talk

Ants are very small.

Resources

paper plates and napkins, celery sticks (or pretzel logs), peanut butter or soft cream cheese, raisins, plastic knives

Let the children make "ants on a log" by spreading peanut butter or cream cheese on celery sticks or pretzel logs and placing ants (raisins) on the peanut butter or cream cheese.

Sand Table

Teacher Talk

Ants are very small.

Resources

sand/water table, sand, sticks, plastic ants

Place sand in the table (or use a dish pan). Add plastic ants and sticks. Let the children make ant trails and anthills with the sticks and ants.

Math Center

Teacher Talk

God created ants.

Resources

craft sticks, ant or dot stickers, markers, basket, empty cans, construction paper

Place ant stickers or dot stickers to represent ants on twenty or thirty craft sticks. Place the ant sticks in a basket. Cover five empty cans with construction paper. Write a number (one through five) on each can. The children can count out the correct number of ant sticks and place them in the can.

Science Center

Teacher Talk

Ants carry things that weigh more than they do.

Resources

several buckets, rocks, scale

Fill buckets with varying weights of rocks, from one pound to twenty pounds. Let the children try lifting the buckets. Talk about how much weight an ant carries when it carries food to its home. Weigh each child. Can each child carry things that weigh more than he or she does?

Note: Don't let the children hurt themselves trying!

Worship Center

Teacher Talk

God created ants.

Resources

picture of ant (or an ant farm in a container)

Set the picture or ant farm on a table for children to examine.

Say: God created many different kinds of creatures. This is one of God's special little creatures. They live outside and we see them in many different places. Ants were made by God, just like you were made by God.

Pray: Thank you, God, for ants and all the creatures you made. Amen.

Wonder Time

Call the children together for wonder time.

Wonder Question: I wonder if an ant is an insect?

Say: An insect is a bug that has three body parts and six legs. Let's look at the picture of an ant and see if it is an insect.

Hold up a picture of an ant, and count its body parts and legs. Begin an "Insect Chart" on a large piece of paper. Ask the children to describe the ant, then write what the children say on the paper. Add to the chart each day.

Play: "Follow the Queen Ant"—play the same as "Follow the Leader." Be sure children take turns as the "Queen Ant."

Read the Bible verse.

Say: Ants gather food during most of the year. They can carry very heavy weights even though they are so small. In the winter they stay in the ground and eat the food they have stored. That is God's plan.

Pray: Thank you, God, for the special plan you have for ants and the plan you have for me. Amen.

The Ants Go Marching

The ants go marching one by one,
Hurrah! Hurrah!
The ants go marching one by one,
Hurrah! Hurrah!
The ants go marching one by one,
The little one stops to suck his thumb.
And they all go marching down
To the ground, to get out of the rain,
Boom, boom, boom.

Verses:
Two by two—tie his shoe
Three by three—climb a tree
Four by four—shut the door
Five by five—scratch his thigh
Six by six—pick up sticks
Seven by seven—point to heaven
Eight by eight—shut the gate
Nine by nine—say, "I'm behind!"
Ten by ten—shout, "Amen!"

Group Fun

Resources

brown construction paper, chenille sticks, stapler, tape

Let the children make ant headbands. Cut the construction paper before class to create a headband for each child (one or two inches wide and long enough to go around the head). Give each child a headband piece and two chenille sticks. Have the children shape the chenille sticks into antennae and tape them in place. Staple the headbands together. Children can wear their ant headbands as they sing "The Ants Go Marching."

Goodbye Circle

Let the children talk about the things they enjoyed doing today. Encourage each child to say "I'm as strong as an ant" and show his or her muscles.

Pray: Thank you, God, for ants. Amen.

Evaluation

Were the children able to determine if an ant met the "insect criteria?" Did children enjoy wearing their ant headbands and singing and doing the ant song? Be sensitive this week to any child's discomfort with the bug study.

Open the Bible to Proverbs 6:8.

Say: "Ants store up their food during the summer, getting ready for winter. (Proverbs 6:8, *Good News Bible*, adapted).

Have the children repeat the Bible verse.

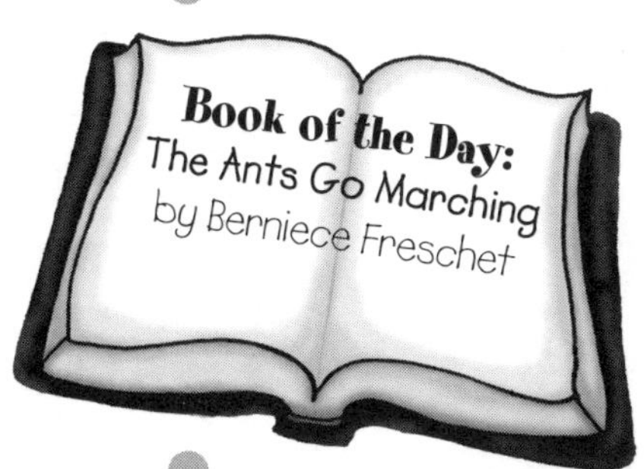

Lesson 47

Bees

Goals:

To help children learn about bugs.

To know that God created bugs.

To learn that there are many different kinds of bugs.

To learn the characteristics of a variety of different bugs.

Teacher Talk:

God created bees.

There are many different kinds of bugs.

Insects have three body parts and six legs.

Bees make honey.

Bees only sting if something bothers them.

Objectives:

By the end of this session the children will:

Determine if a bee is an insect.

Dictate sentences about bees.

Faith Connections

Bible verse: God commanded, "Let the earth produce all kinds of animal life, large and small."

(Genesis 1:24, *Good News Bible*, adapted)

Bees are part of the smaller animal life that God created. We enjoy watching them buzz around flowers and enjoy eating the honey they create. And we try to stay away from the stinging end of these little creatures. Your children can learn that bees are an important part of God's creation, something to be watched and admired, but not touched!

Teacher's Prayer

Dear God, do I "sting" when I am disturbed? Help me to stay calm during times of stress, and not to take any frustration I might be feeling out on the children in my care. Amen.

Center Time

Continue the centers from Lesson 46.
For this lesson add or change the following:

> As children arrive, play Rimsky-Korsakov's "Flight of the Bumblebee."

Art Center

Teacher Talk

God created bees.

Resources

wax (example: Gulfwax), paper, watercolors, paintbrushes

Encourage each child to draw a picture or design with the wax. The children can then paint over the wax; the paint will not stick to wax. Explain to children that bees create wax similar to this as part of their hives.

Manipulatives Center

Teacher Talk

Bees make honey.

Resources

egg cartons, stapler, staples, tape, pipe cleaners

Cut the egg cartons into individual sections. Let the children use the egg carton sections to build honeycombs.

Cooking Center

Teacher Talk

Bees make honey.

Resources

crackers, juice and cups, honey in a small bowl with spoon, plastic knives

Encourage the children to enjoy a "bee tea." Let the children spread a small amount of honey on a cracker and pour a cup of juice (nectar). They can then eat and enjoy their snacks.

Math Center

Teacher Talk

God created bees.

Resources

construction paper, hexagon pattern, scissors

Use the hexagon pattern to cut a number of hexagons from a variety of different colored construction paper. Let the children use the hexagons to make honey comb designs.

Science Center

Teacher Talk

Bees make honey.

Resources

honeycomb, magnifying glass

Let the children examine the honeycomb with and without the magnifying glass. Talk about the shape (hexagons—six sides).

Writing Center

Teacher Talk

There are many different kinds of bugs.

Resources

index cards, marker, paper, pencils, pictures of bees and ants

Write the words *bee* and *ant* on index cards. Display the cards where children can see them. Place the pictures of the appropriate insects next to the words. Let the children copy the words.

Worship Center

Teacher Talk

God created bees.

Resources

picture of bee, honeycomb or jar of honey, flowers

Encourage the children to look at the objects and discuss them.

Say: Each of these things go together. Bees get nectar from flowers and use it to make honey. That is part of God's plan. When bees go to plants to gather nectar, they help the plants grow. That is also part of God's plan. All living things were made by God and God has a special plan for each thing—including you!

Pray: Thank you, God, for your plans for bees and your plans for me. Amen.

Open the Bible to Genesis 1:24.

Say: "God commanded, 'Let the earth produce all kinds of animal life, large and small'" (Genesis 1:24, *Good News Bible*, adapted).

Have the children repeat the Bible verse.

Wonder Time

Call the children together for wonder time.

Wonder Question: I wonder if a bee is an insect?

Say: Yesterday we learned that insects are bugs that have three body parts and six legs. Let's look at this picture of a bee and see if it is an insect.

Study the bee picture and count its parts. Write the information on the "Insect Chart" from yesterday.

Sing: "The Bee Song" to the tune of "She'll Be Coming Round the Mountain."

Read the Bible verse.

Say: Bees are an important part of God's world.

Pray: Thank you, God, for bees. Amen.

The Bee Song

Oh, the bees fly 'round the flowers in my yard. Buzz! Buzz!
Oh, the bees fly 'round the flowers in my yard. Buzz! Buzz!
Oh, the bees fly 'round the flowers, yes the bees fly 'round the flowers,
Oh, the bees fly 'round the flowers in my yard. Buzz! Buzz!
(flap hands and walk around in a circle)
Oh, the bees make lots of honey we can eat. Yum! Yum!
Oh, the bees make lots of honey we can eat. Yum! Yum!
Oh, the bees make lots of honey yes the bees make lots of honey,
Oh, the bees make lots of honey we can eat. Yum! Yum!
(rub stomach)

Group Fun

Resources

bubble wrap, crayons, washable yellow tempera paint, shallow container, paper, pencils, markers, stapler, smocks

Help the children make bee books. Give each child a sheet of paper and have each child use the crayons to make a rubbing of the bubble wrap. Pour the yellow paint in a shallow container. Have each child dip a finger in the paint and make several prints on the bubble wrap rubbing. The bubble wrap is the beehive and the prints are the bees. When prints dry, the children can add to the pictures as desired using the crayons or markers. While the children are doing rubbings and prints, ask each child to dictate a sentence telling something about bees. Write each child's sentence on a piece of paper and put his or her name on the paper (or have child write his or her own name if desired). The children can then decorate the papers with their sentences as they choose with the markers and crayons. Staple the "beehive" picture on top of the sentence paper, making the cover to the child's bee book.

Goodbye Circle

Let the children talk about the things they enjoyed doing today. Ask each child to tell something about bees.

Pray: Thank you, God, for special insects in the world, like bees. Amen.

Evaluation

Did each child have the verbal skills to tell something about bees? Were children able to listen and follow directions to create the cover for the bee book?

Lesson 48

Caterpillars and Butterflies

Goals:

To help children learn about bugs.

To know that God created bugs.

To learn that there are many different kinds of bugs.

To learn the characteristics of a variety of different bugs.

Objectives: By the end of this session the children will:

Determine if caterpillars and butterflies are insects.

Examine butterflies and a caterpillars.

Faith Connections

Bible verse: All your creatures, LORD, will praise you.

(Psalm 145:10, *Good News Bible*)

One of the great mysteries we encounter when we are young is that of a hairy caterpillar creating a strange cover, then emerging as a glorious butterfly. Even as adults we can marvel at God's exciting creation. The image of the butterfly epitomizes spring and Easter, with its story of "death" and new life. Preschool children can be introduced to this marvel and enjoy knowing that God has a special plan for each of God's creatures—and that we can praise God for this wonderful world.

Teacher's Prayer

I praise you, Lord, for the wonders of this world. Thank you for all you have given me. Help me to enjoy the gifts as well as the challenges. Amen.

Teacher Talk:

God created caterpillars and butterflies.

Insects have three body parts and six legs.

Caterpillars turn into butterflies.

Center Time

Continue the centers from Lessons 46-47. For this lesson add or change the following:

Art Center

Teacher Talk

Caterpillars turn into butterflies.

Resources

paper, washable tempera paint, plastic spoons, scissors, table covering, smocks

Cover the table and have the children wear smocks. Set out the paints. Place a plastic spoon in each container. Let the children place a small amount of paint in the center of their papers. They can use several colors. When the children are finished adding paint, have them fold their papers in half and press down. The children can open the papers carefully and see their butterfly designs. If desired, the children can cut the papers into a butterfly shape when the paint has dried.

Math Center

Teacher Talk

Caterpillars turn into butterflies.

Resources

egg cartons, scissors, markers, chenille sticks

Cut egg carton cup sections in half lengthwise. Cut sections to create "caterpillars" of different lengths (1 to 6 cups). If desired, decorate the caterpillars with markers and chenille sticks (for antennae). Set the caterpillars on a table, and encourage the children to sort them by length. The children can count each caterpillar's "humps," then count to see how many "humps" the caterpillars have altogether.

Music Center

Teacher Talk

God created caterpillars and butterflies.

Resources

cassette/CD player, cassette/CD (possibly Madame Butterfly), scarfs or lengths of multi-colored crepe paper

Play the music on the cassette/CD player. Encourage the children to move like butterflies using the scarfs or crepe paper. Talk about how butterflies look when they fly.

As children arrive, place a butterfly sticker on the back of each child's hand or on the child's clothing.

Science Center

Teacher Talk

Caterpillars turn into butterflies.

Resources

caterpillar, cocoons, butterfly (real or in pictures), magnifying glass

Place the materials on a table for the children to examine carefully (if real). Talk about each object and how they are different and the same.

A butterfly garden may be ordered from: Insect Lore Products; P.O. Box 1535; Shafter, CA 93263; 1-800-LIVE BUG.

Writing Center

Teacher Talk

Caterpillars turn into butterflies.

Resources

index cards, marker, picture of caterpillar and butterfly, paper, pencils

Write the words *caterpillar* and *butterfly* on index cards and hang them over the table. Hang the appropriate pictures next to the words. Let the children copy the words.

Worship Center

Teacher Talk

God created caterpillars and butterflies.

Resources

caterpillars / cocoon / butterfly (real or pictures), pictures of babies and adults, mirror

Set the butterfly materials together on a table, and set the baby pictures, adult pictures, and mirror on the other end of the table. Encourage the children to look at the materials, and look at themselves in the mirror.

Say: God created caterpillars in a special way. When it's time for them to grow up, they make a cocoon and then become a butterfly. God made people in a special way, too. First they are babies, then they are children like you, then they become grown-ups. That is all part of God's plan.

Pray: Thank you, God, for your plan for caterpillars and your plan for me. Amen.

Wonder Time

Call the children together.

Wonder Question: I wonder if caterpillars and butterflies are insects?

Say: We have learned that insects have three body parts and six legs. Let's look at the pictures of the caterpillar and butterfly and see if they are insects.

Study the pictures and count the parts. Write the information on the "Insect Chart."

Play: Caterpillar Footwork. Have groups of two or three children form a caterpillar by connecting hands to the shoulders of the person ahead in line. Encourage the caterpillars to travel to a specified spot and back without becoming "disconnected."

Sing: "Caterpillar" to the tune of "Do You Know the Muffin Man."

Read the Bible verse.

Say: Caterpillars and butterflies are important parts of spring. When we see caterpillars become butterflies, we are reminded that God does wonderful things.

Pray: Thank you, God, for the wonderful things you do. Amen.

Caterpillar

Caterpillar crawls along, crawls along,
crawls along. (*Inch fingers along arm.*)
Caterpillar crawls along, it eats and
eats the leaves. (*Munch with fingers.*)
When it's full it finds a place, finds a
place, finds a place. (*Hand over eyes.*)
When it's full it finds a place to make
its bed and sleep. (*Rest head on hands.*)
Caterpillar spins around, spins
around, spins around. (*Spin in place.*)
Caterpillar spins around in a cocoon
so tight. (*Wrap arms around body.*)
There it sleeps so quietly, quietly, quietly.
(*Place index finger over mouth for "shh."*)
There it sleeps so quietly for many
days and nights. (*Rest head on hands.*)
No one sees, but right inside, right
inside, right inside. (*Point index finger.*)
No one sees, but right inside God's
making a butterfly! (*Flap "wings."*)

Open the Bible to Psalm 145:10.

Say: "All your creatures, LORD, will praise you" (Psalm 145:10).

Have the children repeat the Bible verse.

Group Fun

Resources

coffee filters, scissors, washable markers, spray bottles filled with water, clothespins with round heads, craft glue, chenille sticks, cardboard tubes

Help the children make cocoons and butterflies. Before class cut the chenille sticks into four-inch lengths, one per child. Give each child a coffee filter to color with the markers. Let each child can lightly mist the colored filter with water. Give each child a clothespin. Help the children put spots of glue on the inside of the clothespins. The children can gather the filters and slide them inside the clothespins. Arrange "wings" as desired. Help the children wrap a chenille sticks around the top of the clothespins to form the antennae. Have the children put the butterflies carefully inside the paper rolls, then pull them out of their "cocoons."

Goodbye Circle

Let the children talk about the things they enjoyed. Ask each child to tell something about caterpillars or butterflies.

Pray: Thank you, God, for caterpillars that turn into butterflies. Amen.

Evaluation

Was each child able to follow directions to create his or her own butterfly and cocoon? Make note of any children having difficulties.

Lesson 49

Spiders

Teacher Talk:

God created spiders.

Insects have three body parts and six legs.

Spiders spin webs.

Spiders help by eating insect pests.

Goals:

To help children learn about bugs.

To know that God created bugs.

To learn that there are many different kinds of bugs.

To learn the characteristics of a variety of different bugs.

Objectives: By the end of this session the children will:

Determine if a spider is an insect.

Sing a song about a spider.

Examine a spider and a web.

Faith Connections

Bible verse: God made everything that creeps upon the ground of every kind.

(Genesis 1:25, adapted)

Spiders are artisans, creating lacy works of art between trees, bushes, and flowers. They work tirelessly as they spin their webs, often to have their work destroyed by a breeze or a careless human hand. Preschool children can learn that spiders are part of God's creation. They can learn that spiders should not be handled, but that we can watch them and admire their work.

Teacher's Prayer

Dear Lord, help me to slow down and take the time to admire the artistry of a spider's web, rather than just brushing it out of my way. Amen.

Center Time

Continue the centers from Lessons 46-48. For this lesson add or change the following:

Art Center

Teacher Talk

Spiders help by eating insect pests.

Resource

yarn pieces, glue, black tempera paint, shallow tray, paper towels, markers, paper plates, picture of spider

Encourage the children to glue pieces of yarn onto the plates to make make spider webs. Fold paper towels and place them in the shallow tray. Pour black tempera onto the towels to make a paint pad. Let the children dip their thumbs onto the paint pad and then onto their plates to make spider bodies. Let the children add legs with markers.

Building Center

Teacher Talk

Spiders spin webs.

Resources

chairs, yarn

Encourage the children to wind yarn around the chair legs to create a giant spider web. The children can then play "spider" in the web they created.

Manipulatives Center

Teacher Talk

Spiders help by eating insect pests.

Resources

plastic spiders, baskets, tweezers

Place the spiders in a basket and set tweezers next to it. Let the children use the tweezers to move the spiders from one basket to another. Have the children count the spiders as they move them.

Writing Center

Teacher Talk

Spiders spin webs.

Resources

photocopies of web (see page 217), pencils

Encourage the children to use the pencils to trace the photocopy of the web, to help develop pencil and writing skills.

As children **arrive,** use yarn and tape to create a spider web over the doorway. Have the children crawl under the web to enter.

Math Center

Teacher Talk

God created spiders.

Resources

plastic spiders, bucket, index cards

Write a number, 1 - 10, on each index card. Place the numbered cards and the spiders on a table. Set the bucket on the floor next to the table. Each child can pick a numbered card, then drop the corresponding number of spiders into the bucket. Have the children count out loud as they do the activity.

Science Center

Teacher Talk

Spiders spin webs.

Resources

spider in a jar (with air holes—release after class), magnifying glass, spider web or picture of web

Encourage the children to observe the spider with and without the magnifying glass. Have the children look at the web and talk about its design.

Worship Center

Teacher Talk

God created spiders.

Resources

black construction paper, shallow pan (approximately 9" x 12"), white tempera paint, marbles, spoon

Have the children place a piece of paper in the pan. They can then use the spoon to dip two marbles into the paint to coat the marbles, then place the marbles in the pan. Encourage children to tip the pan to roll the marbles around, creating a web.

Say: Spiders are a special kind of bug that God created. They spin beautiful webs. When you walk outside you can look around carefully and probably see a web that a spider has created. Spiders are a special part of God's world.

Pray: Thank you, God, for spiders and webs. Amen.

Open the Bible to Genesis 1:25.

Say: "God made everything that creeps upon the ground of every kind." (Genesis 1:25, adapted).

Have the children repeat the Bible verse.

Wonder Time

Call the children together for wonder time.

Wonder Question: I wonder if spiders are insects?

Say: We have been learning about insects all this week. How many body parts does an insect have? Show me how many body parts with your fingers. How many legs? Show me how many legs with your fingers. Let's look at the picture of the spider and see if it is an insect.

Study the picture and count the parts. Write the information on the "Insect Chart."

Sing: "The Itsy Bitsy Spider" (and do the motions)

Read the Bible verse.

Say: There are many different kinds of spiders, but they all have only two body parts and eight legs. They are a special part of God's bug world.

Pray: Thank you God for insects and bugs. Amen.

"The Itsy Bitsy Spider"

The itsy bitsy spider climbed
up the water spout.
Down came the rain and
washed the spider out.
Out came the sun and
dried up all the rain
And the itsy bitsy spider
climbed up the spout again.

Group Fun

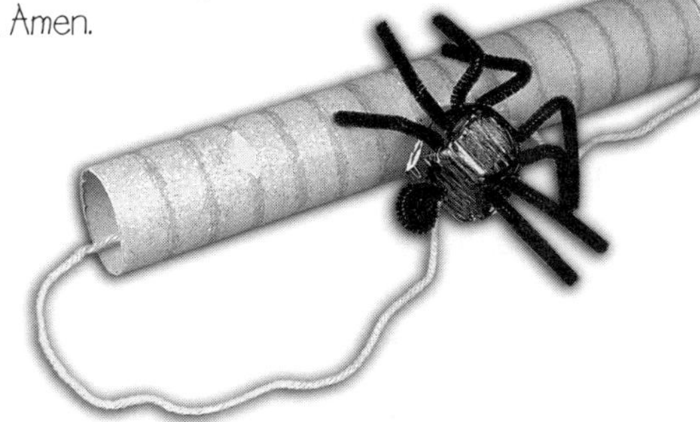

Resources

paper towel tubes, egg carton sections, black chenille sticks (cut in half), glue, yarn, scissors, hole punch

Help the children make itsy bitsy spiders. Before class, cut the yarn into pieces three times the length of the paper towel tubes. Give each child a tube and a piece of yarn. Help the children (if needed) thread the yarn through the tubes. Give each child an egg carton section. The children can stick the chenille sticks into the sides of the egg carton cups to form spider legs. Punch a hole in the front and back of each cup. Help each child tie one end of the yarn through the first hole and the other end of the yarn through the second hole. The children can pull the yarn and pull the spiders up the "water spouts" and then lower them down again. Use the spiders and the "water spouts" as you sing "Itsy Bitsy Spider" again.

Goodbye Circle

Let the children talk about the things they enjoyed doing today. Ask each child to hold up the number of fingers that show how many legs a spider has.

Pray: Thank you, God, for spiders. Amen.

Evaluation

Was each child able to meet the day's objectives? Did each child have the fine motor skills needed to thread the yarn during the group project? Make note of each child's abilities.

Lesson 50

In a Patch of Grass

Goals:

To help children learn about bugs.

To know that God created bugs.

To learn that there are many different kinds of bugs.

To learn the characteristics of a variety of different bugs.

Objectives:

By the end of this session the children will:

Tell how many body parts an insect has.

Tell how many legs an insect has.

Faith Connections

Bible verse: God looked at everything God had made, and God was very pleased.

(Genesis 1:31, Good News Bible, adapted)

It's easy to look at the trees and flowers and birds and be pleased with God's creation. It's sometime harder to do so when we're swatting a fly away from our food or looking at an ant crawling over our picnic. We may not understand God's plan for the world, but we know that God created ALL things, even the creepy crawly ones. Preschoolers need to learn that each of God's creations is important—even little tiny bugs.

Teacher's Prayer

Help me, Lord, to remember that every living thing is your creation. Give me the wisdom to remember that each pesky ant and bee is important in your sight, just as each of the children in my care is. Amen.

Teacher Talk:

God created bugs.

There are many different kinds of bugs.

Insects have three body parts and six legs.

All kinds of creatures live in the grass.

Bugs make many different kinds of noises.

Center Time

Continue the centers from Lessons 46-49. For this lesson add the following:

Art Center

Teacher Talk

There are many different kinds of bugs.

Resources

clay or play dough, pipe cleaners, beads, margarine tubs (1 per child), plastic grass

Have each child place a small amount of plastic grass in a margarine tub; this will be the new bug friend's home. To make a bug friend, children can use the play dough to create a bug, then make legs with the pipe cleaners. Beads can be pressed into the bug to use as eyes.

Home Living Center

Teacher Talk

All kinds of creatures live in the grass.

Resources

paper plates; napkins; plastic knives; plain crackers, cream cheese, sprouts; or white frosting, plain cookies, green tinted coconut

Encourage the children to take crackers and spread them with cream cheese, then place a small amount of sprouts on the cream cheese to make green grass goodies." Or use white frosting on plain cookies, and add green tinted coconut.

Math Center

Teacher Talk

All kinds of creatures live in the grass.

Resources

empty cans or frozen juice containers, green construction paper, scissors, tape, craft sticks, bug stickers (4 or 5 of each bug)

Cover the containers with green construction paper. Add a second shorter layer and fringe it to look like grass. Place a different bug sticker on each can and write the name of the bug on the can. Attach the rest of the bug stickers to the craft sticks. Let the children sort the bugs and put them in the correct cans.

Sand Table Center

Teacher Talk

All kinds of creatures live in the grass.

Resources

sand/water table or dish pan, plastic (Easter-basket type) grass, assorted plastic bugs, magnifying glass

Place the grass and bugs in the sand table. Or use an empty dish pan. The children can explore in the grass to find the bugs, then examine them with the magnifying glass. Have the children describe what they see.

Music Center

Teacher Talk:

Bugs make many different kinds of noises.

Resources:

cassette/CD player, cassette/CD, rhythm instruments

Play the music from the cassette/CD. Encourage the children to accompany the music with the rhythm instruments, and to try to make "bug sounds" with their instruments.

Worship Center

Teacher Talk

God created bugs.

Resources

dish pan, shovel full of dirt with grass, magnifying glass

Place a shovel full of dirt with grass into the dish pan. Set it on a table and place the magnifying glass nearby. Encourage the children to look at, but not touch, any living things that might be in the dirt and grass. Ask the children to describe what they see in the dirt.

Say: Everything you see in this dish pan was created by God. God made all kinds of living things, some big things and some small. All of them are important.

Pray: Thank you, God, for big things and little things that you made. Amen.

Wonder Time

Call the children together for wonder time.

Wonder Question: I wonder how many different kinds of bugs there are?

Say: God made hundreds of different kinds of bugs, but not all of them are insects. Let's look at our Insect Chart and see which of the bugs we studied this week are insects.

Look at chart: Review characteristics of insects—3 body parts and 6 legs.

Sing: "In the Grass" to the tune of "Mary Had a Little Lamb."

Read the Bible Verse.

Say: There are hundreds of different little things that live in the dirt and grass and the sky. God made them all and each one has a specific purpose. That is God's plan.

Pray: Thank you, God, for bugs. Amen.

In the Grass

Little bugs are in the grass,
in the grass, in the grass.
Little bugs are in the grass,
moving all around.

Little ants are in the grass,
in the grass, in the grass.
Little ants are in the grass,
crawling all around.

Little bees are on the grass,
on the grass, on the grass.
Little bees are on the grass,
buzzing all around.

Spiders climbing on the grass,
on the grass, on the grass.
Spiders climbing on the grass,
climbing all around.

Open the Bible to Genesis 1:31.

Say: "God looked at everything God had made, and God was very pleased" (Genesis 1:31, *Good News Bible*, adapted).

Have the children repeat the Bible verse.

Group Fun

Resources

white construction paper (12" x 18"), green and brown washable tempera paint, sponges, green crepe paper, glue, shallow containers (2), shallow tray, bucket of soapy water, towels

Let the children pretend to be barefoot in the grass. Pour the green paint and the glue into separate containers. Have the children sponge green paint on the paper to create "grass." The children can then tear strips of green crepe paper and glue them on the paper. Pour the brown paint into the shallow tray. When the green paint is dry, have each child step into the tray of brown paint and onto his or her picture to leave brown "foot prints." Be sure to have children then immediately wash their feet and dry them on the towels.

Teacher Tip: Cover the work area with newspapers.

Goodbye Circle

Let the children talk about the things they enjoyed. Ask children to show how many body parts an insect has by holding up the correct number of fingers. Do the same for the number of legs.

Pray: Thank you, God, for all the bugs and insects you made. Amen.

Evaluation

Was each child able to listen and follow directions to participate in the group project?

BIRDS

This week the children will have the opportunity to learn more about all kinds of birds. Each day they will participate in a variety of activities and centers that will allow them to discover where different birds live, what they eat, and what different birds look like.

The focus will be on the fact that God created birds, and that God's plan is for us to be friends with each other and with animals—both are an important part of God's world.

Lesson 51

Birds

Teacher Talk:

God created birds.

God cares for the birds, and God cares for you.

Robins are a bird we see in the spring.

Robins lay eggs in the spring.

Goals:

To know that God created birds.

To learn that there are many different kinds of birds.

Objectives: By the end of this session the children will:

Make birds.

Repeat the sound robins make.

Faith Connections

Bible verse: The winter is over. This is the time for singing; the song of doves is heard in the fields.

(Song of Songs, 2:11-12, *Good News Bible*, adapted)

When God created the earth, God created many kinds of animals and birds. Birds exist all over the world. Birds are often associated with beautiful music and bright colors. Preschool children can learn that in many parts of the country, the return of certain birds means winter is over and spring is finally here. It is a time to rejoice in God's plan for the world.

Teacher's Prayer

Dear Lord, you have a plan for every part of your world, including me. Be with me as I try to help the children in my care grow to know and love you. Amen.

Center Time

Set up your centers as described on pages 6–9. For this lesson add the following:

As children arrive, place a bird sticker on the back of each child's hand or on the child's clothing.

Art Center

Teacher Talk

Robins are a bird we see in the spring.

Resources

sponges, washable tempera paint in shades of blue, shallow container, paper

Cut sponges into egg shapes in several sizes. Let the children make designs with the "robin's egg" sponges.

Manipulatives Center

Teacher Talk

God created birds.

Resources

plastic canvas, lengths of thin plastic lacing, marker

Draw a simple bird or egg shape on pieces of plastic canvas. Cut plastic lacing into long lengths. Knot one end of each piece. Let the children weave the lacing in and out of the holes along the shapes.

Math Center

Teacher Talk

Robins lay eggs in the spring.

Resources

egg carton, light blue construction paper, scissors

Cut paper into egg-shaped ovals that will fit in the egg carton cups. Encourage each child to place an "egg" in each cup. Ask the children to count the number of eggs, then take one away. How many are left? Have the children continue to remove eggs and count the remainder.

Music Center

Teacher Talk

God created birds.

Resources

cassette/CD player, cassette/CD of nature sounds

Encourage the children to listen to the nature cassette/CD. The children can make bird sounds to accompany the cassette/CD.

Science Center

Teacher Talk

Robins are a bird we see in the spring.

Resources

pictures of robins, books about robins

Encourage the children to look at the pictures of the robins and look through the books. Ask the children if they have ever seen a robin. Tell the children that in many parts of the country, robins are considered a sign of spring because they fly away for the winter and then fly back when it starts to become warm.

Writing Center

Teacher Talk

Robins are a bird we see in the spring.

Resources

index card, marker, paper and pencils, picture of robins

Write the word *robin* on an index card. Display the picture of the robin. Let the children copy the word.

Worship Center

Teacher Talk

God cares for the birds and God cares for you.

Resources

dead tree branch, healthy growing plant, toy stuffed bird or picture of bird

Place the materials on a table. Talk about the differences between the dead branch and the growing plant.

Say: During the winter, many plants die and leaves fall from the trees. When spring comes, the days get warm and plants begin to grow. In many places, birds leave during the winter, and come back during the spring. When we hear the birds sing in the spring it makes us happy—and it is all part of God's plan.

Pray: Thank you, God, for birds that sing in the spring. Amen.

Open the Bible to Song of Songs 2:11-12.

Say: "The winter is over. This is the time for singing; the song of doves is heard in the fields" (Song of Songs 2:11-12, *Good News Bible*, adapted).

Have the children repeat the Bible verse.

Wonder Time

Call the children together for wonder time.

Wonder Question: I wonder what kinds of birds we can see in the spring?

Say: In many places, robins fly away during the cold weather, then fly back in the spring. Because of this, robins are considered a special spring bird.

Do: Robin Sounds. Make a robin sound, "Cheer-up, Cheerilee,"as described in the book of the day. Have children practice the sound with you.

Read the Bible verse.

Say: When winter is over, people are happy because plants start to grow and birds like doves and robins make nests and sing beautiful songs.

Pray: Thank you, God, for birds that sing in the spring. Amen.

Group Fun

Resources

tongue depressors, craft feathers (shades of brown), markers, wiggly eyes, yellow construction paper, scissors, cotton swabs, glue, shallow container

Help the children make robin friends. Place glue in a shallow container. Give each child a tongue depressor. Have children decorate their sticks with the feathers and markers, using the cotton swabs to apply the glue. Give each child two wiggly eyes to glue to the bird's face. The children can cut beaks (small triangle) from the yellow construction paper and glue them on.

Did You Ever See a Robin?

Did you ever see a robin,
a robin, a robin?
Did you ever see a robin,
flying high in the sky?
(Fly robin friends in the air.)
Did you ever see a robin,
a robin, a robin?
Did you ever see a robin,
sitting up in a tree?
(Hold one arm up for tree branch, perch "robin" on arm.)
Did you ever see a robin,
a robin, a robin?
Did you ever see a robin,
sing "Cheer-up, Cheerilee."?
(Hold robin up high.)

Have children sing the song printed in the box using their robin friends. Sing "Did You Ever See a Robin?" to the tune of "Did You Ever See a Lassie?".

Goodbye Circle

Let the children talk about the things they enjoyed doing today. Have children repeat the robin call they learned.

Pray: Thank you, God, for robins that come in the spring. Amen.

Book of the Day:
My Spring Robin
by Anne Rockwell

Evaluation

Did the children show that they understood that spring is a part of God's plan? Did each child choose to participate in several center activities?

Lesson 52

Inside or Outside

Goals:

To help children learn about birds.

To know that God created birds.

To learn that there are many different kinds of birds.

To learn that birds can live in homes as pets or outside.

Objectives: By the end of this session the children will:

Pretend to be birds.

Weave materials to make a "nesting kite."

Faith Connections

Bible verse: God created all kinds of birds.

(Genesis 1:21, *Good News Bible*, adapted)

During these spring lessons, the children have been learning about different parts of God's creation. From the smallest seed to the largest tree, God created all things on the earth. Children can learn that God created birds also. God takes care of all God's creations—birds, animals, and people, and we are expected to help care for other living things on the planet.

Teacher's Prayer

Dear Lord, you have created all manner of living things. Be with me as I teach those special creations that are in my class. Amen.

Center Time

Continue the centers from Lesson 51. For this lesson add or change the following:

As children arrive, have the children flap their arms like wings and fly into the room.

Art Center

Teacher Talk

Birds have feathers.

Resources

variety of feathers, tempera paints, shallow containers, paper, table covering, smocks

Cover the table and have the children wear smocks. Pour tempera paints into shallow containers. Encourage the children to use the feathers to paint pictures. Feathers can be found at craft stores, or use feathers from an old feather duster.

Manipulatives Center

Teacher Talk

Some people have birds as pets.

Resources

wooden or plastic straw connecting toys (such as Tinker Toys).

Encourage the children to use the materials to build birdcages.

Music Center

Teacher Talk

There are many different kinds of birds.

Resources

cassette/CD player, cassette/CD, paper plates

Play the music. Encourage the children to use the paper plates as wings and "soar like birds" as they listen to the music.

Sand Table Center

Teacher Talk

There are many different kinds of birds.

Resources

sand table or dishpan, birdseed, margarine tubs, scoops, pastry brushes

Put the birdseed inside a dry sand table or dishpan. Encourage the children to scoop, brush, and pour the birdseed.

Science Center

Teacher Talk

Birds can live inside or outside.

Resources

pictures of several different kinds of birds, live bird (if possible)

If possible, have a live bird in a cage. (Check with families and friends.) Be sure the children do not touch the bird, but talk about what the bird looks and sounds like. What does it eat? If you provide pictures, talk about what each bird in the picture looks like and how they are similar and different.

Writing Center

Teacher Talk

Some people have birds as pets.

Resources

cookie sheet, birdseed

Pour a thin layer of birdseed on a cookie sheet. Encourage the children to write in the seed with their fingers. If you have pictures of letters, hang them over the writing area and have the children copy the letters with their fingers in the birdseed.

Worship Center

Teacher Talk

God created all kinds of birds.

Resources

cassette/CD player, cassette/CD of nature sounds

Play the cassette/CD and encourage the children to listen and describe what they hear.

Say: On the cassette you can hear many different sounds. All are made by things God created. If we listen carefully to the cassette, we can hear bird songs. Birds are part of God's creation. Some people keep birds as pets. If we have a pet bird, we need to take good care of it because it is part of God's creation.

Pray: Thank you, God, for birds that are pets and birds that live outside. Amen.

Wonder Time

Call the children together for wonder time.

Wonder Question: I wonder if all birds can live inside people's houses?

Say: Some kinds of birds can live inside, and people keep them as pets. Some kinds of birds live outside. There are many different kinds of birds.

Play: "Drop the Feather." Have the children stand in a circle. Give each child a chance to try dropping feathers into a bucket or bowl. Discuss why this is difficult.

Sing: "Little Bird" to the tune of "Twinkle, Twinkle, Little Star."

> **Little Bird**
>
> I saw a bird go hop, hop,
> hop. *(Move hand up and down in hopping motion.)*
> I asked the bird to stop,
> stop, stop. *(Shake index finger.)*
> I went to the window to say,
> "How do you do?" *(Cup hands around mouth.)*
> It spread its little tail and away
> it flew. *(Flap arms as wings.)*
> I saw another bird go hop, hop,
> hop. *(Move hand in hopping motion.)*
> I hope this bird will stop,
> stop, stop. *(Shake index finger.)*

Read the Bible verse.

Say: God made many kinds of birds, and they live in many different places—some indoors and some outdoors.

Pray: Thank you, God, for indoor birds and outdoor birds. Amen.

Open the Bible to: Genesis 1:21.

Say: "God created all kinds of birds" (Genesis 1:21, *Good News Bible*, adapted).

Have the children repeat the Bible verse.

Group Fun

Resources

plastic berry baskets or plastic needlepoint sheets, scissors, yarn, cotton balls, string, torn tissue paper, raffia, feathers, narrow ribbon, computer paper side strips

Help the children make nesting kites. Before class, cut the sides from the berry baskets or cut needlepoint sheets into 4" x 6" rectangles. Tie a 12" piece of yarn to the top of each rectangle. Set out the assorted materials listed above.

Say: We are going to make a "nesting kite." You can take yours home today and hang it in a tree in your yard or near your home. The birds will use the materials in it to help make their nests.

Encourage the children to choose at least four different items from the materials provided. Have children weave each item in and out at least three times, making sure that items are loose enough for a bird to pull out.

Goodbye Circle

Let the children talk about the things they enjoyed doing today. Ask each child to name something he or she learned about birds today.

Pray: Thank you, God, for all the different kinds of birds. Amen.

Evaluation

Did each child have the fine motor skills to do the weaving for the nesting kite? If you had a pet bird, did each child have the opportunity to see it and talk about it?

Lesson 53

Nests and Eggs

Teacher Talk:

God created birds.

There are many different kinds of birds.

God cares for the birds, and God cares for you.

Birds live in special kinds of houses.

Some birds make nests.

Goals:

To help children learn about birds.

To know that God created birds.

To learn that there are many different kinds of birds.

Objectives:

By the end of this session the children will:

Study a bird nest.

Make collages of nesting materials.

Make edible bird nests.

Faith Connections

Bible verse: Even the sparrow finds a home, and the swallow a nest for herself.

(Psalm 84:3)

Home is an important concept, and God planned a specific kind of home for each living creature. Children can learn that birds live in special kinds of houses, and that different birds live in different kinds of houses.

Teacher's Prayer

Loving God, every person and animal needs a home to live in. Help me to learn about the types of homes my children live in so I can meet any needs they might have. Amen.

Center Time

Continue the centers from Lessons 51-52. For this lesson add the following centers:

Art Center

Teacher Talk

Some birds make nests.

Resources

twigs, yarn, feathers, construction paper, glue

Encourage the children to create collages. Talk about how birds might use each object.

Building Center

Teacher Talk

Birds live in special kinds of houses.

Resources

variety of blocks and building materials

Encourage the children to use blocks and building materials to make houses that birds might like to live in.

Dramatic Play Center

Teacher Talk

God cares for the birds and God cares for you.

Resources

large empty box, straw (or packing peanuts if you have children allergic to straw), plastic eggs, blankets

Place straw or packing peanuts inside the box, with several plastic eggs. Set the blankets nearby. Have the children pretend they are baby birds or mommy and daddy birds living in a nest.

Math Center

Teacher Talk

Some birds make nests.

Resources

plastic bowl, plastic eggs, large basket

Place plastic eggs in a basket. Let the children guess how many eggs they think might fit in the "nest" (plastic bowl). Have children place eggs in the bowl and count to see how many actually fit in the nest.

As children arrive,
say: "Let me hear you chirp like a bird."

Science Center

Teacher Talk

Some birds make nests.

Resources

old bird's nest (clean), magnifying glass

Have the children study the bird's nest with the magnifying glass. What is the nest made of? How big is it? Talk about what other kinds of houses birds might live in.

Writing Center

Teacher Talk

There are many different kinds of birds.

Resources

several feathers, washable black tempera paint, shallow container, paper, smocks, table covering

Cover the table and have the children wear smocks. Pour a small amount of paint in the shallow container. The children can dip the quill end of the feathers into the paint and "write" with the feathers.

Worship Center

Teacher Talk

God created birds.

Resources

bird nest (or picture of bird nest), pictures of different kinds of birds, pictures of "people" houses

Set the nest and pictures on a table for the children to look at.

Say: Birds and people were both created by God, but they look very different and they live in different kinds of houses. Could you live in a bird's nest? Could a bird live in your house like a person? God made each thing special.

Pray: Thank you, God for birds and bird-houses and people and people houses. Amen.

Open the Bible to Psalm 84:3.

Say: "Even the sparrow finds a home, and the swallow a nest for herself" (Psalm 84:3).

Have the children repeat the Bible verse.

Wonder Time

Call the children together for wonder time.

Wonder Question: I wonder what kind of house a bird lives in?

Say: There are many kinds of birds in the world. They live in all kinds of different houses. Some birds live in cages. Some birds live in holes or in the ground. Some birds live in trees and build nests.

Play: "Four Little Eggs" (see page 219). Have the children repeat the words and actions after you.

Read the Bible verse.

Say: God made all kinds of birds, and each bird is special. God planned for each bird to have a special kind of home.

Pray: Thank you, God, for all kinds of birds and all kinds of bird homes. Amen.

Group Fun

Resources

peanut butter chips (12 oz. bag), chow mein noodles (2 - 3 oz. cans), cookie sheet, small resealable bags, plain donuts (1 per child), chocolate frosting, plastic knives, jelly beans

Make edible bird nests with the children. Before class, melt the peanut butter chips over low heat, then add the chow mein noodles and stir until thoroughly coated. Spread mixture on a cookie sheet, separating the clumps as much as possible. When cool, place mixture in plastic bags, making a bag for each child. Hide the bags in the classroom.

Say: When birds want to make a nest, they have to find some materials to make it. Each one of you needs to look around the room until you find a bag with some special "nesting material" in it. When you find it, come and sit at the table. (Help the children if needed.)

When each child has a bag, give each child a donut and a plastic knife. Have the children spread the frosting on the donuts, then top them with the "nesting material." When each nest is completed, give each child several jelly bean "eggs" to place in the nest. The children can then eat and enjoy their special treats. (You could read the book of the day while the children are eating their snacks.)

Goodbye Circle

Let the children talk about the things they enjoyed doing today. Ask each child to name a place where a bird can live.

Pray: Thank you, God, for helping us learn about birds. Amen.

Evaluation

Was each child able to listen to and follow the instructions for the group project? Are the children enjoying the center activities?

Lesson 54

Penguins

Goals:

To help children learn about birds.

To know that God created birds.

To learn that there are many different kinds of birds.

Objectives:

By the end of this session the children will:

Experiment to determine if objects will float or sink.

Look at Antarctica on a map.

Faith Connections

Bible verse: God looked at everything God had made, and God was very pleased.

(Genesis 1:31, *Good News Bible*, adapted)

God's creations are varied and unique. There are hundreds of different types of birds, and each type looks different and has different needs. Children can learn that penguins are a type of bird that God created, and even though they are very different from the birds they may see outside their windows, they are part of God's special world.

Teacher's Prayer

Creator Lord, the creativity of your world never ceases to amaze me and fill me with wonder. Every one of your creations is special. Help me to appreciate the special gifts of each of the children in my care. Amen.

Teacher Talk:

God created birds.

There are many different kinds of birds.

Penguins can float on the water.

Penguins live where it is very cold.

Center Time

Continue the centers from Lessons 51-53. For this lesson add or change the following:

As children arrive, have the children walk like penguins by keeping their legs together and moving their arms and waddling their bodies.

Dramatic Play Center

Teacher Talk

Penguins live where it is very cold.

Resources

dress-up clothes; winter clothing: jackets, hats, mittens, scarves

Encourage the children to play dress-up. Dress-up clothes can be worn, and the children can pretend to have a party—penguins look like they are all dressed up. The winter clothing can be worn, and the children can pretend to go visit where penguins live, a place that is very cold.

Geography Center

Teacher Talk

Penguins live where it is very cold.

Resources

glove, map of world, pushpins, yarn

Set the globe on a table. Hang the map where children can see it. Mark Antarctica with a pushpin. Place another pushpin in the location where you live. Connect the two pins with yarn. Have the children look at the two locations and discuss how far apart they are. Talk about the characteristics of Antarctica.

Science Center

Teacher Talk

Penguins can float on the water.

Resources

dishpan with water; selection of items that float and do not float: corks, penny, paper clips, feather, eraser, and so forth; towel

Place the dishpan of water on a table. Encourage the children to sort the items into two piles—things that they think will float and things that they think won't float. The children can then test the objects to see if their predictions were correct. Items can be dried on the towel after each test.

Water Table Center

Teacher Talk

Penguins live where it is very cold.

Resources

water table (empty), several containers of ice cubes, mittens/gloves, tongs, plastic animals

Let the children play with the animals in the ice. Have the children wear the gloves or mittens or use tongs. Talk about what it would be like to live someplace that is cold all the time.

Writing Center

Teacher Talk

There are many different kinds of birds.

Resources

index card, marker, paper, pencils

Write the word *penguin* on an index card. Hang it where children can see it. Let the children copy the words.

Worship Center

Teacher Talk

God created birds.

Resources

pictures of many different types of birds including penguins; mirror

Hang the pictures at the children's eye level, or set the pictures on a table. Encourage the children to look at the pictures and talk about how the birds are similar and different. Have the children look in the mirror and talk about how the children are the same and different also.

Say: God created many different types of birds, just like God created many different kinds of people. God loves every kind of bird—and God loves every person. God loves you!

Pray: Thank you, God, for special birds and special people. Amen.

Wonder Time

Call the children together for wonder time.

Wonder Question: I wonder what kind of birds live in places where it is very cold?

Say: Penguins are special birds. Some of them live in places where everything is covered with snow and ice. Sometimes we can see penguins at the zoo. They are fun to watch.

Sing: "The Penguin Song" to the tune of "London Bridge."

Read the Bible verse.

Say: God made many kinds of birds. There are different kinds of birds in countries all over the world. God loves every bird that God created just like God loves every person God created.

Pray: Thank you, God, for all the different kinds of birds you love and for loving me. Amen.

The Penguin Song

Penguins waddle side to side,
(Arms flat at sides, hands out, legs together.)
Side to side, side to side.
(Waddle like a penguin.)
Penguins waddle side to side,
Penguins waddling.

Penguins leap up in the air,
(Same position as above, but leap up and down.)
In the air, in the air.
Penguins leap up in the air,
Penguins leaping high.

Open the Bible to Genesis 1:31.

Say: "God looked at everything God had made, and God was very pleased" (Genesis 1:31, *Good News Bible*, adapted).

Have the children repeat the Bible verse.

Group Fun

Resources

picture of penguin, paper, glue, shallow container, cotton swabs, scissors, black and white scraps of paper, black markers, black and white crayons, old newspapers, other black and white collage materials such as: packing peanuts, lace scraps, ribbon, and so forth

Help the children make black and white collages. Pour the glue into the shallow container. Ask students to look at the picture of the penguin and describe the colors they see. Tell the children they are going to make black and white collages that will help them think of penguins. Set out the collage materials listed above. Give each child a sheet of paper. Encourage the children to use the materials and their creativity to create pictures. The children can dip the cotton swabs in the glue to attach the materials.

Goodbye Circle

Let the children talk about the things they enjoyed doing today. Ask each child to name a bird that he or she has learned about this week. Repeat the Bible verse.

Pray: Thank you, God, for special birds all over the world. Amen.

Evaluation

Did each child experiment with the sink or float activity? Was each child able to make a "guess" and then test to determine if it was true or false? Make plans to help those children who had difficulties.

Lesson 55

I'm a Bird Watcher

Teacher Talk:

God created birds.

There are many different kinds of birds.

We can listen and hear bird songs when we are outside.

Birds live in many different places.

Birds eat special kinds of foods.

Goals:

To help children learn about birds.

To know that God created birds.

To learn that there are many different kinds of birds.

Objectives: By the end of this session the children will:

Name a sense organ they might use when looking for birds.

Measure foods to make a trail mix.

Go on a bird walk.

Faith Connections

Bible verse: In the trees near by, the birds make their nests and sing.

(Psalm 104:12, *Good News Bible*)

Spring is a time of new growth. Animals and birds produce young, and bird songs fill the air. Preschool children need the opportunity to explore the outside world and see birds in the real world, not just in pictures. Almost anywhere you live, you can go outside and see birds flying through the air—help your children find them and enjoy watching them.

Teacher's Prayer

Creator Lord, you have made a world full of beauty and joy. Help me to share that world with the children in my care. Amen.

Center Time

Continue the centers from Lessons 51-54. For this lesson add or change the following:

As children arrive, tape a feather to each child's clothing.

Art Center

Teacher Talk

Birds live in many different places.

Resources

magazines with pictures of birds and their homes, scissors, glue, paper

Have the children cut or tear out pictures of birds and homes where birds live. Let the children glue the pictures to their paper.

Cooking Center

Teacher Talk

Birds eat special kinds of foods.

Resources

paper cups, three large bowls, ¼ cup measuring cups, "Cheerios" type cereal, roasted sunflower seeds, raisins

Pour each food item into a bowl. Set the cups, food, and measuring cups on the table. Encourage each child to make "bird seed trail mix" by measuring ¼ cup of each food into his or her paper cup. The children can then eat and enjoy their snack.

Writing Center

Teacher Talk

There are many different kinds of birds.

Resources

cookie sheet, sand, feathers

Pour enough sand on the cookie sheet to cover the bottom. The children can use the end of the feathers to "write" in the sand.

Math Center

Teacher Talk

There are many different kinds of birds.

Resources

index cards, bird stickers

Place a bird sticker on each card, making a set of thirty to forty cards. Be sure there are at least four or five stickers of each bird. Set the cards on a table. Have the children make patterns with the cards.

Science Center

Teacher Talk

There are many different kinds of birds.

Resources

feathers, twigs, birdseed, cotton balls, 3 identical clear plastic jars (example: empty peanut butter containers)

Fill each jar with a different material. Screw the lids on tightly. Let the children shake the jars. Which jar is the lightest? Which is heaviest? What kinds of sounds do the jars make when they are shaken?

Music Center

Teacher Talk

We can listen and hear bird songs when we are outside.

Resources

plastic eggs, sand, spoon, tape, cassette/CD player, cassette/CD

Play a cassette/CD. Each child can spoon a small amount of sand into a plastic egg, then tape the egg together (children may need help taping the egg). Encourage the children to use the egg shakers to accompany the music.

Worship Center

Teacher Talk

We can listen and hear bird songs when we are outside.

Resources

mirror

Hang the mirror. Ask each child to look at his or her face in the mirror.

Say: God created many kinds of birds. Today we are going on a bird walk. What parts of your face will you use to help you see birds? What parts of your face will you use to help you hear birds? God created birds for us to enjoy, and God gave us bodies that help us enjoy this wonderful world.

Pray: Thank you God, for things to see and hear and eyes and ears to see and hear them. Amen.

Open the Bible to Psalm 104:12.

Say: "In the trees near by, the birds make their nests and sing" (Psalm 104:12, *Good News Bible*).

Have the children repeat the Bible verse.

Wonder Time

Call the children together for wonder time.

Wonder Question: I wonder how birds are different from other animals?

Have children talk about the differences. List them on chart paper.

Play: Feather Race. Divide the class into groups of three or four. Give each group a helper tool (choose from feathers, paper fans, straws, and turkey basters). Have them take turns trying to move a feather across the room. Talk about which way works best.

Sing: "Pigeons Peck" to the tune of "Mary Had a Little Lamb."

Read the Bible Verse.

Say: God made a world full of birds. When we go outside, we can hear birds singing and see birds flying in the sky.

Pray: Thank you, God, for this world full of birds to watch. Amen.

Pigeons Peck

Pigeons pecking back and forth,
(Stand with legs stretched apart, arms out like wings, bob head down towards knees and back up.)
Back and forth, back and forth.
Pigeons pecking back and forth,
Trying to find some food.

Pigeons walking, heads bobbing,
(Walk with head bobbing back and forth, arms bent and hands at waist.)
Heads bobbing, heads bobbing.
Pigeons walking, heads bobbing,
Trying to find more food.

Group Fun

Resources

paper, markers and crayons

Take a bird walk with the children. Walk outside and sit on the ground. Do you hear birds singing? Listen quietly. When you hear a specific bird sound, try repeating it back. What happens? Does the bird answer back? Encourage each child to describe what he or she sees and hears. When you come back inside, ask each child to draw a picture of something he or she saw outside.

Goodbye Circle

Let the children talk about the things they enjoyed doing today. Ask each child to name something he or she saw outside.

Pray: Thank you, God, for this special world we live in. Amen.

Book of the Day:
Feathers for Lunch
by Lois Ehlert

Evaluation

Were the children able to sit quietly and listen for birds? Are there children who still have difficulties listening and following directions? Make note of any children having difficulties.

REPTILES

This week the children will have the opportunity to learn about a type of animal they may not have much experience with—reptiles. While reptiles are not warm and fuzzy cute animals, children are fascinated with them and will enjoy the chance to learn more about them, as each day they study a specific reptile species.

The lessons this week focus on learning about reptiles so that children can appreciate them and know that they are a unique part of God's creation.

Week 4

A Reptile Is . . .

Goals:

To learn about four different types of reptiles.

To learn that reptiles are created by God.

Objectives: By the end of this session the children will:

Create "reptiles" using recyclable materials.

Sort pictures of reptiles by size.

Faith Connections

Bible verse: God made everything that creeps upon the ground of every kind. (Genesis 1:25, adapted)

The world is full of a variety of animal life. Every corner of the world has its own unique creatures. We write books and poetry about the beauty of some of them. We adopt them and bring them into our homes. Some, however, are shunned or even feared. Reptiles tend to top that list. Preschool children need the opportunity to learn about all types of animal life, and to know that they are all part of God's creation.

Teacher's Prayer

Dear God, help me to not pass any prejudices that I may have to the children in my care. Give me the words to keep them open-minded and in awe of each of your creations. Amen.

Teacher Talk:

God made many different types of reptiles.

Reptiles like to be in places where it is warm.

Reptiles can be many different colors.

Reptiles can be big or small.

Center Time

Set up your centers as described on pages 6–9. For this lesson add the following:

As children arrive, ask, "What letter does the word reptile start with?"

Building Center

Teacher Talk

God made many different types of reptiles.

Resources

variety of blocks and building materials

Have the children build a home that they think a reptile might like to live in. Talk with the children about the homes they create.

Home Living Center

Teacher Talk

Reptiles like to be in places where it is warm.

Resources

large empty box, blankets, stuffed animals

Place the blankets and stuffed animals inside the box. If possible, set up more than one box. Let the children climb in and pretend they are reptiles warming their bodies.

Science Center

Teacher Talk

God made many different types of reptiles.

Resources

pictures of a variety of animals and reptiles

Set out the pictures. Encourage the children to study them. Ask the children to name those animals they are familiar with. Work with the children to help them sort the reptiles from the other animals.

Puzzle Center

Teacher Talk

God made many different types of reptiles.

Resources

reptiles pictures (see page 218), scissors

Photocopy and cut apart a least two copies of the reptile pictures (see page 218). Mix up the pictures and place them in the center. Have the children match the pictures.

Art Center

Teacher Talk

Reptiles can be many different colors.

Resources

resealable sandwich bags, spoons, variety of colors of finger paint, paper, smocks

Have the children wear smocks. Talk with the children about what colors reptiles might be. Have the children put spoonfuls of two different colors of paint in their sandwich bags. Help them close the bags securely (help if needed). Let each child mix the colors together and decide if the new color would be a good color for reptiles. The children can then paint reptile pictures with their new colors.

Writing Center

Teacher Talk

God made many different types of reptiles.

Resources

index cards, markers, paper and pencils

Write the word *reptile* on a card. Hang it where the children can see it. Encourage the children to copy the word.

Worship Center

Teacher Talk

God made many different types of reptiles.

Resources

book showing pictures of various reptiles (such as *A Child's Book of Snakes, Lizards, and Other Reptiles*, by Kathleen N. Daly)

Set out the book. Let the children look through it. Talk about the reptiles in the book.

Say: Reptiles are special types of animals. They have smooth or scaly skins; they walk or crawl on their bellies; and they can't keep themselves warm—they need to get warm by being near something warm. Reptiles are part of God's creation.

Pray: Thank you, God, for special animals like reptiles. Amen.

Wonder Time

Call the children together for wonder time.

Wonder Question: I wonder what a reptile is?

Say: All reptiles have scaly skins. Sometimes their skin feels smooth. They breathe air, just like we do. They come in many different shapes and colors. Alligators, lizards, snakes, and turtles are all reptiles.

Do: "Reptiles Fingerplay." Have the children stand in a circle and repeat what you say and do.

Read the Bible verse.

Say: Reptiles are a special type of animal. They are part of God's creation.

Pray: Thank you, God, for reptiles. Amen.

Reptiles Fingerplay

Here come the reptiles,
stomping along.
(Stomp feet in place.)
They're all singing
their reptile song.
(Say: "Hiss.")
Some reptiles are tall
and some are wide.
(Hold hands up, then apart.)
Some reptiles have
spikes and a horny hide.
(Pretend to pet a reptile.)
Some reptiles have shells,
and some have claws.
(Hold hands like claws.)
Some reptiles have lots
of teeth in their jaws.
(Show teeth.)
Some reptiles crawl, and
some of them creep.
(Bend over and "creep" in place.)
But when reptiles are tired,
they all go to sleep!
(Lay head on hands.)

Open the Bible to Genesis 1:25.

Say: "God made everything that creeps upon the ground of every kind" (Genesis 1:25, adapted).

Have the children repeat the Bible verse.

Group Fun

Resources

variety of recyclable materials: egg cartons, oatmeal containers, paper tubes, craft sticks, packing "peanuts;" construction paper scraps; scissors; glue; tape; markers and crayons

Help each child create a reptile. Set out the materials listed above. Tell the children that they will be making their own reptiles. Encourage the children to use the materials provided and their imaginations. Have the children talk about their creations as they build them. If desired, the children can paint their reptiles when they are completed. When the reptiles are finished, display them and give the children the opportunity to look at their friends' reptile creations.

Goodbye Circle

Let the children talk about the things they enjoyed doing today. Ask each child to tell something that he or she learned about reptiles today.

Pray: Thank you, God, for animals and especially reptiles. Amen.

Evaluation

Did the children enjoy the opportunity to use their creativity to make reptiles? Was each child able to name something she or he learned about reptiles?

Lesson 57

Alligators and Crocodiles

Teacher Talk:

God made many different types of reptiles.

Alligators and crocodiles have scaly skins.

Reptiles are part of God's creation plan.

God made alligators and crocodiles.

Goals:

To learn about four different types of reptiles.

To learn that reptiles are created by God.

Objectives:

By the end of this session the children will:

Look at pictures of alligators and crocodiles.

Make "alligator tails."

Measure an "alligator's" length.

Faith Connections

Bible verse: God looked at everything God had made, and God was very pleased.

(Genesis 1:31, *Good News Bible*, adapted)

It's easy to see fuzzy, cute little animals as pleasing creations of God, but it can be a little more difficult when we are dealing with reptiles. Reptiles are "cold-blooded" rather than warm, and not often seen as "cute;" but they are an important part of God's creation. Preschool children need to know that all animals were made by God and are important parts of God's world.

Teacher's Prayer

Dear God, help me to remember that all creatures, animal and human, are your children, even though they may seem unlovable at times. Amen.

Center Time

Continue the centers from Lesson 56. For this lesson add or change the following:

As children arrive, ask, "Have you ever seen an alligator or a crocodile?"

Art Center

Teacher Talk

Alligators and crocodiles have scaly skins.

Resources

old bicycle tire, 2" x 18" pieces of newsprint, crayons, markers

Lay the bicycle tire on the table. Help the children as needed to lay their papers over the tread on the tire and make rubbings with the crayons. If desired, the children can turn their rubbings into pictures of alligators or crocodiles using the markers.

Cooking Center

Teacher Talk

God made alligators and crocodiles.

Resources

paper plates, plate of cheese slices

Place the cheese slices on the table. Encourage each child to take a cheese slice and bite it. The children can then study the bite marks they left on the cheese slices. Talk about alligator and crocodile teeth.

Science Center

Teacher Talk

God made alligators and crocodiles.

Resources

pictures of alligators and crocodiles

Place the pictures where the children can easily study them. Encourage the children to describe the two reptiles. How are they the same? How are they different?

Math Center

Teacher Talk

Reptiles are part of God's creation plan.

Resources

string, scissors, craft sticks, paper, marker

Cut a piece of string approximately 7 feet long. Lay the string on the table and set the craft sticks nearby. Tell children that alligators grow to be from 5 feet to 20 feet long. Ask the children to guess how many craft sticks long the string is and record their guesses on the paper. Have the children measure the string with the craft sticks, and record the actual measurement.

Writing Center

Teacher Talk

God made alligators and crocodiles.

Resources

index cards, pictures of an alligator and a crocodile, marker, paper, pencils, tape

Write the word *alligator* and the word *crocodile* on index cards. Hang each card next to the picture of the reptile. Encourage children to copy each word.

Worship Center

Teacher Talk

God made alligators and crocodiles.

Resources

pictures of alligators and crocodiles or book about alligators and crocodiles (such as *All About Alligators*, by Jim Arnosky)

Place the pictures or book on the table. Encourage the children to look at the pictures and discuss the appearance of the alligators and crocodiles.

Say: We have been learning about many different kinds of things that God created. Alligators and crocodiles are reptiles that were created by God. It would be pretty boring if there were only one kind of animal; God created many different kinds of animals that live all over the world.

Pray: Thank you, God, for all the different kinds of animals in this world. Amen.

Open the Bible to Genesis 1:31.

Say: "God looked at everything God had made, and God was very pleased" (Genesis 1:31, *Good News Bible*, adapted).

Have the children repeat the Bible verse.

Wonder Time

Call the children together for wonder time.

Wonder Question: I wonder what alligators and crocodiles are?

Say: Alligators and crocodiles are reptiles. They look a lot alike, but alligators have much broader snouts than crocodiles do. They grow to be pretty long, with long tails.

Sing: "The Alligator Song" to the tune of "This is the Way."

Read the Bible verse.

Say: Alligators and crocodiles live part of the time in water and part of the time on land. They are part of God's creation.

Pray: Thank you, God, for alligators and crocodiles. Amen.

The Alligator Song

This is the way we snap our jaws,
(hold arms straight out in front; move them together and apart)
Snap our jaws, snap our jaws.
This is the way we snap our jaws,
Snap, snap, snap.

This is the way we smack our tail,
(clap hands on thighs)
Smack our tail, smack our tail.
This is the way we smack our tail,
Smack, smack, smack.

This is the way we crawl away,
(stamp feet)
Crawl away, crawl away,
This is the way we crawl away.
Stomp, stomp, stomp.

Group Fun

Resources

paper cups, yarn, scissors, masking tape, two jump ropes

Help the children make alligator tails. Before class, poke a small hole in the bottom of each cup. Cut the yarn into four-foot lengths. Give each child five or six cups and a piece of yarn. Help the child thread the cups on the yarn one at a time and tie a knot in the yarn to hold each cup in place (or use masking tape). When the children have completed their alligator tails, help them tie the tails to their clothes.

Play "Alligator in the Swamp." Have the children wear their alligator tails. Lay two jump ropes about six inches apart. Tell the children that they are alligators walking in the swamp. Have each child walk between the ropes, making alligator growls. The children can stand on one side of the swamp and take turns trying to jump over the swamp. If desired, move the ropes apart after all have jumped and try again.

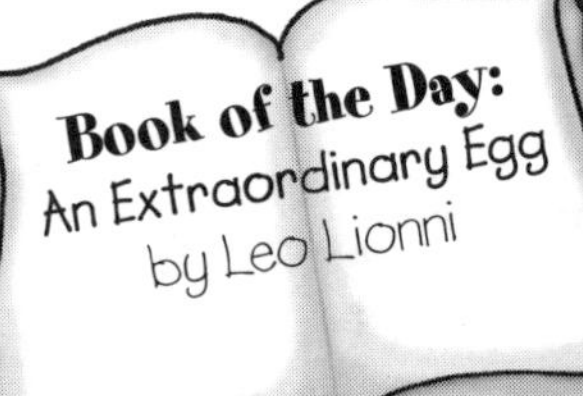

Goodbye Circle

Let the children talk about the things they enjoyed today. Tell them that baby alligators make a special call when they want their mothers to come: "YeeOck! YeeOck!." Have the children repeat the baby alligator sound. Repeat the Bible verse.

Pray: Thank you, God, for all the wonderful alligators and crocodiles you made. Amen.

Evaluation

Were the children able to thread the yarn through the holes in the cups? Make plans to work with children who have not yet developed fine motor skills.

Lesson 58

Lizards

Goals:

To learn about four different types of reptiles.

To learn that reptiles are created by God.

Objectives: By the end of this session the children will:

Create lizard friends.

Compare the sizes of lizards and alligators.

Faith Connections

Bible verse: Lizards are small, but very, very clever.

(Proverbs 30:24, *Good News Bible*, adapted)

In the scripture quoted above, the writer considers lizards to be clever because they can be held in the hand yet can be found in palaces. In the south, lizards find their way into many homes because they are so small. They are often accepted because they eat the bugs in the homes. Preschool children can learn that although reptiles are often very small, the reptiles are an important part of God's creation—just like they are.

Teacher's Prayer

Dear Lord, help me teach the children in my class that size is not important—every creation of God's has purpose and worth. Amen.

Teacher Talk:

God made many different types of reptiles.

Lizards eat vegetables.

God created lizards.

Lizards can be many different colors and sizes.

Iguanas are a type of lizard.

Center Time

Continue the centers from Lessons 56-57. For this lesson add or change the following:

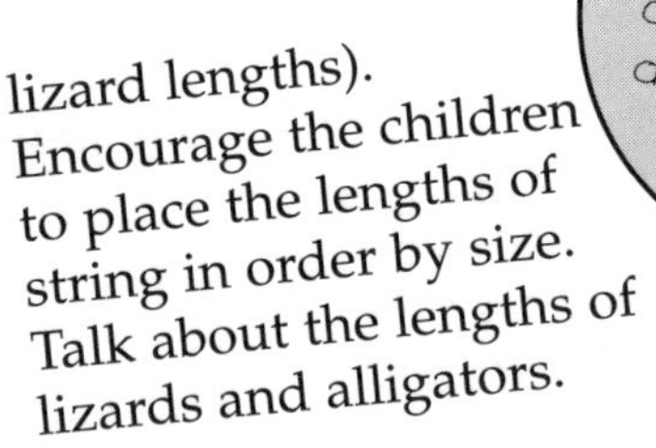

Sand Table

Teacher Talk

Lizards can be many different colors and sizes.

Resources

sand table, plastic grass, plastic or rubber lizards, magnifying glasses

Place plastic grass inside the empty sand table. Add the lizards and magnifying glasses. Let the children search for and find the lizards, then examine them with the magnifying glasses.

Science Table

Teacher Talk

Lizards can be many different colors and sizes.

Resources

live lizards in a cage or pictures of lizards

Place the lizards or pictures on the table. Let the children look at them. Talk about the lizard's appearance and size. How do they compare to the alligator that was discussed yesterday?

Art Center

Teacher Talk

Lizards can be many different colors and sizes.

Resources

chenille sticks, wiggle eyes, glue, construction paper, scissors

Let the children create lizard friends. They can twist chenille sticks together, add eyes, and use construction paper to add features. The lizard friends will be used during the group project.

Math Center

Teacher Talk

Lizards can be many different colors and sizes.

Resources

string or yarn, scissors

Cut string or yarn into a variety of lengths. Cut at least one length five or six feet long (alligator length), and the rest into a variety of sizes from two inches to two feet (average lizard lengths). Encourage the children to place the lengths of string in order by size. Talk about the lengths of lizards and alligators.

Writing Center

Teacher Talk

Iguanas are a type of lizard.

Resources

index cards, marker, paper and pencils, pictures of lizards and iguanas

Write the words *lizard* and *iguana* on index cards. Hang them where children can see them. Place the appropriate pictures nearby. Encourage the children to copy the words.

Cooking Center

Teacher Talk

Lizards eat vegetables.

Resources

raw washed vegetables (broccoli, carrots, squash, zucchini), cutting board, plastic knife, paper plates, bowl

Place raw vegetables in a bowl, with the knife and plates nearby. Let the children cut up the vegetables and taste them. Tell the children that lizards like to eat vegetables.

Worship Center

Teacher Talk

God created lizards.

Resources

pictures of lizards

Place the pictures of lizards on a table. Let the children look at and discuss them.

Say: Nearly all lizards have four legs and can run very fast. Most of them are very small. Some eat bugs, and some eat vegetables. They are all reptiles, and they are all created by God.

Pray: Thank you, God, for special reptiles called lizards. Amen.

Wonder Time

Call the children together for wonder time.

Wonder Question: I wonder what lizards are?

Say: Lizards are a special type of reptile. Almost all of them have four legs, and they can run very fast. Their skins are scaly and they come in all kinds of colors. One type of reptile can even change its color!

Play: "Lizard Race." Have the children imagine that they are lizards. Encourage the children to take turns racing from one predetermined point to another the way they think a lizard might race.

Sing: "I Wish I Were" to the tune of "Did You Ever See a Lassie?" Encourage the children to do the motions as they sing.

Read the Bible verse.

Say: Lizards can be large or small. Some people keep lizards as pets. Lizards are part of God's creation.

Pray: Thank you, God, for lizards. Amen.

I Wish I Were

Oh, I wish I were a lizard,
a lizard, a lizard.
Oh, I wish I were a lizard;
I know what I'd do.
I'd run, and I'd run; then
I'd lie in the sun.
Oh, I wish I were a lizard;
I know what I'd do.

Open the Bible to Proverbs 30:24.

Say: "Lizards are small, but very, very clever" (Proverbs 30:24, *Good News Bible*, adapted).

Have the children repeat the Bible verse.

Group Fun

Resources

rocks, markers, glitter, glue, lizard friends (made in Art Center)

Help the children make lizard rocks. Give each child a rock. Tell the children that lizards like to climb on rocks in the sun and sleep on them to stay warm. They are going to make "lizard rocks" for the lizard friends they made in the Art Center. Encourage the children to decorate their rocks as desired with the materials provided. Children can then put their lizard friends on their new rock homes.

Goodbye Circle

Let the children talk about the things they enjoyed doing today. Ask each child to name an animal that is a reptile.

Pray: Thank you, God, for reptiles, like lizards and alligators and crocodiles. Amen.

Evaluation

Did the children enjoy creating lizard friends? Make note of those children who had difficulties and make plans to help them.

Lesson 59

Snakes

Teacher Talk:

God made many different types of animals.

A snake smells with its tongue and its nose.

God created snakes.

Snakes can be short or long.

Goals:

To learn about four different types of reptiles.

To learn that reptiles are created by God.

Objectives:

By the end of this session the children will:

Make snakes.

Move like snakes.

Identify an object by its smell.

Faith Connections

Bible verse: Let everything that breathes praise the LORD!

(Psalm 150:6)

Snakes are God's creatures, but they are often feared and reviled. Even so, snakes have their purpose in the world. Every creature in the world is a creation of God, and has been given a means to praise God. Preschool children can learn that they can praise God in a number of different ways.

Teacher's Prayer

Lord, I give you praise for all that you have given me. Thank you for the opportunities you present me each day as I work with the children in my care. Amen.

Center Time

Continue the centers from Lessons 56-58. For this lesson add or change the following:

As children arrive, ask, "What letter does the word snake start with?"

Art Center

Teacher Talk

God created snakes.

Resources

clay or play dough, markers or paint

Let the children use clay to create snakes. If they choose, they can decorate their snakes with markers or paint when their creations are dry.

Math Center

Teacher Talk

Snakes can be short or long.

Resources

snakes of various lengths

Teacher Tip: Snakes can be purchased, cut from construction paper, cut from paper tubes, or made from clay.

Set the snakes on the table. Encourage the children to place the snakes in order of length, from shortest to longest and longest to shortest.

Music Center

Teacher Talk

God created snakes.

Resources

cassette/CD player, cassette/CD, rhythm instruments

Play a cassette/CD and set out the instruments. Talk with the children about sounds that snakes make. Let the children use the instruments to try to create snake sounds to accompany the cassette.

Sand Table Center

Teacher Talk

God created snakes.

Resources

sand table, sand, plastic or rubber snakes, magnifying glass

Partially fill the sand table with sand. Hide the snakes in the sand. Have the children search for the snakes. When they find the snakes, have them study the snakes with the magnifying glass.

Science Center

Teacher Talk

A snake smells with its tongue and its nose.

Resources

margarine tubs or film canisters; variety of "smells:" onion, lemon, pickle, cinnamon

Place a "smelly object" in each container. Put the lid on. Poke several holes in the lid so the smell comes through, but the object is hidden. Have the children sniff each container and name the smell.

Writing Center

Teacher Talk

God created snakes.

Resources

shallow container or cookie sheet, sand, twigs

Pour a layer of sand in the container and place the twigs nearby. Encourage the children to use the twigs to trace letters in the sand—especially the letter "S."

Worship Center

Teacher Talk

God made many different types of animals.

Resources

pictures of snakes, mirror

Set out the mirror and the pictures of the snakes. Let the children look at the snake pictures and look at themselves in the mirror. Have the children describe the snakes and themselves.

Say: You and the snakes look very different, but you are the same in one very important way—you were both created by God. Snakes can't talk, so they can't say thank you to God with words like we can, but we can say thank you in a prayer.

Pray: Thank you, God, for creating me and for creating snakes. Amen.

Open the Bible to Psalm 150:6.

Say: "Let everything that breathes praise the LORD!" (Psalm 150:6).

Have the children repeat the Bible verse.

Wonder Time

Call the children together for wonder time.

Wonder Question: I wonder what snakes like to do?

Say: Snakes are a type of reptile. One of their favorite things to do is find a warm place to sleep.

Do "Slither Like a Snake." Remind the children that snakes have no arms or legs. Tell the children they are going to pretend to be snakes. Have them lie on the ground with their arms and legs close to their bodies. Encourage them to slither back and forth like snakes to get across the room.

Sing: "I Wish I Were a Snake" to the tune of "Did You Ever See a Lassie."

Read the Bible verse.

Say: Snakes are part of God's creations. Everything that God made praises God—and we can too. We can praise God when we pray.

Pray: Thank you, God, for all the wonderful things you do. Amen.

I Wish I Were a Snake

I wish I were a snake,
a snake, a snake.
I wish I were a snake;
I know what I'd do.
I'd slither and hiss and
slither and hiss.
(Move hand like snake and make hissing sound.)
Oh, I wish I were a snake;
now that's what I'd do.

Group Fun

Resources

pictures of snakes; washable tempera paint; paintbrushes; paint smocks; large or small paper tubes; construction paper scraps; chenille sticks; tape; paper punch

Help the children make snakes. Have the children look at the pictures of the snakes and discuss their appearance (color, size, shape). Have the children show you how long they want their snakes to be, and give them the appropriate number of tubes. Have children decorate their tubes and let the paint dry. (They can use markers if you want to eliminate waiting time.) When the tubes are dry, have each child hook enough chenille sticks together to match the length of the snake. Insert the chenille sticks into the tubes. Punch a hole at each end of the snakes. Hook the chenille sticks through the holes. The chenille sticks will allow the snake to bend and move. The children can then use the paper scraps to create heads and tails, and tape them to the snakes.

Goodbye Circle

Let the children talk about the things they enjoyed doing today. Have the children say: "Snake starts with 'S.'" Then encourage each child to hiss like a snake.

Pray: Thank you, God, for snakes. Amen.

Evaluation

Did each child have the fine motor skills to twist the chenille sticks together? Did the children enjoy learning about snakes?

Lesson 60

Turtles

Goals:

To learn about four different types of reptiles.

To learn that reptiles are created by God.

Objectives: By the end of this session the children will:

Examine a turtle.

Make turtles.

Faith Connections

Bible verse: Then God commanded, "Let the earth produce all kinds of animal life: large and small."

(Genesis 1:24, *Good News Bible*, adapted)

Turtles can range in size from 4 inches long to the 8-foot-long, 1,500-pound leatherback sea turtle. We keep turtles as pets and joke about how slow they are. But turtles are also part of God's creation, and sea turtles are an endangered species. Preschool children can learn that it is important to respect and care for all of God's creation, especially before it is too late and something no longer even exists.

Teacher's Prayer

Dear Lord, help me to not miss an opportunity to help wherever and whenever it might be needed. Amen.

Teacher Talk:

God created turtles.

Turtles can be large or small.

Some turtles like to eat vegetables.

Turtles have shells that protect them.

Center Time

Continue the centers from Lessons 56-59. For this lesson add the following:

As children arrive, ask, "What letter does the word *turtle* start with?"

Sand Table

Teacher Talk

Turtles have shells that protect them.

Resources

sand table, sand, plastic turtles, plastic eggs, magnifying glass

Place the sand in the sand table. Hide the turtles and eggs in the sand. Let the children search for the turtles and turtle eggs. The children can study the turtles they find with the magnifying glass.

Science Center

Teacher Talk

God created turtles.

Resources

live turtle in an aquarium, magnifying glass

Set the turtle in the aquarium on a table where the children can see it. Let the children study the turtle with the magnifying glass.

Math Center

Teacher Talk

Turtles can be large or small.

Resources

small paper plates, walnut shells or other counters, crayons

Decorate five paper plates to be turtle shells. Write a number from one to five on each paper plate. Set out plates and counters. Have the children count the correct number of items and place them on the appropriate turtle shell.

Cooking Center

Teacher Talk

Many turtles eat vegetables.

Resources

paper plates, lettuce, carrots,

Peel and slice the carrots. Place the carrots and lettuce on a plate. Let the children taste the lettuce and carrots—turtle food!

Art Center

Teacher Talk

Turtles have shells that protect them.

Resources

plastic bubble wrap, green and brown tempera paint, paint brushes, construction paper, scissors, smocks, table covering

Before class, cut paper into large circles for turtle shells. Cover the table and have the children wear smocks. Let the children paint pieces of bubble wrap with green and brown paint, then press their paper shells over the painted bubble wrap to create designs.

Building Center

Teacher Talk

God created turtles.

Resources

assorted blocks

Tell the children that some turtles lay eggs in the sand. When the baby turtles hatch, they have to get to the sea quickly. Let the children use the blocks to build an obstacle course, then have them pretend to be baby turtles going through the course to get to the sea.

Worship Center

Teacher Talk

God created turtles.

Resources

pictures of turtles, book about sea turtles (such as *Tracks in the Sand*, by Loren Leedy)

Place the book and pictures on a table and encourage the children to look at them.

Say: Sea turtles are a special kind of turtle. They are called an "endangered species" because there are not many of them left. They are part of God's world. It is everyone's job to take care of God's world and all the things that live in it.

Pray: Dear God, thank you for turtles and people who help them. Amen.

Wonder Time

Call the children together for wonder time.

Wonder Question: I wonder why turtles have shells?

Say: Turtles carry their houses on their backs. When a turtle is scared it can pull its head and legs inside the shell for protection.

Sing: "Mr. Turtle" to the tune of "London Bridge."

Read the Bible verse.

Say: Turtles are part of God's creation. Some of them are small and can be kept as pets. Some of them are very large. Some turtles live on land and some in the water. No matter what kind of turtle it is, it is an important part of God's world.

Pray: Thank you, God, for all kinds of turtles. Amen.

Mr. Turtle

Mr. Turtle hides his head,
Hides his head, hides his head.
Mr. Turtle hides his head,
So he cannot see.
(Cover eyes with hands.)
But if he poked his head out,
His head out, his head out,
But if he poked his head out,
He would just see me.
(Uncover eyes.)

Group Fun

Resources

paper bowls, construction paper, markers and crayons, glue, scissors

Help the children make turtles. Give each child a paper bowl. Encourage the children to decorate the bowls with the markers and crayons to make turtle shells. Each child can then cut pieces from the construction paper to make legs, a head, and a tail and glue them in place. When the turtles are completed, the children can enter their turtles in the "turtle race."

Turtle Race: Line up the turtles on the edge of a table. Have the children take deep breaths, and blow under and behind their turtles' shells to move the turtles across the table.

Goodbye Circle

Let the children talk about the things they enjoyed doing today. Ask each child to name a type of reptile that he or she learned about this week.

Pray: Thank you, God, for all the different kinds of reptiles. Amen.

Evaluation

Did the children enjoy learning about reptiles this week? Did each child meet the objectives for the week? Make plans to work with those children who need help.

Open the Bible to Genesis 1:24.

Say: "God commanded, 'Let the earth produce all kinds of animal life: large and small'" (Genesis 1:24, *Good News Bible*, adapted).

Have the children repeat the Bible verse.

Seasonal

Seasonal Holidays

Goals:

1. The children will have the opportunity to discover that God plans for spring.
2. The children will have the opportunity to celebrate Easter and to learn some religious symbols of Easter.
3. The children will have the opportunity learn about St. Patrick's Day.
4. The child will have the opportunity to celebrate Mother's Day.
5. The child will have the opportunity to learn about Cinco de Mayo.

The five lessons in the Seasonal Unit are designed to give the children opportunities to celebrate the holidays that happen during the spring season. These lessons are not meant to be used consecutively. Each lesson can be used at the appropriate time in your school's calendar. Simply use one of these lessons instead of one of the regular lessons. Or choose activities form these lessons and add them to the regular lessons.

Bible Stories for This Unit:
Genesis 9:13 (The Rainbow)
Exodus 20:12 (Respect Your Parents)
Ecclesiastes 3:1 (For Everything There Is A Season)
Matthew 5:12 (Be Happy)
Luke 24: 1-12 (The Resurrection)

Lesson 61

Spring

Goals:

To help children understand that spring is a time of planting and new growth.

To help children realize that spring is one of the seasons of the year.

Objectives: By the end of this session the children will:

Sort and recognize objects that represent spring.

Listen for spring sounds.

Make bunny ears.

Faith Connections

Bible verse: For everything there is a season.

(Ecclesiastes 3:1)

God has a plan for the world, and the four seasons are part of that plan. Children need to know that God has created a specific time for every event, and that spring is a time of new growth, and a time for planting things. The days start to get warmer and longer. We can rejoice as we see the world reborn.

Teacher's Prayer

Dearest Lord, thank you for the rebirth of your beautiful world. Help me to renew my spirit as you renew the world in this joyous spring season. Amen.

Teacher Talk:

Seasons are part of God's plan.

It is now the season called spring.

In spring we plant seeds.

We thank God for spring.

Center Time

Set up your centers as described on pages 6–9. To use today:

Art Center

Teacher Talk

It is now the season called spring.

Resources

construction paper, markers, stickers and stamps, stamp pad, tape, glue, stapler

Before class, cut a pair of bunny ears and a 2 by 24-inch rectangle from construction paper for each child. Each child can color his or her bunny ears and decorate the headband. When the children are through decorating the parts, they can glue or tape the ears to the headband. Staple the headband to fit the child.

Cooking Center

Teacher Talk

It is now the season called spring.

Resources

paper plates, pear halves, baby carrots, cottage cheese, spoons

Let the children make bunny snacks. Give each child a pear half on a small paper plate. This will make the body of the bunny. Have the children add baby carrots on either side of the narrow end of the pear to make ears. Let the children add a spoonful of cottage cheese to the wide end to make the bunny's tail.

Music Center

Teacher Talk

It is now the season called spring.

Resources

cassette/CD player, cassette/CD or recording of "The Bunny Hop"

Let the children move to the music. Have them pretend to be growing flowers, plants, spring rain, or any other type of spring thing they choose. Or play "The Bunny Hop" and let the children hop around the room as the music plays. Encourage the children to wear their bunny ears from the Art Center.

As children arrive, ask, "What season is it?"

Spring Center

Teacher Talk

In spring we plant seeds.

Resources

pictures or objects that represent different seasons (mittens, fall leaves, seed packet, flower, rabbit, bathing suit, snowman, and so forth)

Have the children choose which objects represent spring. Talk with them about what each object is and when and how it is used or seen.

Writing Center

Teacher Talk

It is now the season called spring.

Resources

index card, marker, paper and pencils

Write the word *spring* on an index card. Hang it at the children's eye level. Have the children copy the word.

Worship Center

Teacher Talk

Seasons are part of God's plan.

Resources

plants, flowers, seed packets

Set out the plants, flowers, and seed packets. Let the children look at the plants and smell and touch the flowers.

Say: When winter is over, the days get warmer. When that happens, it is time to start planting seeds, and time for flowers and plants to grow. It is a special time of God's year that we call spring.

Pray: Thank you, God, for the time when plants and flowers begin to grow, the time we call spring. Amen.

Wonder Time

Call the children together for wonder time.

Spring Is Here

Spring, spring, spring is here,
Spring is here today.
Plant some seeds and shout Hooray!
Spring is here today.

Wonder Question: I wonder what happens during the season we call spring!

Say: Spring is a very special time of year. We can plant seeds outside, and the plants and flowers start to grow. Leaves grow on the trees. The whole earth becomes green again. People are happy because the days get longer and warmer. Spring is a happy, happy time.

Play: "Spring Into Spring." Tell children that there are two kinds of springs—the season and the kind that looks like a "Slinky" toy that bounces up and down. They are going to pretend to be a "Slinky" spring and bounce up and down because they are happy that it is the spring season! Have children stand in a circle and jump up and down. Tell the children to bend their knees before springing and when landing, with toes coming down first. Practice little springs with soft landings and noisy springs. Practice springs on one foot.

Sing: "Spring Is Here" to the tune of "Row, Row, Row Your Boat."

Read the Bible verse.

Say: God has a special plan for the world. God made four special different seasons. Now it is the season called spring.

Pray: Thank you, God, for spring and all your special seasons. Amen.

Open the Bible to Ecclesiastes 3:1.

Say: "For everything there is a season" (Ecclesiastes 3:1).

Have the children repeat the Bible verse.

Group Fun

Resources

tape recorder, blank tape, microphone, large sheet of paper, marker

Lead the children on a spring listening walk. Talk a walk outside with a blank tape in the tape recorder. Look around for signs of spring. Have the children dictate things they see into the tape recorder. Listen carefully for spring sounds and tape any spring sounds you hear on the tape recorder.

When you return to your room, play the tape. Make a list of the things you saw and the sounds you heard on the large sheet of paper. Write the words "Spring Is Here" on top of the paper and display it in the room.

Goodbye Circle

Let the children talk about the things they enjoyed doing today. Ask each child to name something that happens in the spring. Repeat the Bible verse.

Pray: Thank you, God, for spring. Amen.

Evaluation

If weather didn't allow a spring listening walk, make plans to do it on another day.

Lesson 62

Easter

Teacher Talk:

Easter is a special day to remember Jesus and his life.

Easter comes in the spring.

Eggs are a special part of Easter.

Easter is a time to celebrate.

Goals:

To help children learn some religious symbols of Easter.

To help children know that Easter comes in the springtime.

To teach children that Easter is an important day of celebration for Christians.

Objectives:

By the end of this session the children will:

Name religious symbols of Easter.

Celebrate the joy of Easter.

Faith Connections

Bible verse: Jesus is not here. He has risen.

(Luke 24:6, *Good News Bible*, adapted)

The events of Easter can be difficult for even adults to understand. It is important to reassure the children in the class that it is a happy occasion—Jesus' friends were happy to see him, and the events of the week were part of God's plan. We do not always understand God's plan, but we know that God loves us and wants only good things for us. It is all right to answer a child's question about Easter with "I don't know," and it is important to focus on the resurrection and the joy of that day.

Teacher's Prayer

Dear Lord, we remember the events of Holy Week with mixed feelings. It is hard to imagine the trial and crucifixion, but the week culminates in such joy. We know it was your plan, but we can not always understand. Be with me as I try to share the joy of Easter with the children in my care. Amen.

Center Time

Set up your centers as described on pages 6–9. To use today:

As children arrive,
Have Easter music playing and say, "Happy Easter!"

Art Center

Teacher Talk

Easter comes in the spring.

Resources

washable tempera paint in pastel spring colors: green, blue, pink, yellow, lavender; paintbrushes; paint smocks; paper

Encourage the children to paint with the colors provided to make Easter pictures.

Building Center

Teacher Talk

Easter is a time to celebrate.

Resources

assorted blocks

Let the children use the blocks to build a church.

Dramatic Play Center

Teacher Talk

Easter is a time to celebrate.

Resources

dress-up clothes

Have the children dress-up and pretend to go to church, or have an Easter parade in their special outfits.

Easter Center

Teacher Talk

Easter is a special day to remember Jesus and his life.

Resources

variety of Easter symbols: plastic eggs, cross, butterfly (artificial or picture), lamb (picture or stuffed animal), plant

Place the Easter symbols on a table for the children to look at. Encourage the children to discuss each object. If children ask, explain the symbol's significance to the Easter story.

Cooking Center

Teacher Talk

Eggs are a special part of Easter.

Resources

paper plates and napkins, hard-boiled eggs, plastic knives

Remove the shells of the eggs. Encourage the children to slice and try pieces of the egg.

Writing Center

Teacher Talk

Easter is a time to celebrate.

Resources

old greeting cards, index card, marker, paper, pencils, envelopes

Write the word *Easter* on an index card. Place it at the children's eye level. The children can copy the word or use cards, paper, and envelopes to write Easter cards and letters to friends and family.

Worship Center

Teacher Talk

Easter is a special day to remember Jesus and his life.

Resources

Easter lily in a pot, picture of Jesus

Set the lily on a table and place the picture nearby. Encourage the children to look at and smell the flower.

Say: Many people buy flowers like this at Easter. They are called Easter lilies. They help remind us of what a happy day Easter is for people who believe in Jesus. Easter is the day we remember that God loves all of us very much.

Pray: Thank you, God, for loving (name of child) so much that you sent your Son Jesus to live with us and be with us. Amen.

Open the Bible to Luke 24:6.

Say: "Jesus is not here. He has risen" (Luke 2;46, *Good News Bible*, adapted).

Have the children repeat the Bible verse.

Wonder Time

Call the children together for wonder time.

Wonder Question: I wonder why Easter is a special day?

Say: On Easter we celebrate that Jesus is alive. God had a special plan for Jesus. Easter is the day we celebrate God's special plan. Jesus' friends thought Jesus was dead but he wasn't—Jesus is alive!

Play: Easter Egg Race. Divide the children into three or four teams, based on the number of children. Give the first child in each line a spoon with a plastic egg. Each child must walk to the end of a designated course and back, carrying the egg in the spoon. If it drops, he or she picks it up; puts it back and keeps walking. Emphasize fun and balance.

Sing: "On This Happy Easter Day" to the tune of "The Farmer in the Dell."

Read the Bible verse.

Say: God had a special plan for Jesus. God's plan makes us feel wonder and joy, and on Easter we are happy and say: "He is risen," because Jesus is alive.

Pray: Thank you, God, for Jesus and your special plan. Amen.

On This Happy Easter Day

O we remember Jesus.
O we remember Jesus.
On this happy Easter day,
O we remember Jesus.

O Jesus is alive.
O Jesus is alive.
O on this happy Easter day,
O Jesus is alive.

Words: Daphna Flegal

Group Fun

Resources

plastic rings (from soft-drink cans cut apart, or lids from margarine tubs with centers cut out), spools of curling ribbon in pastel colors, scissors, tape player, tape (children's Christian music)

Help the children make Hosanna streamers. Before class, cut a 3-foot length of each color ribbon for each child. Lay the ribbons in piles. Give each child a plastic ring. Show each child how to fold a ribbon in half, put the folded edge through the ring, then pull the loose ends of the ribbon over the ring and through the folded end, pulling them tightly. Older preschoolers will be able to do this, while younger preschoolers may need help. When the children have finished creating their streamers, encourage them to wave them as you listen to the music on the tape. Have the children say "He is risen" as they wave their ribbons and dance as they desire. Celebrate Easter!

"Easter Party"

Resources: refreshments children bring from home - cookies or cupcakes, jelly beans, juice

If desired, enjoy an Easter party with your children.

Goodbye Circle

Let the children talk about the things they enjoyed doing today. Have children wave their Hosanna streamers and say "He is risen, Happy Easter!"

Pray: Thank you, God, for Jesus, and Easter, and loving us. Amen.

Evaluation

Were there questions you could not answer? Did the children feel comfortable with your responses? Were children able to celebrate the joy of the Easter story? Make plans to spend time with those children who had difficulties.

Lesson 63

St. Patrick's Day

Goals:

To celebrate St. Patrick's Day.

To help children learn that St. Patrick's Day is a special day people in March can celebrate.

Objectives:

By the end of this session the children will:

Make shamrock headbands.

Talk about St. Patrick's Day.

Faith Connections

Bible verse: God said, I have set my rainbow in the clouds.

(Genesis 9:13, adapted)

Children enjoy parties and special foods, so St. Patrick's Day can be a fun spring celebration. They will enjoy the stories of leprechauns and the "pot of gold at the end of the rainbow," so focus on those fun aspects of the holiday. It's also a good time to review the color green!

Teacher's Prayer

Thank you, God, for special days where we can just have fun imagining a "pot of gold at the end of a rainbow." Help me to remember, though, the real meaning of the rainbow—your covenant with the world. Amen.

Teacher Talk:

St. Patrick's Day is a holiday that people celebrate in March.

People in Ireland began the celebration of St. Patrick's Day.

Green is a special color of St. Patrick's Day.

We can thank God for special celebrations in the spring.

Center Time

Set up your centers as described on pages 6–9. To use today:

As children arrive, play Irish folk music.

Art Center

Teacher Talk
Green is a special color of St. Patrick's Day.

Resources
shamrock shapes or patterns (see page 212), pencils, green construction paper, scissors, stickers, markers and crayons, 2" x 24" pieces of tagboard or posterboard (headband), stapler

Before class, cut shamrock shapes (see page 212) from green construction paper or make patterns for the children to use. Let the children trace and cut shamrocks from paper. Each child can decorate a headband as desired then attach shamrocks to make a "St. Patrick's Day" headband. Staple the headband to fit each child's head.

Geography Center

Teacher Talk
People in Ireland began the celebration of St. Patrick's Day.

Resources
globe, map of Ireland, marker or shamrock sticker, book with pictures of Ireland

Display a world map. Place a shamrock sticker on Ireland. Or use a marker to draw a shamrock on the country. Let the children look at the book. Talk about where Ireland is located and where you are now.

Math Center

Teacher Talk
People in Ireland began the celebration of St. Patrick's Day.

Resources
variety of coins, empty coffee cans, black construction paper, tape

Before class, cover coffee cans with black paper to make "Leprechauns' Pots" (one for each type of coin). Have the children count and sort the coins into the pots.

Writing Center

Teacher Talk
People in Ireland began the celebration of St. Patrick's Day.

Resources
index cards, paper, green markers, pencils, old greeting cards

Write the word *Ireland* on an index card with a green marker. Place it at the children's eye level. Let the children copy the word with a green marker, or write a card or letter to send to a leprechaun.

Building Center

Teacher Talk
People in Ireland began the celebration of St. Patrick's Day.

Resources
picture of leprechaun, variety of blocks

Hang the picture of the leprechaun. Let the children build a house a leprechaun might live in.

Worship Center

Teacher Talk
We can thank God for special celebrations in the spring.

Resources
picture of a rainbow, green plants

Hang the picture of the rainbow. Place the plants nearby.

Say: Spring is a time of green things because plants and trees grow and have new leaves. St. Patrick's Day is a fun spring holiday when people wear green and talk about little people called leprechauns who hide gold at the end of rainbows. God made springtime as a time to rejoice and celebrate.

Pray: Thank you, God, for celebrations in the spring. Amen.

Wonder Time

Call the children together for wonder time.

Riggedy, Higgedy

Riggedy, higgedy, wiggedy, rig.
Paddy dances an Irish jig.
Riggedy, higgedy, wiggedy, rig.
He feeds potatoes to his pig.
Riggedy, higgedy, wiggedy, rig.
Let's all dance an Irish jig.

Wonder Question: I wonder why people celebrate St. Patrick's Day.

Say: St. Patrick's Day is a special holiday that started in Ireland, a country way across the ocean. It is a fun day when people wear green, eat special foods, and have parties! One of the fun parts of the day are the stories about leprechauns. They are little pretend people with pointed ears who hide pots of gold at the end of rainbows.

Play: Leprechaun Leap. Have the children pretend they are little leprechauns. The children can "leap" (like frogs) and hide behind pretend bushes. Allow the children several opportunities to do leprechaun leaps.

Sing: "Riggedy, Higgedy" (Traditional words to the tune of "Twinkle, Twinkle Little Star").

Read the Bible verse.

Say: Rainbows are a part of St. Patrick's Day. They are also a special part of God's world. When we see them we can remember how much God loves us and cares for us.

Pray: Thank you, God, for rainbows. Amen.

Open the Bible to Genesis 9:13.

Say: God said, "I have set my rainbow in the clouds" (Genesis 9:13, adapted).

Have the children repeat the Bible verse.

Group Fun

Resources

instant pistachio pudding mix, milk, whipped topping (1 container per 2 pudding mixes), drained crushed pineapple, green cherries (sliced in half), measuring cups, large spoon, cups, plastic spoons, can opener, large bowl, lemonade, yellow food coloring, blue powdered drink mix, cups

Help the children make a leprechaun salad. Set out the ingredients. Have the children help you measure and make the pudding according to the package directions. Add whipped topping and crushed pineapple. Make sure all the children have a chance to stir the materials. Allow each child to spoon some "Leprechaun Salad" into a cup, then place a green cherry on top. Eat the salads and enjoy.

Serve a green beverage. You can mix lemonade (with some yellow food coloring) and blue powdered drink mix to create a green drink.

Goodbye Circle

Let the children talk about the things they enjoyed doing today. Ask each child to name something that they remember about St. Patrick's Day.

Pray: Thank you, God, for spring, and St. Patrick's Day, and rainbows. Amen.

Evaluation

Were the children able to work together to create the group snack? Did the children enjoy the fun of St. Patrick's Day?

Lesson 64

Mother's Day

Teacher Talk:

God plans for mothers.

God created all kinds of families.

Mothers are part of a family.

Mother's Day is a special day to celebrate people who take care of us.

Goals:

To celebrate mothers.

To learn what kinds of things mothers do.

To understand that God plans for mothers.

Objectives: By the end of this session the children will:

Talk about their families.

Make presents for their mothers.

Faith Connections

Bible verse: Respect your father and your mother.

(Exodus 20:12, *Good News Bible*)

Mother's Day can be difficult for any child who may not have a mother living in her or his family. Be sensitive to children who are living in different types of families. Emphasize that God loves all kinds of families, and that while mothers are wonderful, not all families have mothers living with them. When you do, this is a special day to say thank you to your mother.

Teacher's Prayer

Thank you, God, for the families of the children in my care. Help me to help those children who do not have mothers in their families, and help me to get to know the mothers who are part of my class. Amen.

Center Time

Set up your centers as described on pages 6–9.
To use today:

Art Center

Teacher Talk

Mother's Day is a special day to celebrate people who take care of us.

Resources

old puzzle pieces (from puzzles that are missing pieces—preferably large pieces), glue, glitter, sequins and fake jewels, pin backs, craft glue or glue gun

Before class, use the craft glue or glue gun to attach a pin back to each puzzle piece. Glue it to the front (picture) side of the puzzle piece. Give each child a puzzle pin. Let the children decorate the pins with the materials provided.

Home Living Center

Teacher Talk

Mothers are part of a family.

Resources

baby dolls and clothes, baby blankets, doll bed, high chair, adult dress up clothes

Set out the materials and encourage the children to play families. Encourage the children to play mommy and daddy with the clothing provided.

Puzzle Center

Teacher Talk

God created all kinds of families.

Resources

puzzles of families (purchased or teacher-made)

To make a family puzzle, cut out pictures from magazines and attach them to posterboard or cardboard. Laminate the puzzles or cover them with clear self-adhesive paper. Cut each puzzle into four or five pieces. Encourage the children to put the puzzles together and talk about their pictures.

As children arrive, ask, "Who takes care of you and loves you?"

Water Table Center

Teacher Talk

Mother's Day is a special day to celebrate people who take care of us.

Resources

water table or dishpan, water, dolls, towels

Partially fill the table or dishpan with water. Let the children bathe their dolls and dry them with the towels.

Writing Center

Teacher Talk

Mother's Day is a special day to celebrate people who take care of us.

Resources

old greeting cards, paper, pencils, markers, envelopes

Before class, type the words "You are an important 'piece' of my life" on a piece of paper. Make enough copies so each child can have one. The children can use the papers to make cards to go with the puzzle pins. Or use the children can use the greeting cards and paper to make Mother's Day cards.

Worship Center

Teacher Talk

God created mothers.

Resources

pictures of families

Place the family pictures on a table. Encourage the children to look at and talk about the pictures.

Say: God created all kinds of families. All families are different. Mothers can be important parts of the family.

Pray: Thank you, God, for families and mothers. Amen.

Open the Bible to Exodus 20:12.

Say: "Respect your father and your mother" (Exodus 20:12, *Good News Bible*).

Have the children repeat the Bible verse.

Wonder Time

Call the children together for wonder time.

Wonder Question: I wonder why God planned for mothers?

Say: God made all kinds of families, and every family is special. Some families have mommies that live with them. Mother's Day is a special day when we say thank you to mommies and other special people who love us and take care of us. (Encourage the children to talk about their families.)

Sing: M-O-M-M-Y to the tune of "B-I-N-G-O."

Read the Bible verse.

Say: God has a special plan for each person. God wants children to live in families and have people who love them and take care of them.

Pray: Thank you, God, for families and people who love me. Amen.

M-O-M-M-Y

I love her, and she loves me,
And mommy is her name-o.
M-O-M-M-Y,
M-O-M-M-Y,
M-O-M-M-Y.
And mommy is her name-o.

Group Fun

Resources

unfrosted cupcakes (two per child), canned frosting, sprinkles, plastic knives, small paper plates, plastic wrap, lunch-size paper bags, crayons, markers, stickers, glue, lace and ribbon scraps, yarn, paper punch

Give each child two cupcakes to decorate—one to eat and one to take home. The children can frost their cupcakes and decorate them as desired. Have each child choose which cupcake she or he wants to take home to give to a family member. Place that cupcake on a plate and cover it with plastic wrap. The children can then eat and enjoy their classroom cupcake treats.

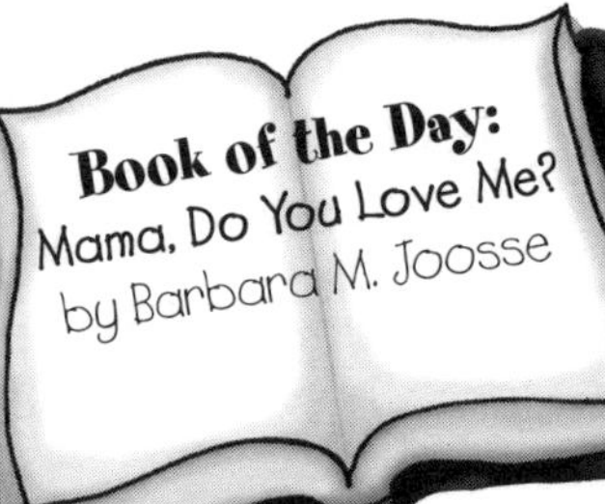

Let the children decorate lunch-size paper bags as gift bags for the cupcakes or the puzzle pins. Give each child a bag. Let the children decorate the bags with the crayons, markers, stickers, and scraps. Place the cupcake or pin inside the bag. Help each child fold over the top of the bag. Use a paper punch to make two holes through the fold. Help the child thread yarn through the holes and tie the yarn in a bow to hold the bag shut.

Goodbye Circle

Let the children talk about the things they enjoyed doing today. Ask each child to name a special person in his or her family.

Pray: Thank you, God, for my special family. Amen.

Evaluation

Were children able to talk about their families? Have there been any changes in your children's families over this school year? Make a note of any changes in the children's records.

Lesson 65

Cinco de Mayo

Goals:

To help children know that people all over the world have special celebrations.

To learn about a part of the Mexican culture.

Objectives: By the end of this session the children will:

Make paintings using the colors of the Mexican flag.

Taste a Mexican food.

Play a traditional Mexican game.

Faith Connections

Bible verse: Be happy and glad.

(Matthew 5:12, *Good News Bible*)

Cinco de Mayo (May 5) is a national holiday in Mexico, when people commemorate the anniversary of a victorious military battle. It is a time of parties, parades, and dance—fiesta time. Preschool children can learn that people all over the world enjoy celebrating special times by having parties. They can also learn that God loves us and wants us to be happy and have special times together.

Teacher's Prayer

Thank you, God, for special times to celebrate with friends, family, and the children in my care. Amen.

Teacher Talk:

Cinco de Mayo is a special day people celebrate in Mexico.

Cinco means five in Spanish.

God wants us to be happy.

Center Time

Set up your centers as described on pages 6–9. To use today:

As children arrive, play traditional Mexican music.

Cooking Center

Teacher Talk:

Cinco de Mayo is a special day people celebrate in Mexico.

Resources

paper plates, nacho chips, cheese dip, napkins, basket

Set out plates, napkins, dip, and the basket of nacho chips. Encourage the children to dip chips into the dip and enjoy their snack.

Geography Center

Teacher Talk

Cinco de Mayo is a special day people celebrate in Mexico.

Resources

globe, star stickers, world map, yarn, thumbtacks

Place the globe on a table. Place stickers on Mexico and where you live. Hang the map at the children's eye level. Place a thumbtack on Mexico and where you live. Connect the two thumbtacks with yarn. Let the children look at the map and globe and talk about Mexico.

Math Center

Teacher Talk

The Mexican flag is green, red, and white.

Resources

craft sticks or another type of "marker;" red, yellow, and white paint; large can such as an empty coffee can; paintbrushes

Paint markers or craft sticks red, white, and green. If you are using craft sticks, dip the ends in paint and allow them to dry. Place the markers in the can. Let the children shake several markers out of the can. Have the children count the number of each color that landed on the table. The children can place the markers back in the can and repeat the activity.

Science Center

Teacher Talk

The Mexican flag is green, red, and white

Resources

red, blue, and yellow fingerpaint; white construction paper or fingerpaint paper

Let the children use the colors to paint and mix colors. Talk about how the colors look when they are mixed. Have the children experiment to see which colors mix together to make green.

Writing Center

Teacher Talk:

Cinco means five in Spanish.

Resources

index cards, marker, paper, pencils, small stickers

Write the numbers one through five in both English and Spanish on cards: one—uno, two—dos, three—tres, four—cuatro, five—cinco. Place the corresponding number of stickers on each card. Let the children copy the words.

Worship Center

Teacher Talk

God wants us to be happy.

Resources

globe, variety of traditional party favors that would be familiar to children

Place the party favors next to the globe on the table. Encourage the children to look at the globe and the items.

Say: People all over the world enjoy having parties for special times, just like we do. God created all the different people in the world, and God wants each of us to be happy.

Pray: Thank you, God, for special people and special days. Amen.

Wonder Time

Call the children together for wonder time. Point out Mexico on the globe and name the country.

Cinco de Mayo

Cinco de Mayo,
Cinco de Mayo,
Is lots of fun, lots of fun.
Parades and celebrations;
Parades and celebrations.
Join the fun,
Join the fun.

Wonder Question: I wonder what kinds of parties people in Mexico might have?

Say: In Mexico, people celebrate a special day called Cinco de Mayo, which means the fifth of May. They celebrate it by having parades, parties, and special foods and music.

Sing: "Cinco de Mayo" to the tune of "Are You Sleeping?".

Read the Bible verse.

Say: Cinco de Mayo is a special holiday in Mexico. We have special days where we live also. People all over the world celebrate special days and have fun. God wants us to be happy and celebrate with our friends.

Pray: Thank you, God, for special days and friends. Amen.

Open the Bible to Matthew 5:12.

Say: "Be happy and glad." (Matthew 5:12, *Good News Bible*).

Have the children repeat the Bible verse.

Group Fun

Resources
two kickballs

Teach the children how to play native Mexican kickball. Tell the children that this is a game children play in parts of Mexico. Set up an obstacle course using elements of your room, or, preferably, the playground. Divide the class into two groups. Give each group a kickball and have the children take turns kicking the ball through the obstacle course. Focus on the fun of the activity, rather than making it a competition.

Teacher Tip: If you wish, this would be an appropriate time to have a piñata. These can often be purchased at party supply stores, or easily made by decorating a paper grocery bag. Fill the piñata with candies and small toys and hang it in an easily accessible spot. Children can take turns using a stick or bat to try to break the piñata. (Be sure other children are out of the way!)

Goodbye Circle

Let the children talk about the things the enjoyed doing today. Have the children squat down. Tell them that you are going to count down backwards from 5 - 1. When you reach one they are to jump as high as they can and yell, "Cinco de Mayo!"

Pray: Thank you, God, for Cinco de Mayo fun. Amen.

Evaluation

Make note of each child's large motor skills as he or she tried to kick the ball around the course. Think of ways to help those children who had difficulties.

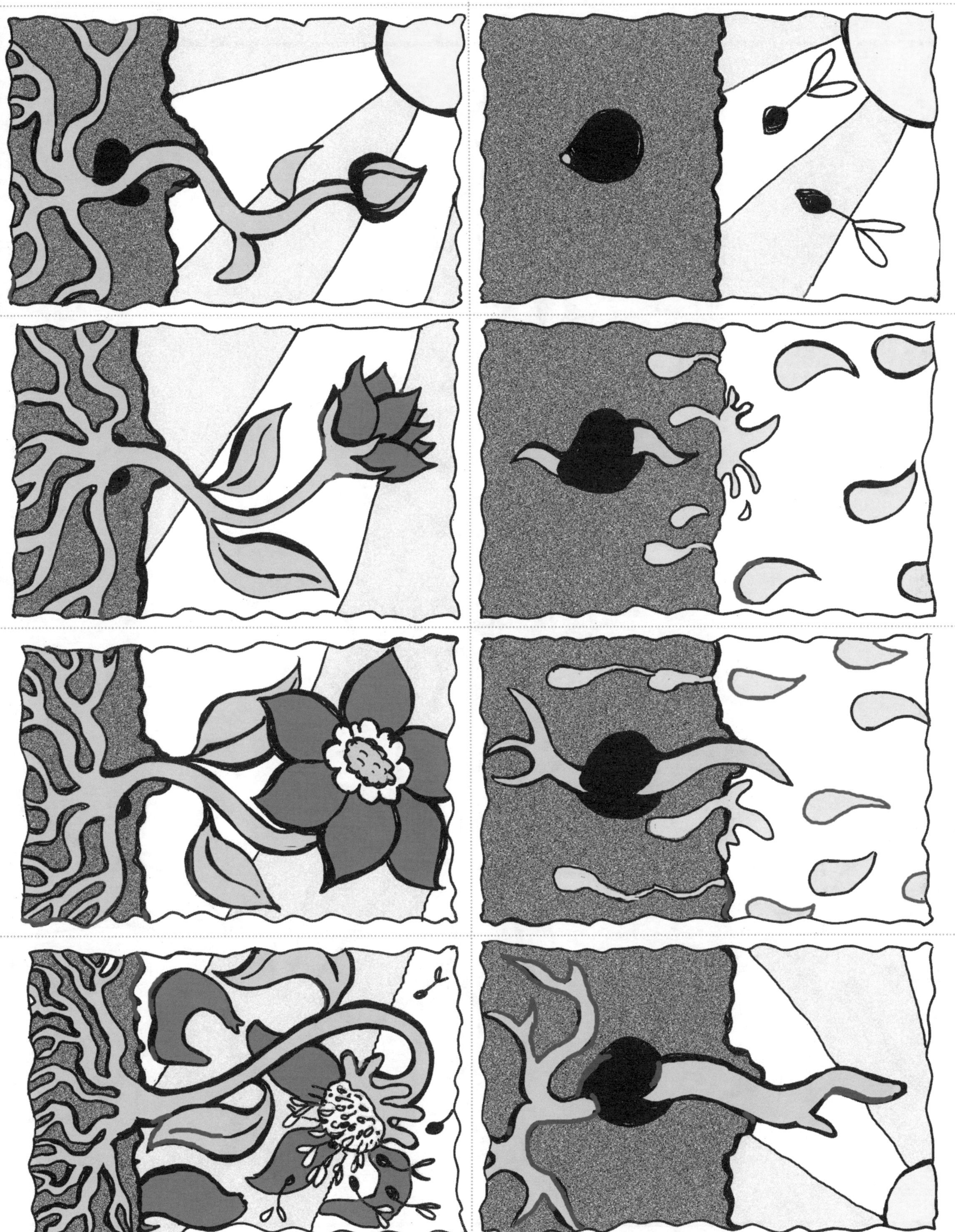

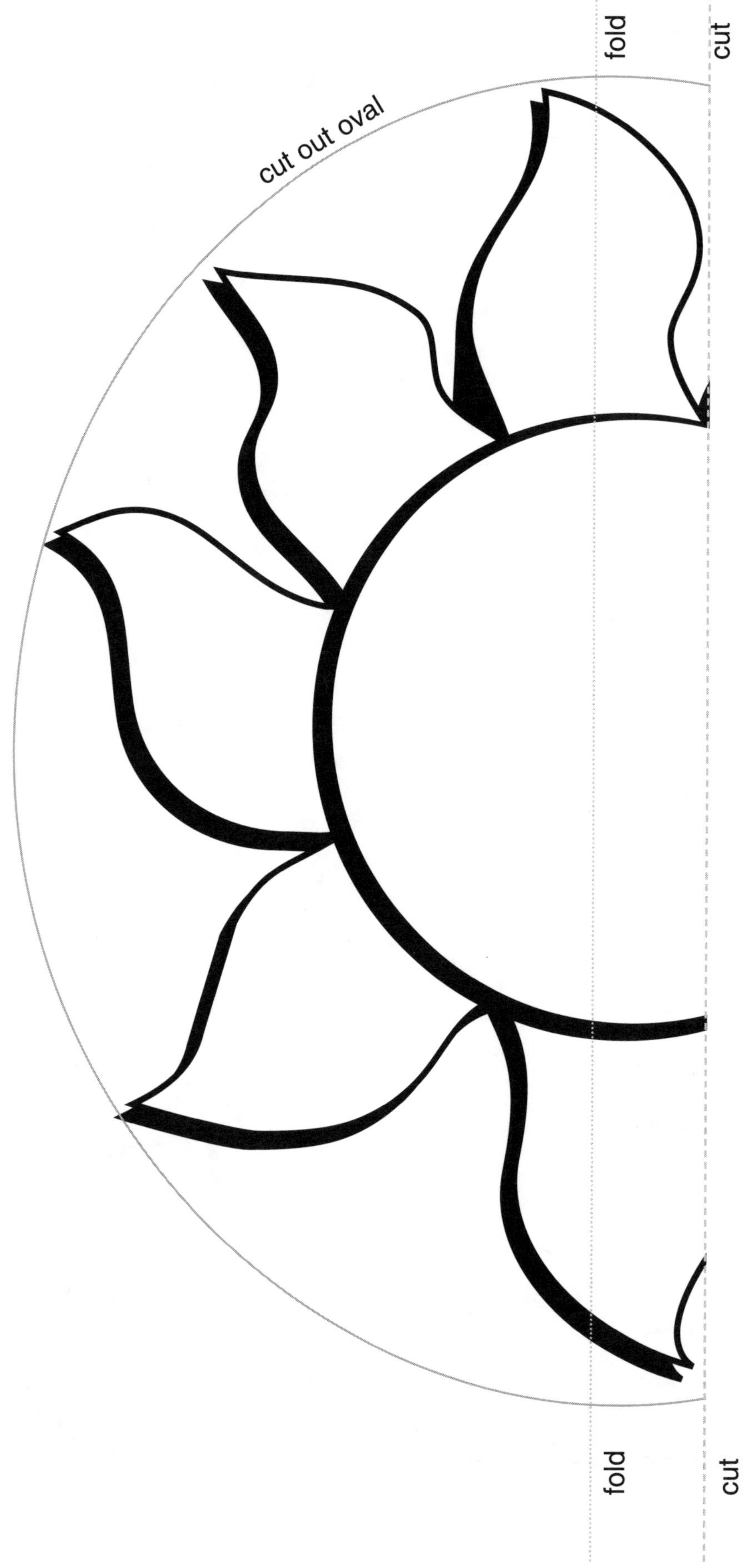
cut out oval
fold
cut
fold
cut

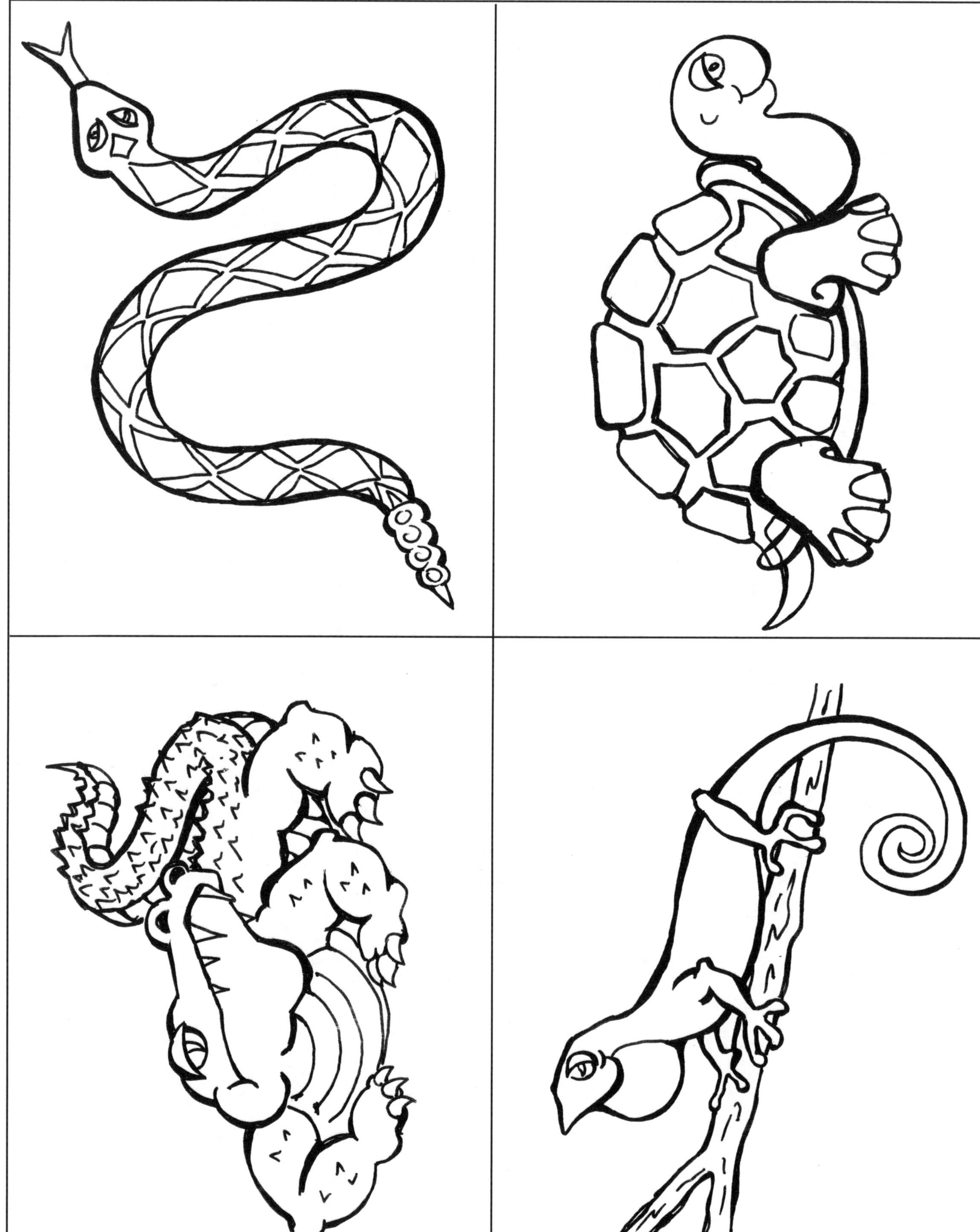

Fingerplays

Four Little Eggs

Four little eggs in the robin's nest
(Hold up four fingers.)
High up in a tree.
(Hold arms up like a tree.)
All of a sudden one did hatch!
(Throw arms up and out.)
Now there are only three.
(Hold up three fingers.)

Three little eggs in the robin's nest,
(Hold up three fingers.)
All a lovely blue.
(Cup hands to form nest.)
All of a sudden one did hatch!
(Throw arms up and out.)
Now there are only two.
(Hold up two fingers.)

Two little eggs in the robin's nest
(Hold up two fingers.)
In the bright warm sun.
(Wiggle fingers downward as sun's rays.)
All of a sudden one did hatch!
(Throw arms up and out.)
Now there is only one.
(Hold up one finger.)

One little egg in the robin's nest
(Hold up one finger.)
Not having any fun.
(Shake head sadly side to side.)
All of a sudden it did hatch!
(Throw arms up and out.)
Now look—there are none!
(Make a zero with fingers.)

Four little birdies up in a tree.
(Hold up four fingers.)
Their mommy is very proud.
(Flap arms as wings.)
Tweet, tweet, tweet the birdies say
(Flap hands like baby wings.)
As they sing their song out loud.
(Cup hands around mouth.)

Mary, Mary, Quite Contrary

(traditional)

Mary, Mary,
(Make smiling face.)
Quite contrary,
(Make scowling face.)
How does your garden grow?
With silver bells
(Hold puppet down low.)
And cockle shells
(Hold puppet at waist line.)
And pretty maids all in a row.
(Hold puppet up high.)

Mary, Mary, tell us Mary,
(Make smiling face.)
How does your garden grow?
With small, small flowers
(Hold puppet low.)
And tall, tall flowers
(Hold puppet as high as possible.)
And smiling faces all in a row.
(Hold puppet up next to face.)

Week of ____________________ **Theme** ____________________

Weekly Notes		Bible Verse/Book	Art	Math/Writing
Observations:	MONDAY			
	TUESDAY			
Learning Centers:	WEDNESDAY			
Evaluations:	THURSDAY			
	FRIDAY			

Science/Cooking	Building/Home Living	Music/Movement	Additional Centers

Dear Parents,

This week your child is learning about colors. Please encourage your child to wear an article of clothing that matches the color of the day.

Also please allow your child to bring an object (one that can be handled by children) that is the color of the day. The objects will be used in our learning centers.

Colors of the Day:
Monday —red
Tuesday—yellow
Wednesday—blue
Thursday—green
Friday—rainbow colors

Sincerely yours,

Dear Parents,

This week your child is learning about shapes. Please allow your child to bring an object (one that can be handled by children) that is the shape of the day. The objects will be used in our learning centers.

Shapes of the Day:
Monday —rectangles
Tuesday—circles
Wednesday—squares
Thursday—triangles
Friday—diamonds

Sincerely yours,

Dear Parents,

Tomorrow your child will hear the story **Stone Soup** and make vegetable soup. Please send a can of vegetables with your child to add to the soup.

Sincerely yours,

Dear Parents,

Tomorrow your child will make a fruit salad. Please send fresh fruit with your child to add to the salad.

Sincerely yours,

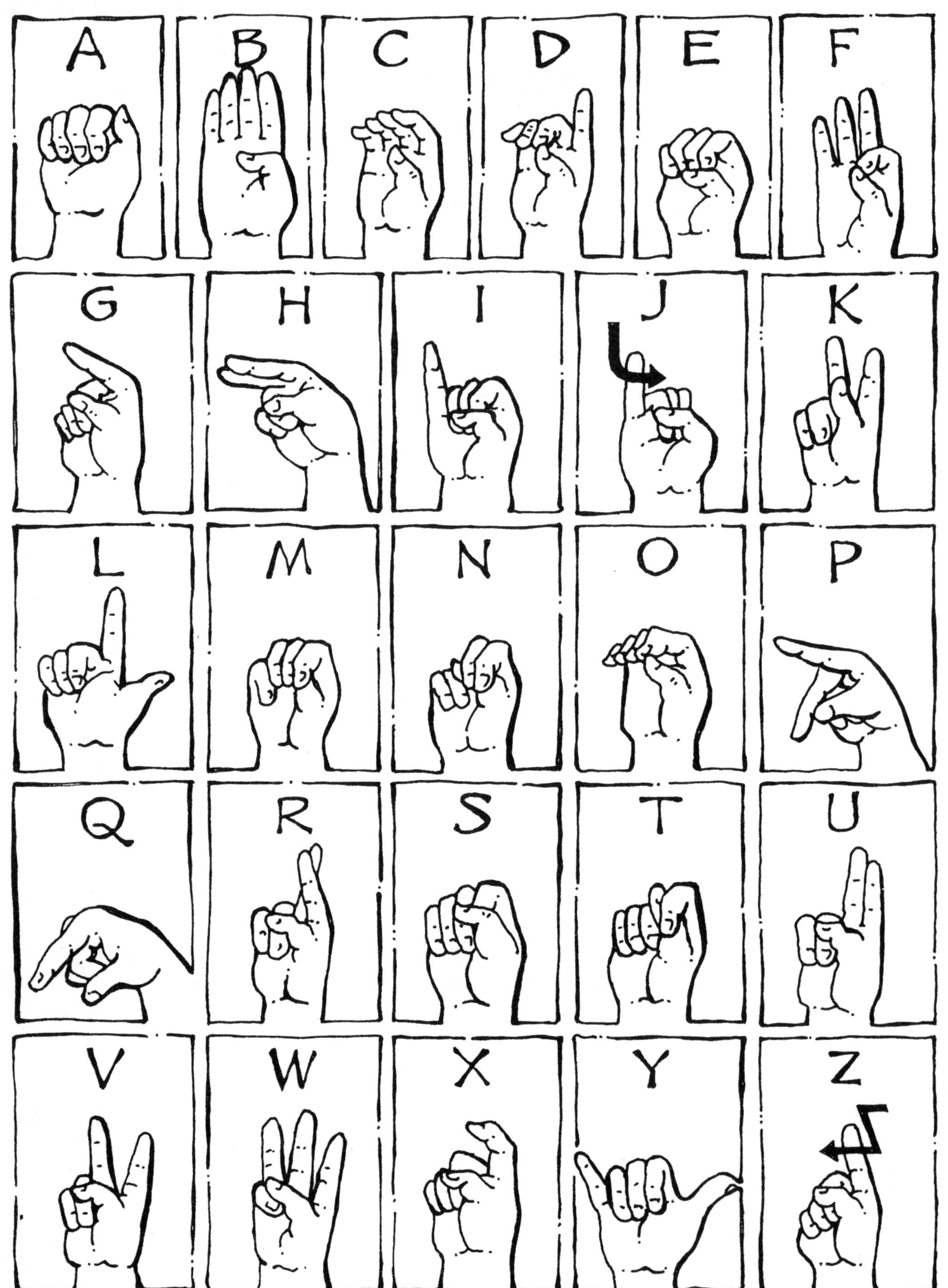
A
B
C
D
E
F
G
H
I
J
K
L
M
N
O
P
Q
R
S
T
U
V
W
X
Y
Z